WORLD SERIAL KILLERS

WORLD
SERIAL KILLERS

Nigel Cawthorne

canary
press

Foul deeds will rise,
Though all the earth o'erwhelm
them, to men's eyes.

William Shakespeare, *Hamlet Act 1, Scene 2*

[*o'erwhelm them* i.e., cover them up.
From Middle English *whelmen* to cover up or engulf.]

...

Serial murder may, in fact, be a much older
phenomenon than we realize. The stories
and legends that have filtered down about
witches and werewolves and vampires may
have been a way of explaining outrages so
hideous that no one in the small and close-
knit towns of Europe and early America could
comprehend the perversities we now take for
granted. Monsters had to be supernatural
creatures. They couldn't be just like us.

John E. Douglas, *Mindhunter:*
Inside the FBI's Elite Serial Crime Unit

CONTENTS

CONTENTS

PART 2. EUROPEAN SERIAL KILLERS

PART 3. ASIAN SERIAL KILLERS

PART 4. AUSTRALIAN SERIAL KILLERS

PART 5. SOUTH AFRICAN SERIAL KILLERS

AFTERWORD

INTRODUCTION

Serial murder is neither a new phenomenon, nor is it uniquely American. Dating back to ancient times, serial murderers have been chronicled around the world. In nineteenth century Europe, Dr Richard von Krafft-Ebing conducted some of the first documented research on violent, sexual offenders and the crimes they committed. Best known for his 1886 textbook *Psychopathia Sexualis*, Dr Krafft-Ebing described numerous case studies of sexual homicide, serial murder, and other areas of sexual proclivity.

Serial murder is a relatively rare event, estimated to comprise less than one percent of all murders committed in any given year. However, there is a macabre interest in the topic that far exceeds its scope and has generated countless articles, books, and movies. This broad-based public fascination began in the late 1880s, after a series of unsolved prostitute murders occurred in the Whitechapel area of London. These murders were committed by an unknown individual who named himself "Jack the Ripper."

These murders and the *nom de guerre* "Jack the Ripper" have become synonymous with serial murder. This case spawned many legends concerning serial murder and the killers who commit it. In the 1970s and 1980s serial murder cases such as the Green River Killer, Ted Bundy, and BTK sparked a renewed public interest in serial murder, which blossomed in the 1990s after the release of films such as *Silence of the Lambs*.

The relative rarity of serial murder combined with inaccurate, anecdotal information and fictional portrayals of serial killers has resulted in many common myths and misconceptions. In fact, many serial killers hide in plain sight within their communities. Serial murderers often have families and homes, are gainfully employed, and appear to be normal members of the community. Because many serial murderers can blend in so effortlessly, they are oftentimes overlooked by law enforcement and the public.

This Introduction is produced courtesy of the FBI's National Center for the Analysis of Violent Crime. Extracted from Behaviour Analysis Unit-2, Symposium Agenda, San Antonio, Texas, USA, 2005.

PART 1

AMERICAN SERIAL KILLERS

RODNEY ALCALA
The Dating Game Killer

Serial killer Rodney James Alcala earned his sobriquet because in 1978, he took time out from his criminal career to appear as a contestant on ABC's popular TV show *The Dating Game*.

The host introduced him with the words: "Bachelor No. 1 is a successful photographer who got his start when his father found him in the darkroom at the age of thirteen, fully developed. Between takes you might find him skydiving or motorcycling. Please welcome Rodney Alcala."

However, fellow contestant actor Jed Mills described

Alcala as "creepy, definitely creepy". He felt there was something wrong with Alcala instantly when they met in the Green Room before the first take. "He was quiet, but at the same time he would interrupt and impose when he felt like it," Mills said. "And he was very obnoxious and creepy – he became very unlikeable and rude and imposing as though he was trying to intimidate. I wound up not only not liking this guy … I could not be near him … He was a standout creepy guy in my life."

SEXUAL PREDATOR

Plainly female contestant Cheryl Bradshaw did not feel the same. She picked Alcala as her date. Criminal profiler Pat Brown later studied the tapes.

"He was aware that he could say things that were considered sexy and funny and the girl would like that," Brown said. "But a psychopath's true nature comes seeping through … He had already committed a crime, raped a little girl. Here is a man portraying himself as a desirable young man when he is a violent sexual predator of children."

Eventually Cheryl Bradshaw found things different off camera. "He is showing his psychopathic personality in the green room," she said. "This guy was going on the show to prove how special and wonderful he was. And his ego was riding on it." When the time came to go out on a date with him she refused. Brown thought that this rejection may have pushed Alcala over the edge.

Born Rodrigo Jacques Alcala Buquor in San Antonio, Texas, in 1943, the Dating Game Killer spent part of his childhood in Mexico before moving back to the US in 1954, living in Los Angeles with his mother and sisters. At seventeen, he joined the US Army, but was diagnosed with a severe anti-social personality and given a medical discharge in 1964.

Enrolled at the UCLA School of Fine Arts, he was awarded a bachelor's degree in 1968. But a motorist spotted him on Sunset Boulevard luring eight-year-old Tali Shapiro into his car. Tailing them back to Alcala's Hollywood apartment, he called the police.

The cops kicked the door in and found the girl lying on the kitchen floor. She had been raped, beaten with an iron bar and throttled. She was not dead though. While they applied emergency CPR, Alcala slipped out of the back door and fled.

IRISH EYES

Crossing the country, he enrolled at New York University's film school under the name John Berger. There, he said he studied under Roman Polanski. Otherwise, he passed himself off as a fashion photographer to get women to pose for him, giving him the opportunity to rape and kill his would-be models.

Forty years after the event the police tied Alcala to the

murder of twenty-three-year-old TWA flight attendant Cornelia Crilley in 1971. When the police broke in to her Upper East Side apartment, they found her slumped against an overturned bed with a rope around her neck. She had been raped and strangled. Her bra had been pulled up over her head and there was a bite mark on her left breast. Saliva was collected, but DNA profiling had yet to be invented. At the time the police suspected Crilley's boyfriend, Leon Borstein, but the murder remained unsolved. It was only in 2011 that a dental impression from Alcala was found to match the bite mark on her body.

"I am now almost seventy-one, and this occurred forty years ago, and I am still affected by it," Borstein said. "I was devastated by her death. She was beautiful, charming, with a great sense of humour. She had the Irish eyes and the Irish hair."

TOYING WITH HIS VICTIMS

Altering his alias slightly to John Burger, Alcala worked at a childrens' summer drama camp in New Hampshire where two students recognized Alcala from the FBI's Most Wanted poster in the post office. He was arrested and shipped back to LA where he was charged with rape, kidnapping, assault and attempted murder.

But the Shapiro family had moved back to Mexico and refused to let Tali testify. Without their principal witness, the prosecution were forced to plea bargain. Alcala pleaded guilty to molesting a child. The other charges were dropped. Sentenced to three years, he was paroled after seventeen months.

Within weeks, Alcala was found with a thirteen-year-old girl who accused him of kidnapping her and supplying her with marijuana. He was sent back to jail for violating his parole, but was out again in 1977.

Soon after, his parole officer gave Alcala permission to visit relatives in New York. When the daughter of the owner of Ciro's nightclub, socialite Ellen Jane Hover, disappeared, the name "John Berger" was found written on her calendar on the date she vanished. The twenty-three-year-old was last seen with a ponytailed photographer named John Burger.

Back in LA, Alcala was picked up and questioned after the Burger/Berger connection was made. But Ellen Hover's body had not been found by then, so he was released. Her remains were later found on the wooded Rockefeller Estate.

On December 16, 1977, two days after Alcala had been released, the body of twenty-seven-year-old nurse Georgia Wixted was found in her studio apartment in Malibu. The night before she had attended a birthday party at Brennan's Pub in Santa Monica. She had been raped, sodomized, and sexually abused with a claw hammer, which had then been used to smash her head in after she had been strangled with a nylon stocking. Her body was left posed.

The next murder connected to Alcala was that of thirty-three-year-old legal secretary Charlotte Lamb, whose naked body was found in a laundry room of an El Segundo apartment complex on June 24, 1978. She had been raped, beaten, and strangled with her own shoelace. Once again the body was left posed. It appeared that the perpetrator liked to toy with his victims, choking them until they lost consciousness, then reviving them, only to throttle them once more.

That summer Alcala appeared on *The Dating Game*.

POSING FOR PICTURES

Early in 1979, a fifteen-year-old hitchhiker called the police from a motel in Riverside County in Southern California saying she had been kidnapped and raped, but had escaped. Alcala was charged but his mother put up a $10,000 bail.

Out on bail, he raped and murdered twenty-one-year-old computer keypunch operator Jill Parenteau in her Burbank apartment. Blood was found after he had cut himself breaking a window to get in. He was charged with murdering Parenteau but the case was dropped due to lack of evidence.

Six days later, on June 20, 1979, twelve-year-old Robin Samsoe disappeared. She had been with her friend Bridget Wilvert at Huntington Beach when a man asked them to pose for pictures in their swimsuits. A neighbour intervened and the photographer took off. Later Bridget lent Robin her yellow bike to go to her ballet class. Her decomposing body was found twelve days later in the foothills of Los Angeles.

Detectives circulated a sketch of the photographer to the media and Alcala's parole officer recognized him. Arrested at his mother's house in Monterey Park on June 24, Alcala claimed that he had been applying for a job as a photographer for a disco contest at the time of Samsoe's disappearance.

However, in a search of the house, police found a receipt for a locker. In it were photographs of young girls. One of them showed Lorraine Werts posing for him on Huntington Beach, near where Robin and Bridget had been approached. The police also found earrings that belonged to Charlotte Lamb and Robin Samsoe.

CHARGING ALCALA

In 1980, Alcala was convicted of Robin Samsoe's murder and sentenced to death, but the verdict was overturned by the California Supreme Court because the jurors had been improperly informed of his previous sexual offences. A second conviction was thrown out in 2001 because the judge did not allow a witness to back up the defence's allegation that the US Forest Service ranger who found Robin's body in the mountains had been hypnotized by the police.

By 2003, DNA analysis had developed to a point that the semen found on the bodies of Jill Barcomb, Georgia Wixted, and Charlotte Lamb could be matched to Alcala's. At his third trial, the murder of Robin Samsoe was added to the murder of Jill Barcomb, Georgia Wixted, Charlotte Lamb, and Jill Parenteau.

He pleaded not guilty by reason of insanity. Acting as his own attorney, he even cross-questioned himself in the witness box. He was convicted of five counts of first-degree murder. During the penalty stage of the proceedings, Tali Shapiro made a surprise appearance and Alcala was sentenced to death once more.

Some one hundred and twenty of the photographs found in Alcala's locker were published. Twenty-one women came forward to identify themselves. Other people recognized family members who had disappeared. Alcala was then charged with the murder of Christine Thornton in Sweetwater County, Wyoming, in the summer of 1977.

In 2012, Alcala was extradited to New York where he was convicted of the murders of Cornelia Crilley and Ellen Hover, earning him another twenty-five years to life. Alcala is also thought to be responsible for murders in San Francisco, Seattle, New York, New Hampshire and Arizona. There were thought to be hundreds of victims, making Alcala one of America's most prolific serial killers.

2

CHARLES ALBRIGHT
The Eyeball Killer

On December 13, 1990, the semi-naked body of thirty-three-year-old hooker Mary Lou Pratt was found in the 8800 block of Beckleyview in the Oak Cliff district of Dallas, Texas, a neighbourhood known for drugs and prostitution. She had been shot in the back of the head. When a post-mortem was performed, the medical examiner found that her eyes had been removed with almost surgical precision, leaving barely a mark on the surrounding tissue. They had not been gouged out in a fight, but had seemingly been taken as a bizarre memento.

There were few leads to go on, but it was rumoured that

Mary Lou and another prostitute named Susan Peterson had stolen goods from the warehouse of a customer who may have had a grudge against them. However detectives were unable to find out who that was and the trail went cold.

HER EYES WERE GONE

Around the same time another prostitute named Veronica reported that a man had raped her and tried to kill her. She had managed to escape but was left with a vicious head wound. On December 15, she was seen in a light-blue truck. Figuring that the driver may be the man who had attacked her, the police stopped the vehicle.

But Veronica insisted that the man had actually rescued her from her attacker. He called himself "SpeeDee" and his driver's licence gave his address as Eldorado Avenue nearby. He said he lived there with his wife Dixie and maintained that he and Veronica were just friends.

On February 10, 1991, the half-naked body of twenty-seven-year-old prostitute Susan Peterson was found. Her top had been pulled up to reveal her breasts in the same way that Pratt's had been. She too had been shot – once in the back of the head, once in the top of the head, and once more in the left breast with the bullet entering her heart. Again her eyes were gone, they had been surgically extracted. Two days before she died, she had told patrol officers that she might know who Mary Lou's killer was.

Veronica then claimed that she had actually witnessed Pratt's murder, but she was a known liar.

Pratt and Peterson were white, but on March 10, 1991, the body of forty-one-year-old part-time prostitute Shirley Williams was found. She was black. She had been shot in the top of the head and through the face. Once more the eyes had been removed, but this time more roughly and the broken tip of an X-Acto precision knife was found. Shirley's face had been slashed. She was badly bruised and her nose was broken.

DESPERATE FOR LEADS

That night it appears Williams had been getting high on drugs with friends before going out. It had been raining so she had put on a yellow raincoat. She was last seen getting into a car. Earlier she had told her daughter that she would be home that night, but she did not return. In none of these three cases were any fingerprints or semen found. However, among Williams' pubic hairs forensics found the hair of a Caucasian, and the ballistics lab discovered that the same gun had been used to kill Williams and Pratt.

Desperate for a lead, the police thought they would follow up on "SpeeDee." The address on his driver's licence, they discovered, was a property registered in the name of Fred Albright. But he was dead.

A woman then came forward with her suspicions. She knew Charles Albright, Fred's son. He had told her that he was a professional con man and showered her with gifts. Although he was a married man, he moved her into a love nest, but she became increasingly disturbed by his behaviour, particularly his unhealthy obsessions with eyes and knives. Eventually she moved out and moved on. She also said that Albright had known Mary Lou Pratt.

Veronica and another prostitute who had escaped by spraying an attacker with Mace were shown a photograph of Albright and both recognized him as the man who had attacked them. On the night of March 22, 1991, the police went to Albright's house on Eldorado Avenue and arrested him for attempted murder and assault. They also took in his wife Dixie. But "SpeeDee" did not live there. He only used that address for his driver's licence.

In Albright's actual home, the police found red condoms – similar to one that had been found by Shirley Williams' body. They also found some X-Acto knives suitable for removing the eye balls of the victims. Albright denied having a gun, but the police found a .44 Smith & Wesson revolver.

Dixie was shocked that her husband was wanted in connection with such horrendous crimes and provided him with an alibi. On the nights concerned he had been at home in bed with her, though he did have an early morning paper round. She did not know why he had condoms as she had passed her menopause. Nor did she know he already had a criminal record, including a conviction for sexual assault.

Albright denied knowing anything about the murders, nor did he consort with prostitutes, he said. "SpeeDee," it turned out, was one of Albright's tenants, but he denied that Albright was the man he had rescued Veronica from. But detectives kept digging.

EYES OF THE DEAD

It seemed that Albright had been seeing prostitutes behind his wife's back, though he had once said he hated prostitutes and wanted to kill them. He had a fierce temper and, apart from his paper round, he lived off Dixie, who was a widow. Clearly he was a manipulative, intelligent charmer.

Born on August 10, 1933, Charles Albright had been adopted as a child. When he got his first gun, he would kill small animals and stuff them. He told his doting adoptive mother that he wanted to be a taxidermist. She encouraged him but would never let him complete his taxidermy projects, making him leave his stuffed dead animals without eyes because the glass eyes in the local taxidermy shop were too expensive.

Albright graduated from high school and enrolled at North Texas State University. But he was arrested for stealing some money, a rifle, and two handguns and was sentenced to a year in jail.

At Arkansas State Teacher's College, he cheated in exams and bragged of his sexual prowess. When a football teammate broke up with a girl with distinctive almond eyes, he cut the eyes out of her photograph and pasted them on the photograph of his friend's new girlfriend. Other pictures of eyes were stuck on the ceiling and in the bathroom of their apartment.

He was expelled from college for stealing before graduating, so he forged a bachelor's and master's degree. When the forged degrees were discovered, he was sacked from a teaching job. He married his college girlfriend and they had a daughter, but the marriage soon fell apart and they divorced.

Caught stealing again, he was sentenced to two years, but served only six months. Visiting friends, he was accused of molesting their nine-year-old daughter. He claimed he was innocent, but pleaded guilty to avoid the hassle of having to defend himself, and he escaped with probation. His probation officer said he lied so readily that he often convinced himself he was telling the truth.

Having inherited property from his father, Albright squandered the money on prostitutes. He also gave them things he stole. After he met Dixie in Arkansas in 1985, she invited him to come and live with her. He accepted and let her pay all the bills. His only contribution came from his paper round which was largely an excuse to get out of the house to visit hookers.

CASE UNRAVELS

Despite his shady behaviour, the case against him began unravelling. The .44 Smith & Wesson found in his house was not the one used to kill Mary Pratt and Shirley Williams. No blood or any other evidence of murder was found in his house, and Dixie produced garage bills showing that their car was off the road when the first two murders occurred.

A stash of pornographic material was found in "SpeeDee's" house. Albright had a key and, it seems, used the place when "SpeeDee" was away. Hairs on blankets from Albright's truck and in his vacuum cleaner came from an African-American, but there were not enough to identify them as coming from Shirley Williams, given the DNA technology at the time. Even so, on March 26, 1991, capital charges were brought against Albright for the murders of Mary Pratt, Susan Peterson, and Shirley Williams.

Then Mary Beth, a prostitute currently in custody, told the police that on the night Mary Pratt had been killed, a man had forced her into a car at knife point. He drove her out to a field, threw her to the ground and kept punching her. Then he opened a case, got out a knife and slashed open her blouse. He discarded the blade. While he searched for another one, she passed out. When she came round, he was gone.

Interviewing other prostitutes in the area, the police

came across Tina, who had beautiful eyes and said Albright had once been a regular client, but she dropped him when he got rough. On the night Shirley Williams died, Albright had driven by them. Tina got into another car, so did not see if Albright picked up Williams. But when she got back, Williams was gone. She took the police to a field where Albright used to take her. There they found a yellow raincoat like the one Williams had been wearing on the night she disappeared. It had blood on it.

Willie Upshaw, who was serving time for the illegal possession of a firearm, said that Albright had another .44 which the police had not found. He had bought it using his father's name. Upshaw had also been with Albright the day his car had broken down and said that he did have a car on the night Shirley Williams was killed.

SAVAGELY BEATEN

A grand jury was called. They reduced the capital charges to murder in the second degree, taking the death penalty off the table. The district attorney then decided only to go ahead with the case of Shirley Williams.

The trial began on December 2, 1991, with the judge ruling that the other cases could be brought up in court to show a pattern of behaviour. The prosecution maintained that Albright was enraged after Mary Pratt and another prostitute had ripped him off. Another prostitute testified that she had been with Susan Peterson when Albright picked them up and beat them savagely.

However, the yellow raincoat the police had found had gone missing. Neighbours testified that Albright did not have a car at the time of the murder. Upshaw changed his story and Veronica appeared for the defence.

The case depended on the forensics and the scientific evidence concerning the hair. But it was enough for the jury to find Charles Albright guilty of the murder of Shirley Williams. The life imprisonment verdict was not reversed on appeal. Albright died in prison in Lubbock, Texas, on August 22, 2020. He was eighty-seven years old.

3

RICHARD CHASE
The Vampire of Sacramento

At 6:00 p.m. on January 23, 1978, twenty-four-year-old laundry-truck driver David Wallin returned to his modest suburban home in Sacramento, California, to find his twenty-two-year-old wife Terry, who was three months pregnant, dead and horribly violated. Screaming in horror, he ran to the house of a neighbour who called the police.

Terry Wallin had been shot with a .22 pistol and stabbed repeatedly before and after she was dead. The killer had raped her dead body, cut off her left nipple and slashed open her belly. He appeared to have drunk her blood and body parts were missing. Dog faeces had been collected from the yard and forced down her throat.

PARANOID PSYCHOSIS

The local police called Russ Vorpagel, a veteran cop with the FBI's Behavioral Science Unit on the West Coast who, in turn, contacted Robert Ressler, a pioneer in psychological profiling. Clearly such a killer was not going to be satisfied with one homicide. Unless caught quickly, he was bound to kill again.

Ressler immediately came up with a profile of the suspect: "White male, aged 25 – 27 years; thin, undernourished appearance. Residence will be extremely slovenly and unkempt and evidence of the crime will be found at the residence. History of mental illness, and will have been involved in use of drugs. Will be a loner who does not associate with either males or females, and will probably spend a great deal of time in his own home, where he lives alone. Unemployed. Possibly receives some form of disability money. If residing with anyone, it would be with his parents; however, this is unlikely. No prior military record; high school or college dropout. Probably suffering from one or more forms of paranoid psychosis."

THREE MORE BODIES

Four days after the slaughter of Terry Wallin, three more bodies were found in another suburban house not far away. Thirty-eight-year-old mother of three Evelyn Miroth, her six-year-old son Jason, and fifty-two-year-old family friend Daniel J. Meredith had all been shot with a .22. Evelyn had been babysitting her twenty-two-month-old nephew David (Michael) Ferreira, who was missing.

While Jason and Meredith were otherwise unmolested, Evelyn Miroth was found naked on her bed. She had been sodomized. There were multiple stab wounds all over her body, especially around her face and anus. Her belly had also been slashed open and organs removed.

In Michael Ferreira's playpen, there was a blood-soaked pillow and an expended bullet. Detectives did not expect to find the child alive. Meredith's wallet and car keys were missing. His red station wagon was found abandoned nearby with the driver's door open and the keys in the ignition.

Ressler concluded that the killer was a "disorganized" type who lived within a mile of where he had left the car. He also believed that the perpetrator had committed "fetish burglaries" in the area – that is, he had stolen jewellery or articles of women's clothing for auto-erotic purposes.

THIN AND DISHEVELLED
Sixty-five police officers began combing the area and discovered that a dog had been shot and disembowelled at a country club nearby. Then a woman came forward to say that she had seen a man she had known at high school

in the shopping centre which Terry Wallin had visited on the morning of her murder.

He had looked thin and dishevelled. When he had tried to engage her in conversation by pulling on the door handle of her car, she took fright and drove away. The man's name was Richard Trenton Chase.

Chase had graduated from the same high school as the woman in 1968 and lived just a block from where the station wagon had been abandoned, and a mile from both the shopping centre and the country club. So the police staked out Chase's apartment and waited for him.

When Chase emerged, he was carrying a box. Seeing the officers, he made a dash for his truck. They went after him and brought him down. As they grappled on the ground, a .22 fell from the shoulder holster Chase was wearing. A quick search found Daniel Meredith's wallet in his back pocket. The box he was carrying was full of bloody rags.

In a toolbox in his truck, there was a twelve-inch butcher's knife, along with a pair of rubber boots with blood on them. In his apartment, the police found newspaper articles about Terry Wallin's murder, blood-stained clothing, pet collars and leads, and food blenders with blood in them.

TODAY IS THE DAY

Knives taken from the Wallins' house were found in the kitchen drawer. Brain tissue and other body parts were found in the fridge. On the wall was a calendar with the word "Today" scrawled on the days of the murders – as well as another forty-four days spread out over the year.

The bullets from Chase's gun matched a bullet taken from the body of fifty-one-year-old Ambrose Griffin. On December 28, 1977, he had just returned from the supermarket when Chase had driven by and fired two shots. One hit Griffin in the chest and killed him. Then the decapitated body of the missing infant Michael Ferreira was found not far from Chase's apartment.

Chase also matched the description of the perpetrator of fetish burglaries in the area and the collars and leads found in his apartment belonged to dogs and cats that had gone missing. The previous August, he had been arrested near Lake Tahoe. He had blood on his clothes, but said he had been hunting rabbits. There were a number of guns and a bucket of animal's blood in his truck.

Born in 1950, Chase was said to have been a sweet and cooperative child, though he wet the bed until the age of eight. When he was about twelve, his parents fell out. His mother accused his father of being unfaithful, taking drugs, and trying to poison her. Ressler described Mrs Chase as the classic mother of a schizophrenic – "highly aggressive ... hostile ... provocative".

SMEARED WITH BLOOD

At school Chase had no close friends and was unable to keep a girlfriend when they found he could not sustain an erection. He began drinking heavily and smoking marijuana. Caught in possession, he was sentenced to community service. Unable to hold down a job, he dropped out of junior college and lived alternately with his mother and father who supported him.

In 1972, he was arrested for drunk-driving and stopped drinking afterwards. The following year, he was arrested for carrying a gun without a licence and resisting arrest. He had been thrown out of a party after trying to grab a girl's breast. When two men restrained him after he returned, a .22 fell out of his waistband. The police were called and he was fined $50.

After injecting himself with rabbit's blood in 1976, he was sent to a nursing home where he frightened other patients by breaking the necks of two birds he caught and drinking their blood. He was often found smeared with blood and the staff called him Dracula.

When he was discharged, his mother found him an apartment. After an argument with his mother, he killed her cat. More pets went missing. In October, he bought two dogs from the ASPCA for $15 a piece. On October 20, he tried driving out of a gas station without paying for $20 of petrol. After being stopped and questioned, he was allowed to drive on.

He bought more dogs and tormented a family who had placed an ad in a newspaper asking if anyone had seen their missing pooch. Meanwhile police reports of missing pets backed up. He then began taking pot shots at the home of the Phares family. They lived across the street from Ambrose Griffin. Chase kept a cutting from the *Sacramento Bee* about the murder.

CONFESSING ALL

Earlier on January 23, the day he killed Terry Wallin, he was spotted entering the home of a neighbour, but escaped before the police arrived. Entering a nearby house, he stole a few items, urinated on clothes in a drawer and defecated in a child's cot.

An hour later he was at the shopping centre where he met the woman who had known him at high school. After she snubbed him, he left the shopping centre, entered the Wallins' home and killed Terry.

Chase was uncooperative with the police, but began confessing all to a prison psychiatrist. On May 6, 1979, he went on trial for six counts of first-degree murder. Again he confessed. His excuse was that he was being poisoned via his soap dish. The toxin pulverized the blood so he had to drink more fresh blood to stay alive. Rambling on about the Nazis and UFOs, he claimed that he had murdered in self-defence.

On death row, the other inmates taunted him. He saved up his antidepressant pills and killed himself with an overdose in San Quentin State Prison on December 26, 1980, at age thirty.

4

RICHARD COTTINGHAM
The Torso Killer

He seemed an unlikely serial killer. Thirty-four-year-old Richard Cottingham was a married father-of-three living in suburban Bergen County, New Jersey, just over the George Washington Bridge from Manhattan. Neighbours described him as a doting father who always took his children out "trick-or-treating" on Halloween.

He had been a high-school athlete and was the son of an insurance executive. He followed his father into the business. For sixteen years he had worked as a computer technician at Empire Blue Cross Blue Shield, a medical insurance company on Third Avenue in midtown

Manhattan, where he was considered a valued and dependable employee.

However, in April 1980, Cottingham's wife had filed for divorce, alleging "extreme cruelty" and his refusal to engage in marital sex since late 1976. She said Cottingham was an habitual patron of gay bars and homosexual bathhouses in Manhattan.

DUMPED NAKED

In reality, he spent his time targeting prostitutes. Cottingham would pick up his victims in bars or on the streets of Manhattan. Then he would buy them drinks or dinner and spike their glass with a date-rape drug. Once he got his semiconscious victim to his car, he would drive them across the Hudson River to New Jersey and take them to one of the cheap motels that lined the highways there.

He would carry them in through the back door, then molest and torture them. Lucky ones would wake up to find they had been raped and sodomized and covered with horrific wounds. They would either have been left on the floor of the motel room or dumped naked by a roadside with little memory of what had happened.

Cottingham did not care whether his victim lived or died. He got his pleasure from torturing his victim. If they died before he was satisfied, he would continue abusing their corpse until he was done. Then he would abandon the victim like trash, whether she was alive or dead.

FEMALE TORSOS

The police did not realize that they had a serial killer on their hands until he moved the crime scene to Manhattan. On December 2, 1979, firefighters were called to a rundown hotel near Times Square where one of the rooms was on fire. Once they had doused the flames, they discovered two female torsos. Both were missing their heads and hands, which were never found.

The victims' clothes were found neatly folded in the bathtub with their then-fashionable platform shoes topping each pile. Except for blood soaked into the mattresses, the hotel room was remarkably free of any bloodstains, fingerprints or any other evidence. The killer had taken with him the weapon he had used to kill them and dismember the bodies. Aside from the mutilation, the bodies showed signs of horrific torture. There were cigarette burns, welts from beatings, and bite marks around the breasts.

From x-rays, one was identified as Deedeh Goodarzi, a twenty-two-year-old immigrant from Kuwait who was working as a prostitute to support her four-month-old baby. The other victim was never identified, though she appeared to be a teenager.

Although there was little to go on, detectives linked the killings to the case of teenage hooker Helen Sikes who had disappeared from Times Square in January 1979. Her torso turned up in Queens with her throat slashed so deeply that she was nearly decapitated. Her severed legs were found a block away laid side-by-side as if still attached to the body.

CLEAR-CUT CONNECTIONS

Then on May 5, 1980, nineteen-year-old prostitute Valerie Street was found beaten and strangled, and jammed under a bed at a Quality Inn in Hasbrouck Heights, New Jersey. She had been savagely beaten and her breasts had been gnawed so violently that one nipple was nearly severed. Around her mouth were traces of the adhesive tape used to gag her. The tape had been taken away, but the handcuffs used to restrain her had been left. A fingerprint was found on the inner ratchet.

Detectives recalled that the body of twenty-six-year-old radiologist Mary Ann Carr had been dumped by a chain-link fence near the parking lot of the same motel on December 16, 1977. She had been beaten with a blunt instrument. Her body was covered in bites and bruises, and there were cuts to her chest and legs. Her wrists showed marks from handcuffs and there were traces of adhesive tape around her mouth too. The connections were clear-cut but took them no nearer to finding the killer.

On May 15, twenty-five-year-old prostitute Jean Reyner was found in the Seville Hotel on 29th Street near Times Square. She had been stabbed to death. Her breasts had been hacked off and set down side-by-side on the headboard, then the room had been set on fire.

ESCAPING THE PIMPS

A week later, Cottingham was arrested. On May 22, 1980, he had picked up eighteen-year-old Leslie Ann O'Dell, who was soliciting on the corner of Lexington Avenue and 25th Street. She had arrived in New York on a bus from Washington state four days earlier and was quickly lured into prostitution by pimps at the bus station.

Cottingham appeared kind. He bought her drinks and told her about his job and his house in the suburbs. It was about 3:00 a.m. when he then offered to take her to the bus terminal in New Jersey to escape the pimps in Manhattan. Leslie eagerly accepted.

After crossing the George Washington Bridge, he bought her a steak at an all-night diner. She then agreed to have sex with him for $100. It was around dawn when they checked into the same Quality Inn in Hasbrouck Heights where he had left the mutilated body of Valerie Street eighteen days earlier. But no-one at reception recognized Cottingham.

After securing a room, Cottingham drove around the back of the motel and they entered through the rear door. Leaving the girl in the room, Cottingham returned to his car. He came back carrying a paper bag containing a bottle of whiskey and an attaché case. It was then nearly 5:00 a.m.

TORTURE AT KNIFE POINT

He offered to give her a massage and she rolled over onto her stomach. Straddling her, he pulled a knife from the attaché case and put it to her throat, then snapped a pair of handcuffs on her wrists. While Leslie tried to persuade Cottingham that this was unnecessary as she would do what he wanted anyway, he began torturing her, nearly biting off one of her nipples.

She later testified that he said: "You have to take it. The other girls did, you have to take it too. You're a whore and you have to be punished."

The motel staff heard a girl screaming and called the police. When they arrived they caught a man trying to flee the room. Entering the room they found a young woman handcuffed to the bed. She was in hysterics, saying she had been beaten, raped, sodomized, and forced at knife point to give the man oral sex. He had stabbed her and bitten almost right through her nipples.

Although Cottingham denied everything, when he was arrested he was carrying handcuffs, a leather gag, two slave collars, a switchblade, a replica pistol, and a large number of pills. In the basement of his house the police found a trophy room where he kept some personal effects of his victims.

ONE HUNDRED HOMICIDES

In the case of Leslie Ann O'Dell, he was charged with

kidnapping, attempted murder, aggravated assault, aggravated assault with deadly weapon, three counts of aggravated sexual assault while armed for rape, sodomy and forced fellatio, possession of a weapon, possession of controlled dangerous substances, Secobarbital and Amobarbital, or Tuinal, and possession of controlled dangerous substance, Diazepam or Valium.

Conviction on those charges alone earned him 173 to 197 years in prison. In the trials in New Jersey and New York that followed, he was also found guilty of four second-degree murders. These brought him another twenty years, and seventy-five years to life. In 2010 he pleaded guilty to the 1967 murder of twenty-nine-year-old housewife Nancy Vogel, whose naked body was found bound in her car. They had been neighbours and knew each other.

In 2021, he pleaded guilty to kidnapping, raping and drowning a pair of teenage girls in 1974. He also confessed to three murders of New Jersey school girls in 1968 – 69 in return for immunity from prosecution. Though he claimed to be responsible for up to one hundred homicides, he has only been officially linked to eleven.

"I have a problem with women," he said.

5

JOSEPH JAMES DEÁNGELO
The Golden State Killer

Wifile "The Night Stalker" Richard Ramirez, who terrorized southern California in 1985, languished on death row in San Quentin, "The Original Night Stalker" remained at large. He had started out as the "East Area Rapist", then became the "Orange Coast Serial Killer", before being dubbed "The Original Night Stalker" because his *modus operandi* closely resembled that of Ramirez, raping and killing his victims in their own homes.

As the East Area Rapist he committed fifty rapes in northern California between 1976 and 1986 and killed at least thirteen. He began by raping women who were at home alone. Victims included a sixteen-year-old girl and an eighteen-year-old youth who he shot in the stomach when he confronted the prowler.

A reward of $2,500 was offered for information leading to his arrest. That was later increased to $25,000, with a local dentist adding $10,000 to the $15,000 offered by the *Sacramento Bee*.

SEXUAL ASSAULTS

The suspect attacked single storey, single family dwellings in middle-class neighbourhoods, usually where there was open ground nearby so he could make his approach and his exit without being spotted. Entering at night through a sliding glass door or window, he threatened the victim with a knife, gun or club, then tied them up.

He would prolong his attacks for between one and three hours in the house, sexually assaulting the victim several times. In between the assaults, he would wander about the house eating and drinking, looking through photograph albums and lingerie drawers, and stealing small items.

In one case, he raped two sisters who were at home alone together. He also molested a thirteen-year-old girl while her mother was tied up, and raped a fifteen-year-old babysitter in front of her eight-year-old ward.

After April 1977 he began attacking couples. The male was left bound on the floor with perfume bottles or dishes on top of him while he raped the female, warning if a bottle fell or the dishes rattled, he would kill both of them. It became plain to the police that the attacker had detailed knowledge of the movements and schedules of his victims.

CONFRONTING THE PROWLER

On May 7, 1977, while attacking a couple in Carmichael, a suburb of Sacramento, the rapist said that he would kill his next two victims. This was what the police had long feared. But he stayed his hand when he attacked a couple in the South Area of Sacramento, near the office of the dentist who had put up the $10,000 reward. Sales of guns and locks soared.

Old footprints from herringbone-pattern tennis shoes were discovered under the bathroom window in numerous cases where he could have overheard conversations. He also returned to the same area repeatedly, making maximum use of the intelligence he had gathered.

The police almost caught the attacker on December 12, 1977, when officers spotted a man wearing a ski mask on a stolen bicycle on the Watt Avenue Bridge in East Sacramento. He was seen again two hours later by city patrolmen near an apartment complex on La Riviera Drive near Watt, a place where he had struck three times before.

As the rapes increased in number, he grew more violent and threatening. Then on February 2, 1978, he shot dead Brian K. Maggiore, a sergeant at Rancho Cordova Air Force Base, and his wife of eighteen months Katie when they confronted a prowler. The suspect was spotted by residents as he fled the scene.

EXTREME VIOLENCE

He then moved on to Stockton, Modesto, Danville, Fremont, Concord, San Ramon, Davis, and Walnut Creek, attacking couples and, occasionally, women on their own. A student at UC Davis was attacked in her apartment with extreme violence on June 7, 1978. A month later another woman was attacked in Davis and raped in front of her two sons. And on June 25, 1979, a thirteen-year-old girl was attacked while her parents were at home asleep.

On October 1, 1979, a man in a ski mask entered the home of a couple in Goleta, Santa Barbara County. They were awakened with a flashlight shining in their eyes. The woman was ordered to tie up her boyfriend with cord that the attacker had brought with him. While the masked intruder ransacked the house, the woman tried to escape.

The intruder pulled her back inside. While he was doing this, the man escaped into the backyard. As the intruder pursued the man, the woman escaped again, running to a neighbour who had been woken by her screams. The intruder then fled on a bicycle down a creek bed.

CHINESE KNOT

Two months later, on December 30, 1979, another couple was attacked a few blocks away. Dr Robert Offerman and Debra Alexandria Manning were found shot dead. Both of them were tied up and Manning had been raped. Neighbours who heard the gunshots dismissed them as firecrackers.

On March 13, 1980, the Stalker moved down the coast to Ventura, where he killed Lyman and Charlene Smith. Charlene was raped and both were bludgeoned to death. They were found by their twelve-year-old son. Their wrists and ankles had been tied using an ornate "Chinese knot."

Keith and Patrice Harrington were the next to die, also bludgeoned to death in their home in Dana Point on August 19, as the killer moved south of Los Angeles for the first time. Patrice had been brutally raped. Law enforcement agencies theorized that the male victims had been bludgeoned to death first to terrify female victims who were raped before they were killed too.

Next the killer attacked twenty-eight-year-old Manuela Witthuhn on February 5, 1981, while her husband was ill in the hospital. Her killer entered her home in Irvine, Orange County. He raped her and beat her to death. As in the Smith's case, burnt matches were found in Witthuhn's home.

Cheri Domingo and Gregory Sanchez were killed on July 27, 1981, in Goleta, just a half-mile from the scene of the Offerman-Manning murders. Sanchez had been shot once in the face, then bludgeoned. Cheri Domingo was bludgeoned. The attacker's familiarity with the area lead police to believe he lived nearby.

BEATEN TO DEATH

Then for five years, the killer lay low. He struck one last time on May 4, 1986, killing Janelle Lisa Cruz only a mile from Witthuhn's home in Irvine. Her family was away on vacation in Mexico at the time. Cruz was raped and beaten to death like the previous victims shortly after a male friend left her house.

It was not until 2001 that his rapes as the East Area Rapist earlier and his murders as the Original Night Stalker, then known as the Golden State Killer, were linked by DNA evidence. It is thought that this prodigious criminal committed many other crimes, including two other home-invasion attacks where couples were killed in Goleta, California, from 1979 to 1981. In these crimes, a gun and bludgeoning were used and the victims were bound, but no sexual assault took place.

DeÁngelo was eventually identified on April 24, 2018, when one of his relatives sent a DNA sample to a heritage site. Detectives trawled through the family tree and via forensic genetic genealogy they ruled out other family members until only Joseph James DeÁngelo was left. On August 21, 2020, DeÁngelo was sentenced to twelve life sentences, plus eight years without the possibility of parole.

6

ED GEIN
The Plainfield Ghoul

Although by serial-killer standards he did not kill many people, Ed Gein is one of the most celebrated murderers to grace the silver screen. He is the inspiration behind Norman Bates in Alfred Hitchcock's thriller *Psycho*, Leatherface in *The Texas Chainsaw Massacre* and Buffalo Bill in *The Silence of the Lambs*.

The horror of what he had done was discovered by Sheriff Arthur Schley on the evening of November 17, 1957, when he was investigating the disappearance of fifty-eight-year-old shopkeeper Bernice Worden who had gone missing from her hardware store in Plainfield,

Wisconsin. The cash register was missing and there was blood on the floor. Beside it was a receipt made out to fifty-one-year-old Ed Gein.

UNHAPPY IN HIS OWN SKIN

Sheriff Schley drove out to Gein's remote farmhouse, he was not in but Schley had a search warrant. Inside, the place was a complete mess with sacks full of garbage everywhere. Making his way through the trash-strewn kitchen, Schley brushed against something in the dark. When he turned his flashlight on it, he discovered a carcass hanging upside down from a ceiling beam. It had been decapitated, slit open and gutted like a deer in hunting season. But this was no deer. This was Mrs Worden.

The headless body of the butchered woman was only the beginning. Elsewhere in the house her head was found in a burlap sack. Nails through her ears had a string tied to them so they could be hung up as a gruesome trophy. Elsewhere there was a bowl made from the top of a human skull. There were lampshades, a wastepaper bin and a chair made from human skin. Masks were made from faces peeled from cadavers. Gein had skulls on his bedposts.

There were ten female skulls with the tops sawn off, human organs in the refrigerator, a belt make from female nipples, nine vulvas in a shoe box, four severed noses, and a pair of lips on the drawstring of a window shade. Most bizarrely of all, there was a suit made from a female skin complete with breasts and vulva, which Gein wore so he could feel what it was like to be a woman.

Detectives did not know how many murders to charge him with.

GRAVE ROBBER

Later Gein admitted to killing fifty-four-year-old tavern owner Mary Hogan who, like Mrs Worden, had been shot with a .22 rifle and butchered. The other bodies, he said, had come from local graveyards. Gein would read the obituaries pages of the local papers so he would know where to find fresh corpses. He and a friend named Gus would dig them up at night. Gein said he had only begun killing when Gus was sent to an old people's home and he could not undertake the exertion of exhumation by himself.

Gein could not remember details of the murders. He said that he went into a daze-like trance. That happened during his grave-robbing missions too. Sometimes, he said, he went into the daze while in the cemetery and came home empty-handed. Later graves that Gein said he had interfered with were revisited by the authorities. Body parts and sometimes whole bodies were missing, substantiating Gein's story.

There were also other missing people in the area. Eight-year-old Georgia Weckler had gone missing on her way home from school and fifteen-year-old Evelyn Hartley had been abducted while babysitting. Also listed as missing were two deer hunters, Victor Travis and Ray Burgess, who vanished in December 1952. However, all the body parts found around Gein's farmhouse were of adult women. He said he did not have sex with the corpses because "they smelled too bad."

While he could not remember the details of his crimes, he was clear about his motivation. After his beloved mother died, he wanted to change sex. This was when he began making skin-suits stripped from bodies of women who resembled his mother and wearing them around the house.

INSTRUMENTS OF THE DEVIL

Gein's mother Augusta seems to be the cause of all his problems. She was a martinet who ran a small grocery store in Plainfield. She had a deep contempt for her husband George – a weak character with a drink problem – but stayed with him because of her religious objections to divorce. They had two children – Henry and Ed who was seven years younger. A fervent Lutheran she believed that the world was innately immoral and all women were prostitutes and instruments of the devil.

When she had saved up enough money, she bought a 195-acre farm a quarter-of-a-mile from the nearest habitation so that she could protect her sons from the evils of the world and stop them turning into wastrels like their father. She imbued them with her strict moral code and read the Bible to them daily, usually passages where a vengeful god took divine retribution on sinners.

Ed was shy and effeminate and did not do well at school. He looked up to his older brother as a man of strong character and a hard worker. They did odd jobs around Plainfield and Ed did some babysitting. He seemed to get on better with children than with his own peer group. He was considered reliable and trustworthy, and brought in much needed income after their father died in 1940.

As he grew older Henry sought freedom from the stern discipline his mother imposed. He openly mocked her behind her back. In March 1944, a bush fire threatened the farm. Henry and Ed went their separate ways in an attempt to stamp it out. By the end of the day, Henry had disappeared. Ed called the police, asking them to organize a search party. But when the police arrived, Ed took them directly to Henry's body. There was some bruising to his head and he lay on a piece of ground untouched by the fire, but the county coroner recorded the cause of death as asphyxiation.

Ed was now alone with his mother. She would alternately chastise him and dote on him, even letting him sleep with her in her bed. Augusta finally died on December 29, 1945, when Ed was thirty-nine. He boarded up the rooms that she had lived in – the parlour, the living room and the entire upper floor – and confined himself to the kitchen and a small utility room which he converted into a bedroom.

COME SEE THE GHOUL CAR!

Lonely Ed spent his spare time reading pulp magazines and anatomy books. He became obsessed with the Nazis, head-hunters, and shipwrecks. The occasional visitor to the farm spotted some of Gein's bizarre collection, but he passed them off as shrunken heads brought back from the South Seas by cousins who had fought in World War II or ghoulish Halloween costumes.

After Sheriff Schley's discoveries, Gein was arrested but found mentally unfit to plead. During questioning, Schley, traumatized by the horror of Gein's crimes, banged Gein's head and face into the wall, rendering his first confession inadmissible. Nevertheless, Gein was sent to the Central State Hospital for the Criminally Insane. While he was there the farmhouse burned down. Gein commented: "Just as well."

Gein's possessions that survived the fire were sold off as grim mementoes. These included his 1949 sedan which was exhibited at state fairs, displayed under the banner: "Come and see the Ghoul Car, in which Ed Gein transported his victims." Visitors paid twenty-five cents for the privilege.

By November 1968, Gein was found to be well enough to stand trial. After a week he was found guilty of first-degree murder. Schley died of a heart attack shortly after the ordeal of giving his testimony. Gein was sentenced to spend the rest of his life in a mental hospital where he was a model patient. He died of cancer in 1984 and was buried next to his mother, near some of the graves he had desecrated. His headstone was later vandalized.

7

ISRAEL KEYES
The Anchorage Killer

Confessing to as many as twelve murders, Israel Keyes was asked why he did it. He replied: "Why not?" His motivation was enjoyment, said Monique Doll, an Anchorage homicide detective who worked on the case. "Israel Keyes didn't kidnap and kill people because he was crazy," she told a news conference, "He didn't kidnap and kill people because his deity told him to or because he had a bad childhood. Israel Keyes did this because he got an immense amount of enjoyment out of it, much like an addict gets an immense amount of enjoyment out of drugs."

He also preferred flying below the radar and off the grid, officials said. An admirer of Ted Bundy, he targeted total strangers, avoiding anyone he had any possible connection to, travelling hundreds of miles to target random victims in secluded parks and other remote locations. Keyes told investigators, "Once I started, you know ... there was nothing else like it."

KILLING KITS

Born in 1978, Israel Keyes grew up in Washington state in a fundamentalist Christian family that attended a white-supremacist, anti-Semitic church. Later they moved out of the region and became affiliated with other congregations. Keyes admitted torturing animals as a child and raping a teenager in Oregon in the late 1990s. He managed to lure the girl, aged between fourteen and eighteen, away from her friends. He had intended to kill her, but in the end let her go.

Keyes served in the US Army between 1998 and 2000, but quit so that he could travel freely and commit murder. He worked as a handyman, paying for his travel with burglary and robbing banks. In 2007, he moved to Anchorage, Alaska, with his girlfriend and their daughter, where he set up a construction business.

He hid secret "killing kits" near his home in Anchorage and in New York state, where he had a rundown cabin on ten acres of land. The kit found in Alaska included a shovel, plastic bags, and bottles of Drano, which he told authorities would speed the decomposition of bodies. The kit found in upstate New York contained weapon parts, a silencer, ligatures, ammunition, and garbage bags. Keyes said other kits were hidden in Washington state, Wyoming, Texas, and somewhere in the Southwest, possibly Arizona. There was also one in Vermont, which he had hidden two years before he went on to commit a double murder nearby.

KILLING SAMANTHA KOENIG

But despite all his meticulous planning, he got careless one night when his desire to kill was too much for him. On the spur of the moment, on February 1, 2012, he kidnapped eighteen-year-old barista Samantha Koenig in Anchorage. CCTV footage caught him approaching her coffee kiosk as she was closing up at around 8:00 p.m. and ordering an Americano.

While Koenig was making the coffee, he pulled a gun. He climbed into the kiosk and bound her hands behind her back with zip ties, before leading her out. She had not pushed the panic button because he told her that he would let her go if her parents paid a ransom. This was never his intention.

The FBI said Koenig broke away trying to escape. Keyes chased her and tackled her to bring her to the ground. Pointing his gun at her, he said she should not do anything to make him kill her.

More video footage showed him forcing her into the back of his 2004 Chevrolet Silverado in the parking lot of Home Depot. The police drew up a list of 750 white trucks of the same make in the area, but the licence plate, toolboxes, and a ladder rack he usually carried had been removed before the abduction. They were reinstalled afterwards, effectively disguising the vehicle.

Samantha Koenig was sexually assaulted and strangled. Her body was left in a cold shed for two weeks while her killer went on a cruise.

EYES SEWN OPEN

When he returned, he photographed her posed body with her eyes sewn open to make it look like she was still alive, alongside an issue of the *Anchorage Daily News* dated February 13, twelve days after the abduction. On the back of the photograph he wrote a ransom note demanding $30,000 from her family.

He then sent a text to her boyfriend from her cell phone telling him where to find the note in a nearby dog park. At other times, the batteries were removed from the cell phone so it could not be traced. He dismembered her corpse and over the course of a three-day "fishing trip" he dropped the weighed down, chopped up body parts into the frozen Matanuska Lake, north of Anchorage, through a hole he had cut in the ice with a chainsaw.

Then he made the mistake of using her debit card. Even though he was 4,000 miles away from Anchorage, his rental car was caught on video when he was using the card at an ATM in Texas. Then he was stopped for speeding, federal agents were already on his trail.

Extradited back to Alaska, he admitted a series of burglaries, bank robberies, and murders, although he fell silent after his name was leaked to the press.

The authorities had difficulty identifying all the murder victims as Keyes rarely knew who they were. But he did give the names of a married couple in Vermont. They were Bill and Lorraine Currier who lived in Essex, Vermont, and had been missing for some time.

PULLING THE TRIGGER

Keyes had flown from Anchorage to Chicago and then started driving. He was going to kill someone ... he just didn't know who or where. A thousand miles east of Chicago he stayed at a hotel in Essex, Vermont, where a few years before he had buried a killing kit. He dug up the weapons and went out looking for victims.

Keyes said: "I decided I was going to look for a house with a couple in it ... I was looking for a fairly easy way to get into the garage. And theirs was the first house I found that had all those things." There was no evidence of children or a dog, and he was familiar with that style of house. He knew where the master bedroom was, and the attached garage gave easy access to the house.

Keyes broke into the house through the garage and into the Curriers' bedroom on June 8, 2011. He bound the couple with zip ties, forced them into their car, and drove them to an abandoned farmhouse. The Curriers fought for their lives.

Bill Currier broke free and started a struggle with Keyes who later said in a police interview: "So, I knew I was going to have to knock him out or just kill him … He saw the gun. And he started to say something, and it just pissed me off and I just started pulling the trigger." After the killing Keyes sexually assaulted and strangled Lorraine, and left the bodies in the abandoned farmhouse basement.

The farmhouse had since been torn down and taken to a landfill site. So the bodies were never found despite a ten to twelve week search. However, Samantha Koenig's body was recovered from the frozen lake. It took the FBI's dive team ten hours to recover all the body parts on April 2, 2012.

IDEAS FROM THE WILDERNESS

To get into the mind of Israel Keyes, you have to go back to the remote wilderness of Washington state where he grew up poor in a large family. Keyes said, "For as far back as I can remember, you know, that's where I get a lot of the ideas. Either fishing or out hunting. … See somebody in the woods …"

After an exemplary three years in the army, Keyes settled down and married a member of the Makah tribe in Neah Bay, at the farthest northwestern tip of Washington state. They started a family. Superficially he was a great family guy, a smart guy, a gifted carpenter, an upstanding member of the community, but beneath the surface he was always a killer.

Keyes said in 2012: " I would do something *[a murder]* and then I would go back like business as usual and go out with friends, go out to bars … You know, for all the years they've known me, they actually don't know me at all, really."

In the annals of serial killers, Israel Keyes is a rare bird. He was never convicted of murder and he went on to administer his own capital punishment. On December 1, 2012, while awaiting trial in the Anchorage Correctional Complex, he slit his wrist and strangled himself. He was thirty-four when he died. With no one to try, the case had to be dropped.

8

SAMUEL LITTLE
America's Most Prolific Serial Killer?

Convicted in 2014 for three murders in Los Angeles a quarter of a century earlier, Samuel Little was sentenced to life imprisonment without the possibility of parole. While Little still protested his innocence, detectives across the US had opened their cold-case files and in 2018 Little began confessing to more slayings, boasting in the end that he had killed more that ninety-three victims which would have made him America's most prolific serial killer. However, the authorities could only link him to sixty-one, just eight of which have been confirmed.

VIOLENT STREAK

Born in 1940, Little was a poor student and was first convicted for burglary in Omaha, Nebraska, at the age of sixteen. This earned him time in an institution for juvenile offenders. Only months after he was released, he was arrested again for breaking and entering.

Having been brought up by his grandmother in Lorain, Ohio, Little went to live with his mother in Florida in his late twenties. Using the name Samuel McDowell, he began travelling more widely and often had run-ins with the law. Between 1971 and 1975, Little was arrested twenty-six times in eleven states for crimes that included assault, armed robbery, rape, theft, solicitation of a prostitute, breaking and entering, shoplifting, driving under the influence, aggravated assault on a police officer, and fraud. Always displaying a "dark, violent streak" in his crimes, one veteran detective said that Little had "the craziest rap sheet I've ever seen".

Then in 1976, Pamela Kay Smith knocked on the back door of a home in Sunset Hills, Missouri. She was naked from the waist down and her hands were tied behind her back with electrical cable.

The homeowners called 911 and Smith told the police that Little had attacked her. He had picked her up in St Louis, some fifteen miles away. She said he had choked her with the cable, forced her into his car, beat her until she was unconscious, then drove her to Sunset Hills where he raped her.

Little was found sitting in his car nearby with items of her clothing and jewellery. He denied raping her, telling officers: "I only beat her." He was found guilty of assault with the intent to ravish-rape and was sentenced to just three months in the county jail.

UNBURIED IN A CEMETERY

In October 1982, the skeletal remains of twenty-two-year-old Melinda "Mindy" LaPree were found unburied in a cemetery in Gautier, Mississippi. She was last seen in nearby Pascagoula a month before, getting into a brown wood-panelled station wagon with a man identified as Little. During the investigation two prostitutes came forward, saying they had also been assaulted by Little.

In November, Little was arrested for shoplifting. The police spotted he matched the description of the suspect in the LaPree slaying. He was charged with murder and the aggravated assaults of the two prostitutes, but a grand jury failed to indict him.

He was extradited to Florida to face another murder charge. In September 1982, the body of twenty-six-year-old Patricia Ann Mount had been found in the countryside outside Gainesville. Mount, who was mentally disabled, was last seen leaving a tavern with a man identified as Little in a wood-panelled station wagon.

However, the trial hinged on hairs found on Mount's

clothes that "had the same characteristics as head hairs taken from" Little. But when cross-examined the forensic analyst said: "It was also possible for hairs to be transferred if two people bumped together." Little was acquitted.

In October 1984, Little was back in custody in San Diego, accused of the attempted murder of two prostitutes who were kidnapped a month apart. They had been driven to the same abandoned dirt lot, assaulted and choked. The first woman was left unconscious on a pile of trash, but survived. Officers found Little in a car with the second woman and arrested him.

The two cases were tried together, but the jury failed to reach a verdict. Pleading guilty to lesser charges of assault with great bodily injury and false imprisonment, Little served about thirty months of a four-year sentence and was released on parole in February 1987.

He then moved to Los Angeles, and soon after two women were found dead. They were forty-one-year-old Carol Alford, found in an alley in South LA, and thirty-five-year-old Audrey Nelson, dumped in a trash can downtown. Both had been strangled and were naked below the waist. In 1989, forty-six-year-old Guadalupe Apodaca was found dead in similar circumstances in an abandoned garage. DNA was collected from the bodies.

DEAD WHITE GIRL

For the next sixteen years, Little continued to have brushes with the law in seven states for numerous offences, but evaded justice by moving on. It was not until 2012 that the LAPD matched the DNA in the Alford, Nelson, and Apodaca murder cases to Little. Then, early in 2013, he was arrested for the possession of a crack pipe at a homeless shelter in Louisville, Kentucky. Charged with three counts of murder, he was returned to California.

The scope of the trial was broadened when two prostitutes testified about their narrow escapes from Little. In her early twenties, Leila Johnson escaped strangling to flee topless into heavy shipyard traffic in November 1981. She did not report her attack at the time.

Another Pascagoula prostitute who sought anonymity was badly injured. In July 1980, she said he entered her home, knocked her unconscious, pulled a scarf tightly around her neck, and tried to drown her in a bathtub.

"I guess the only reason he didn't kill me is because a friend of mine came and knocked on my door," she said.

Her case was not investigated, however, until a dead white girl turned up two years later. That was Mindy LaPree whose murder case was re-opened in Mississippi. Little was then being investigated for the murder of sixty women in various states.

Four years after his first murder convictions, Little began making his confessions in exchange for a transfer out of the Los Angeles County prison.

NO STOPPING HIM

Once Little started confessing, there was no stopping him. He admitted strangling Melissa Thomas in Opelousas, Louisiana, in 1996. He pleaded guilty to the murder of Denise Christie Brothers in Odessa, Texas, in 1994 and was given another life sentence. He admitted murdering twenty-three-year-old Brenda Alexander, whose naked body was found on a dirt road in Phenix City, Alabama, in 1979.

In Macon, Georgia, he said he had strangled eighteen-year-old Fredonia Smith and an unidentified woman in 1977. Little also confessed to the 1982 murder of fifty-five-year-old Dorothy Richards and the 1996 murder of forty-year-old Daisy McGuire. Their bodies were found in Houma, Louisiana.

Little strangled thirty-six-year-old mother-of-four Julia Critchfield in Harrison County, Mississippi, in 1978 and her body was dumped off a cliff. He admitted to killing forty-six-year-old Nancy Carol Stevens in Tupelo, Mississippi, nineteen-year-old Evelyn Weston, whose body was found near Fort Jackson, South Carolina, in 1978, and twenty-year-old Rosie Hill in Marion County, Florida, in 1982.

In 2018, the FBI's Violent Criminal Apprehension Program team had confirmed thirty-four of Little's confessions and was working to match the remainder of the known murders or suspicious deaths, though Little often did not know the name or age of the victim.

In December 2018, Little was indicted for the murder of twenty-three-year-old Linda Sue Boards in Warren Country, Kentucky, in May 1981. In May 2019, he was indicted on four counts of aggravated murder and six counts of kidnapping in Cuyahoga County, Ohio.

Serving three consecutive life sentences, Samuel Little died in prison in 2020, he was eighty years old.

9

RICHARD RAMIREZ
The Night Stalker

Richard Ramirez, the Night Stalker who terrorized Los Angeles for two years in the 1980s, was a devil worshipper. A scrawled pentagram – a satanic symbol – was his calling card and he made his rape victims declare their love of Satan before he slaughtered them.

The Night Stalker's murder career began ordinarily enough. On the night of June 28, 1984, the mutilated body of seventy-nine-year-old Jennie Vincow was found spread-eagled on the bed of her one-bedroom apartment in the Eagle Rock district of Los Angeles. She had been raped and her throat had been slashed so violently that she had almost been decapitated. There was blood on the walls of the bedroom and bathroom, and her flat had been ransacked.

HIGHWAY TO HELL

Nine months later the killer struck again. Maria Hernandez had just parked her car in her garage in the Rosemeade suburb of Los Angeles and was walking towards her apartment when she heard footsteps behind her. She turned to be confronted by a man with a gun. He shot her but, miraculously, the bullet ricocheted off her car keys. Even so, the impact of the bullet was enough to knock her to the ground. The gunman gave her a vicious kicking and made his way into her apartment. From inside, Maria heard a gunshot. She staggered to her feet, only to be confronted by the gunman running from the house.

"Please don't shoot me again," she begged. The gunman took to his heels.

Inside the apartment Maria Hernandez found her boyfriend, thirty-four-year-old Hawaiian-born traffic manager Dayle Okazaki, lying dead on the kitchen floor, shot through the head.

There was only one clue to the murder. The gunman had worn a baseball cap with an AC/DC logo. The Australian rock band had recently released an album called *Highway to Hell*. On it, there was a track called "Night Prowler". This was the alias Ramirez preferred. He was annoyed that the newspapers insisted on calling him The Night Stalker.

Less than an hour later, on his way home, the killer pulled thirty-year-old Taiwanese law student Tsai Lian Yu from her car and shot her repeatedly. She died before the ambulance arrived.

EYES GOUGED OUT

Ten days later, Ramirez entered the home of Vincent and Maxine Zazzara, half a mile from the San Gabriel freeway. Maxine was a successful lawyer and Vincent had just fulfilled a lifetime ambition to open his own pizzeria. Both of them were shot at point-blank range and Maxine Zazzara's naked body was mutilated after death. Ramirez stabbed her repeatedly and gouged her eyes out. The bodies were found by their son Peter when he called in at the house the next day.

On May 14, Ramirez broke into the home of William and Lillie Doi. He shot sixty-six-year-old William in the head while he lay sleeping. His wife, sixty-three-year-old Lillie who was in bed next to him, was beaten repeatedly around the head. Then he handcuffed her and ransacked the house. Later he returned to rape her.

INVERTED PENTAGRAM

A fortnight later, eighty-three-year-old Mabel Bell and her eighty-year-old sister Florence Long, an invalid, were attacked in their home in the suburb of Monrovia. Two days later their gardener Carlos Venwezala dropped round. He found Florence lying on her bed in a coma.

Mabel was lying on the bedroom floor in a pool of her own blood. Both women had been beaten with a hammer. They had been cut and tortured. There were even signs that Ramirez had tried to rape Mabel, who died six weeks after the attack.

Along with the hammer, the attacker had left a half-eaten banana on the dining table. He had also left what was to become his trademark – an inverted pentagram, the encircled five-point star that is used in witchcraft. One was scrawled in lipstick on Mabel's thigh. Another was drawn on Florence's bedroom wall.

The next day, Carol Kyle was awoken in her Burbank flat by a torch shining in her eyes. A man pointed a gun at her and dragged her out of bed. In the next room, Carol's terrified twelve-year-old son was handcuffed and locked in a cupboard, as the intruder raped his mother.

"You must have had a very unhappy life to have done this to me," she said to him. He trashed the apartment looking for valuables, before finally departing and leaving Carol and her son alive.

On the night of June 27, 1985, Ramirez slashed the throat of thirty-two-year-old Patty Elaine Higgins in her home in Arcadia. The same fate befell Mary Louise Cannon five days later. Three days afterwards, again in Arcadia, Ramirez savagely beat sixteen-year-old Whitney Bennett with a crowbar. She survived.

On July 7, Ramirez turned his attention back to Monterey Park, where Tsai Lian Yu and William and Lillie Doi had been attacked. Sixty-one-year-old Joyce Lucille Nelson was found beaten to death in her home and sixty-three-year-old Sophie Dickmann was raped and robbed in her apartment.

On July 20, Ramirez murdered sixty-six-year-old Maxson Kneiding and his sixty-four-year-old wife Lela in their Glendale home, then went on to murder thirty-two-year-old Chainarong Khovananth at his home in Sun Valley. After shooting him as he lay asleep in his bed, Ramirez raped and beat Chainarong's twenty-nine-year-old wife Somkid. He forced her to perform oral sex on him and stole $30,000 in cash and jewellery. Forcing Somkid to swear in Satan's name that she would not cry out, he raped their eight-year-old son.

JACK THE KNIFE

The police had concluded long ago that they had a serial killer on their hands. The problem was that he had no clear *modus operandi*. He killed with guns, hammers, and knives. He raped orally, anally, and genitally both children and women, young and old. The LAPD quipped that he was an equal-opportunity monster.

On the night of August 5, postal worker Virginia Petersen was woken by the sound of an intruder. She sat up in bed and cried out: "Who are you? What do you want?"

The burglar laughed, then shot her in the face. Miraculously, she survived.

Her husband Christopher, who was lying beside her, was woken by the shot. He leapt to his wife's defence. This earned him a bullet in the temple. Nevertheless he dived out of bed. The intruder panicked and ran.

Three days later, Ramirez shot another thirty-five-year-old Asian man and beat and raped his twenty-six-year-old wife, but left their two young children unharmed.

Gun shops in Los Angeles quickly sold out and local residents set up neighbourhood watch committees. So Ramirez took a vacation in San Francisco. On the night of August 17, he attacked sixty-six-year-old Asian accountant Peter Pan and his sixty-four-year-old wife Barbara. Both were shot through the head. The bullets matched the rounds found in the Los Angeles murders. An inverted pentagram was drawn in lipstick on the bedroom wall, and under it, Ramirez wrote "Jack the Knife."

IT'S THE NIGHT STALKER!

A week later, Ramirez visited the small town of Mission Viego, south of Los Angeles. He shot twenty-nine-year-old computer engineer William Carns three times in the head and raped his fiancée Inez Erickson, also twenty-nine, twice. He forced her to say "I love Satan" during the ordeal. Afterwards, she spotted Ramirez's rusty old orange Toyota driving away.

Another witness noted its licence-plate number. The police put out an all-points bulletin. Two days later, the car was found in a parking lot in Los Angeles.

Forensic scientists examining the car found one fingerprint. It matched to that of twenty-five-year-old Ricardo Ramirez, who had been arrested three times for marijuana possession. Soon Ramirez's photograph was on the front page of every newspaper in California.

Ramirez was quite unaware of this when he walked into a drugstore to buy a Pepsi. Then at the checkout desk he saw his own face splashed across the Spanish language paper *La Opinion*. The checkout clerk recognized him too. Ramirez made a run for it.

In the street, someone yelled: "It's the Night Stalker!" He tried to pull a woman from her car, but bystanders rushed to her rescue. He tried to steal a red 1966 Mustang, but fifty-six-year-old Faustin Pinon, who was working on the transmission, grabbed him in a headlock.

Ramirez broke free, but across the street fifty-five-year-old construction worker Jose Burgoin heard Pinon's shouts. He picked up a steel rod and hit Ramirez with it. Ramirez stumbled on but Burgoin soon caught up with him. At that moment Deputy Sheriff Andres Ramirez pulled up in a patrol car.

Handcuffed, Ramirez said: "Thank God you came. I am the one you want. Save me before they kill me."

LUCIFER DWELLS IN US ALL

In custody, Ramirez told the police: "I love to kill people. I love watching them die. I would shoot them in the head and they would wiggle and squirm all over the place, and then just stop. Or I would cut them with a knife and watch their faces turn real white. I love all that blood. I told one lady one time to give me all her money. She said no. So I cut her and pulled her eyes out."

In court, Ramirez made satanic signs and even appeared with the inverted pentagram scratched in his palm. He told the judge: "You maggots make me sick. Hypocrites one and all. You don't understand me. You are not expected to. You are not capable of it. I am beyond your experience. I am beyond good and evil. I will be avenged. Lucifer dwells in us all."

Ramirez was found guilty on sixty-three counts, including thirteen murders. He was sentenced to twelve death penalties and over a hundred years imprisonment. He died in jail of natural causes in 2013, at age fifty-three.

10

MELVIN REES
The Sex Beast

On June 26, 1957, an unnamed US Army sergeant was driving in the countryside in Maryland with his girlfriend Margaret Harold when they were forced off the road by a green Chrysler. The driver walked over to them and indicated that they should wind the window down. He asked for cigarettes and money. When they refused, he shot Margaret Harold in the face.

Realizing that his life was in danger, the sergeant fled. Finding refuge in an isolated farmhouse a mile away, he called the police. When they arrived at the scene of the shooting, they found that Margaret had been stripped naked and her dead body had been sexually abused.

The sergeant gave a good description of the slim, dark-haired assailant. Searching the area, the police found a deserted building with a broken basement window. Inside they found violent pornography and pictures of murdered women taped to the walls.

Among them was a picture of a woman taken from a class yearbook from the University of Maryland. This was Wanda Tipton who was still alive and had graduated in 1955. Detectives located her, but she said she knew no one who matched the description given by the sergeant.

MISSING FAMILY

On January 11, 1959, Carroll and Mildred Jackson, and their two little daughters, eighteen-month-old Janet and five-year-old Susan went missing. Driving home to Falls Church, Virginia, a relative spotted their car abandoned at the side of the road. The car was empty and, when they were called, the police could find no sign of a struggle.

Soon after the Jacksons' disappearance, a local couple came forward to report that the same afternoon a blue Chevrolet had driven up behind them, flashing its headlights and forcing them off the road. A dark-haired man got out of his car and approached the couple. Sensing danger, they reversed and fled. The man's description matched that which the Army sergeant had given two years previously.

Two months later, Carroll Jackson's body was found in a ditch. His hands were tied behind his back and he had been shot in the back of the head. Under him was baby Janet who had been dumped in the ditch alive and suffocated by the weight of her father's body.

Two weeks after that, two boys out squirrel hunting found a shallow grave. In it were the bodies of Mildred and five-year-old Susan Jackson. Both had been raped and bludgeoned to death. Mildred had also been tortured and forced to perform oral sex on her assailant. In a shack nearby, the police found a red button from Mildred's dress. Outside the shack there were tyre marks from a Chevrolet.

TRACKING REES

The police then received an anonymous letter naming twenty-six-year-old jazz musician Melvin Rees as a possible suspect. It had come from Glen Moser who said he had a conversation with Rees the night before the Jacksons disappeared.

High on benzedrine, Rees had outlined his views on the then fashionable existential philosophy, asserting: "You can't say it's wrong to kill. Only individual standards make it right or wrong."

He also named Rees as a suspect in the Margaret Harold case. They had been working together in the area at the time. The police tried to track down Rees, but he had moved, leaving no forwarding address. But they learned that he had been to the University of Maryland, so they reached out one more time to Wanda Tipton whose photo had been in the University Yearbook. She admitted this time that Rees had been her boyfriend, but she had broken it off after he said he was married.

Unable to find Rees, the police called in Dutch psychic Peter Hurkos who had been involved in the hunt for the Boston Strangler and investigation of the Manson Family. He named a different suspect, but the man he picked lived at Rees's former address.

Moser then relinquished his anonymity. He went to the police with a letter he had received from his old friend Rees who was then living in Hyattsville, Arkansas, and working in a piano store in West Memphis where the FBI arrested him.

SADISTIC TORTURE

In Rees's home they found a .38 calibre handgun in a saxophone case. It was the gun that had been used to kill Carroll Jackson and Margaret Harold. Along with it was a newspaper cutting carrying a picture of Mildred Jackson and a note, saying: "Now the mother and daughter are all mine." It went on to describe the sadistic torture of Mildred, concluding: "Then tied and gagged, led her to a place of execution and hung [sic] her. I was her master."

Tried in Maryland, Rees was found guilty of the murder of Margaret Harold and sentenced to life imprisonment.

Then in Virginia, he was convicted of the murders of the Jackson family and sentenced to death, but capital punishment had been suspended in the US before the death sentence was carried out. The police also suspected Rees of the murders of four adolescent girls in Maryland. He reportedly told a journalist that he had killed two of them. He died in prison in 1995.

11

GARY RIDGWAY
The Green River Killer

Gary Leon Ridgway is famous for admitting to the most serial killings ever, saying: "I killed so many women I have a hard time keeping them straight." He is linked to the deaths of forty-nine young women but there may have been many more, as Ridgway considered murdering young women his "career"; most were strangled to death around Seattle and Tacoma, Washington state.

It took nearly twenty years for Ridgway to be caught and brought to justice. The task force hunting him even accepted advice from notorious killer Ted Bundy, then on death row, in an effort to track him down. Ridgway committed the majority of his murders between 1982 and 1983, during which time the bodies of his victims were found near Green River in Washington state. This earned the then unknown assailant the title of "The Green River Killer".

JOINING THE DOTS

On July 15, 1982, the body of sixteen-year-old Wendy Lee Coffield was found in the Green River east of Seattle. On August 12, the corpse of Deborah Bonner, twenty-three, was pulled from the same river, about half-a-mile upstream from where Wendy's body had been dumped. Detective Dave Reichert was assigned to the case. Three days later three more bodies – Marcia Faye Chapman, thirty-one, Opal Charmaine Mills, sixteen, and Cynthia Jean Hinds, seventeen – were found. They had all been strangled and a task force was set up to join the dots in what appeared to be a series of linked crimes.

Two earlier killings were not initially recognized as part of the series. On January 21, 1982, the body of sixteen-year-old Leanne Wilcox was found in a field near Tacoma several miles from the river. A friend of Wendy Coffield, she too had been strangled. Then on July 7, 1982, thirty-six-year-old Amina Agisheff disappeared. Her skeletal remains were not found until April 1984.

They kept on coming. Sixteen-year-old Kasee Ann Lee disappeared on August 28. Ridgway admitted strangling her, but her body has never been found. Terry Rene Milligan went missing the following day. Three more teenagers disappeared in September. The killer claimed three more victims in October and another two in December.

He killed twice the following March, five times in April and four more times in May. Between June 1983 and March 1984, he killed at least another fifteen.

By 1986, Dave Reichert had been working on the Green River case for four years. With the body count close to forty, Reichert was still no closer to an arrest than when he started. Suddenly out of the blue, a proposition of assistance arrived from an unexpected source – the serial killer Ted Bundy.

INSIDE A KILLER'S MIND

During his 1970s killing spree, Ted Bundy had become one of the most notorious serial murderers in American history. He had admitted killing thirty-six women, but was suspected of at least a hundred more. According to *The New York Times*, Bundy wrote to Reichert from his death row cell in a Florida jail, where he had been waiting six years for his sentence, saying, "Don't ask me why I believe I'm an expert in this area, just accept that I am and we'll start from there."

It was a long shot, but if anyone knew the inner workings of a killer's mind it was Bundy. With few other plausible leads Reichert was struggling to get off square one, so he flew to Florida to find out what Bundy had to say.

Reichert soon realized that Bundy had much in common with the killer he was hunting. Both were sexual predators, with no feelings or remorse, doing their killing while sexually assaulting their victims. Bundy forewarned Reichert of future actions he expected from the killer, but the reality was they were confessions of Bundy's own past actions. Bundy craved attention and was jealous of the media coverage the Green River killings were getting.

Bundy went to the electric chair in January 1989 before Reichert got anywhere near the killer, however, he did pass on one gruesome piece of insider knowledge: the task force should keep constant watch on any of the recent murder sites. According to Bundy, the Green River Killer would be returning to his victims to have sex with the corpses.

HIDING IN PLAIN SIGHT

For the Green River Task Force, Gary Ridgway's name had been in the frame since the beginning. In 1980, he was interviewed after a prostitute accused him of trying to throttle her. He said that she had bitten him and choked her to make her stop. The police picked him up with prostitute Kelly McGuinness in 1982. She disappeared a year later. Her body was never found.

Following the disappearance of eighteen-year-old prostitute Maria Malvar on April 30, 1983, Ridgway became a leading suspect. The police questioned him and he denied all knowledge of her, even though a friend of hers had seen her get into a truck that was thought to be Ridgway's. Her body was not found until September 2003 after he confessed.

In May 1984 he took a lie detector test, but the polygraph cleared him. Nevertheless, he remained "a person of interest". Then the murders became more sporadic, with one in 1987, one in 1990, and one in 1998.

The killings had tailed off after Ridgway began dating Judith Mawson who became his third wife in 1988. Interviewed later in prison, he said that his urge to kill declined once he was in a relationship with Mawson. It did not leave him completely though. When she moved into his house while they were dating, she noticed there was no carpet. The police later told her he had probably used the carpet to wrap up a body.

Mawson said Ridgway left for work early in the morning some days and, later, assumed that he must have committed some of the murders while supposedly working early shifts. She claimed that she had not suspected Ridgway before she was first contacted by authorities in 1987 and had not even heard of the Green River Killer because she did not watch the TV news.

In 1988, the police obtained a warrant to search his house, but found nothing incriminating. They also got permission to take a saliva sample to determine his blood group. Although DNA fingerprinting had been introduced in 1985, it was still an unreliable procedure if the amount of DNA was small. However, forensic scientists would very soon develop much more dependable analytical methods for establishing the pathology of death. It was just a matter of time. Ridgway was hiding in plain sight.

THE NECROPHILIAC PSYCHOLOGY

With an IQ of just eighty-two, Ridgway was a bed-wetter as a boy. His mother used this to belittle and shame him in front of his family. He admitted, from a young age, of having conflicted feelings of anger and sexual attraction towards her. At sixteen, he stabbed a six-year-old boy, saying he wanted to feel what it was like to kill someone.

At eighteen, he joined the US Navy. Away from home a lot, he began to use prostitutes and his first wife also began to stray. His second wife accused him of trying to choke her. He became a religious zealot, while still using prostitutes. He also had an insatiable appetite for sex, forcing his wife to have sex with him in public places near where his victims' bodies were later discovered.

Ridgway had a particular way of killing. After having sex with his victim, he strangled the woman from behind. Initially he did this manually. But when victims, trying to defend themselves, started inflicting possibly incriminating wounds and bruises on his arm, he began to use ligatures.

Most victims were killed in his home, in his truck, or in a secluded area. The bodies were often posed naked. They were left in clusters around certain areas, which gave him a thrill when he drove by. Sometimes, just as Ted Bundy predicted, he would return to a body and have sex with the corpse.

SPINE CHILLING

By November 2001, DNA analysis had come a long way. So Ridgway's samples saved from the earlier blood tests were subjected to forensic re-analysis and they got a DNA match with the semen recovered from the bodies of four victims of the Green River Killer – the killer was Gary Ridgway.

Ridgway was arrested and charged with the murder of Marcia Chapman, Opal Mills, Cynthia Hinds, and twenty-one-year-old Carol Ann Christensen, who went missing on May 4, 1983, and was found four days later by a family picking mushrooms.

Carol Ann's body had been displayed in a particularly spine-chilling way. Her head was covered by a paper bag. Under it was a fish that had been placed on top of her neck. There was another fish on her left breast and a bottle between her legs. Her hands were crossed over her stomach with freshly ground beef placed on top of them. Her body showed signs of having been in water, even though the river was miles away. Ridgway pleaded not guilty to all the charges.

In March 2003, three more murders were added after a forensic scientist identified microscopic spheres of spray paint of the type used at the truck factory where Ridgway worked as a spray painter. Deborah Bonner, Wendy Coffield, and fifteen-year-old Debra Estes, who went missing on September 20, 1982, and was not found until May 30, 1988, were now identified as victims of the Green River Killer. Again Ridgway pleaded not guilty.

FORTY-NINE MURDERS

Suddenly just before his trial in November 2003, Gary Ridgway changed his mind. As part of a plea-bargain to avoid the death penalty, he decided to confess. He confessed to forty-eight killings – although he said the total might be more than sixty. As it was, the number he confessed to was more than the forty-one on the Green River Task Force's list, but less than the seventy-one he was actually suspected of killing.

On November 5, 2003, Ridgway pleaded guilty to forty-eight counts of aggravated first-degree murder, saying that he had been motivated by a deep hatred for prostitutes. But not all his victims were prostitutes. Some were teenage runaways and drug addicts. Others seem to have been picked at random.

Before his sentencing, the families of Ridgway's victims were allowed to address the court. He appeared largely unaffected by their words until Robert Rule approached the microphone. Ridgway had murdered his sixteen-year-old daughter, Linda, in 1982.

"Mr Ridgway, there are people here that hate you," Mr Rule said. "I'm not one of them. I forgive you for what you have done."

As he spoke, Ridgway wiped away tears. The judge dismissed Ridgway's emotions as "Teflon-coated". Ridgway was given forty-eight life sentences without possibility of parole, plus another ten years for each victim for tampering with the evidence – giving him another 480 years.

In 2011, Ridgway pleaded guilty to a forty-ninth murder – that of Rebecca "Becky" Marrero, a twenty-year-old mother last seen on December 3, 1982. Her skull was found in December 2010, not far from where Maria Malvar had been unearthed. Ridgway had already confessed to murdering her, but there was no evidence to charge him. Once the body part was identified by dental records, he entered a guilty plea under the plea-bargain he had entered into in 2003.

Gary Ridgway is now seventy-three years old and remains imprisoned at Washington State Penitentiary, Walla Walla, WA.

12

LONNIE DAVID FRANKLIN JR
The Grim Sleeper

Lonnie David Franklin Jr's chilling nickname, The Grim Sleeper, came from the fourteen-year break he took from serial killing between 1988 and 2002 when, presumably he slept, grimly. He seems to have begun killing in the spring of 1984 when twenty-one-year-old Laura Moore accepted a lift from him at a bus stop in Los Angeles. When she refused to put her seat belt on, he pulled out a gun and shot her six times. Miraculously she did not die and made her escape. He was never charged with this assault, but Laura appeared at the trial in 2016, when he was sentenced to death for the murder of nine women and one teenage girl. Prosecutors connected him to several other slayings and attempted slayings, and detectives believe he may have killed at least twenty-five women.

SOUTHSIDE SLAYERS

Born in 1952, Franklin grew up in South Central Los Angeles, where he married and had two children. He served in the US Army until 1975 when he was discharged. Then he worked as a mechanic for the LAPD and, between 1981 and 1989, as a sanitation worker.

In the 1980s there was a spate of murders of young women in South Los Angeles whose bodies were dumped in alleyways and dumpsters. Most of the victims tested positive for narcotics and some worked as prostitutes. The police set up a unit looking for the so-called "Southside Slayer". But soon it became clear that there was more than one killer on the loose.

Serial killers Michael Hughes and Chester Turner were active at the time. Caught in 1993 and 2003 respectively, they were convicted and were sent to death row. Both strangled their victims. But there was another killer who used a gun.

BLACK WOMEN TARGETS

The shooter's victims were thought to have begun with twenty-nine-year-old waitress Debra Jackson who was shot three times in the chest and dumped in an alley in the summer of 1985. Over the next three years, there were seven more killings, each using the same handgun.

The body of thirty-five-year-old Henrietta Wright was found under a mattress in an alleyway in 1986. Twenty-three-year-old Barbara Ware was killed in January 1987. Someone called 911 saying they had seen a man dump the body out of the back of a van and gave the vehicle's licence plate number before hanging up. The van was traced back to a church in the area, but the authorities did not follow up for another twenty years.

Twenty-five-year-old Bernita Sparks was the next victim in April 1987, then twenty-six-year-old Mary Lowe that November. Twenty-two-year-old Lachrica Jefferson was killed in January 1988 and in September the naked body of eighteen-year-old Alice Monique Alexander was found under a mattress in an alley.

The killing then stopped after an attack on Enietra "Margette" Washington on November 20, 1988. She said she was approached by a neatly dressed Black man in his early thirties who offered her a lift. When she refused, he said: "What is wrong with you Black women?"

He persisted and she relented. They drove to a residential area where the man went into the house and emerged ten minutes later.

An argument broke out. He pulled a small handgun and shot her in the chest. She blacked out, but was awoken by a flash. The man had taken her picture with a Polaroid camera. Then he sexually assaulted her. Afterwards he pushed her out of the car and left her for dead.

DUMPED IN THE TRASH

In March 2002 the murders started again with the killing of fifteen-year-old Princess Berthomieux. But she was not shot dead. Rather she was strangled. Thirty-five-year-old Valerie McCorvey's half-naked body was left in the street with ligature marks on her neck in July 2003. The body of Janecia Peters was folded into the foetal position in a garbage bag and dumped in a trash bin where she was found on January 1, 2007.

Distinctly different in method to the shootings of 1988, what linked these new murders to the earlier slayings was DNA, and a new task force was set up. One possibility for the hiatus from 1988 to 2002 was because the killer had been in jail. In that case his DNA profile should be on file, but no match could be found.

Indeed Franklin's DNA should have been somewhere on the database as he had a criminal record dating back to 1989. However the probation service was under-resourced and officers did not get around to collecting samples until August 2005. But then in 2009 Franklin's son Christopher was arrested for the illegal possession of a weapon, a felony. His DNA provided a partial, or familial, match.

PIZZA CRUST DNA

To close the case, the police needed a sample of Franklin's DNA. They followed him to a birthday party in an LA restaurant where an officer took the place of a bus boy. He collected Franklin's plate, cup, and pizza crust with enough DNA to match to that found on the victims.

Franklin was arrested. Guns matching the murder weapons were found in his home, along with pictures and video tapes of some of his victims. They were usually nude, partially clothed or in overtly sexual positions. Among the pictures were at least fifty-five women who remain unidentified. It seems that the Grim Sleeper had not been asleep at all. As a garbage worker with the sanitation department he knew landfill sights where bodies could be disposed of with very little chance of it being found.

Franklin was convicted of all ten counts of murder he had been charged with and was sentenced to death. On March 28, 2020, Franklin was found dead in his cell at San Quentin State Prison.

13

ÁNGEL MATURINO RESÉNDIZ
The Railroad Killer

In 1998, the Mexican serial killer Ángel Maturino Reséndiz was convicted of just one murder but was linked, by confession or evidence, to twenty-two others. These all took place near the railroads Reséndiz used to keep ahead of the law. Riding the rails across the United States and Mexico gave rise to his nickname "the Railroad Killer".

BORDERING ON THE CRIMINAL

Born in Puebla, Mexico, on August 1, 1959, Ángel Maturino Reséndiz had a broken childhood. His mother, Virginia

Reséndiz de Maturino, never married his father, and as a boy Reséndiz suffered a history of abuse at her hands. At age six, he was sent to live with his maternal uncle, and ended up being raped by him. By the age of eleven, he had escaped his uncle and was living on the street, sniffing glue.

As a teenager he became isolated and took to travelling on the railroads alone, roaming from town to town, first to Acapulco, then on to Florida. In September 1976, he was arrested for trespassing and was deported back to Mexico. The following month, he was arrested at the US-Mexican border illegally trying to cross back into the US, and was deported again.

But by 1977 he was back in the US, and was convicted of destroying private property and leaving the scene of a crime in Corinth, Mississippi. He was deported once more. Two years later, he broke into a house in Miami, ransacked it and beat up the eighty-eight-year-old owner, fleeing in the victim's car. This earned him a sentence of twenty years of which he went on to serve only six. He was paroled in 1985 and deported again.

THE KILLING BEGINS
Soon after, he returned to the US where he began killing. His first victim was an unidentified African American female, whose badly decomposed body was found in an abandoned farmhouse near San Antonio, Texas, on March

26, 1986. Reséndiz said that she was from Florida and that her name may have been Norma. He had shot her repeatedly with a .38 handgun three months earlier, he said, because she cast a spell on him. Later, he also killed her boyfriend, a Cuban who Reséndiz said was involved in black magic. He dumped his body in a creek somewhere between San Antonio and Uvalde. It has never been found.

In December 1986, he was sentenced to eighteen months for claiming to be a US citizen and once again deported to Mexico, only to be arrested again crossing the border at Laredo, with bogus documents. This earned Reséndiz another eighteen months in prison and another deportation.

Four months later, he was sentenced to another thirty months, this time in New Orleans, for a series of crimes committed under a number of aliases. Deported in May 1991, he was back in the US in June when he murdered twenty-two-year-old Michael White at an abandoned house in San Antonio, supposedly for being homosexual.

The following year, Reséndiz pleaded guilty to a burglary in Las Cruces, New Mexico, and was sentenced to three years and deported again. Later in 1992 he was arrested in Albuquerque, New Mexico, driving a car he had stolen two days earlier in Missouri and was sent back to jail.

In December 1994, he was arrested again in Albuquerque, driving another car stolen in Arizona. The following May he was indicted for receiving a stolen vehicle. In August Reséndiz was arrested for trespassing on railroad property in San Bernardo, California, and was found to be carrying a stolen handgun. Sentenced to thirty days, he was again returned to Mexico.

A warning was issued against him for trespassing at the Norfolk Southern Railroad yard in Macon, Georgia, on August 4, 1996. Ignoring the warning, two days later Reséndiz was arrested for trespassing at a railroad yard at Science Hill, Kentucky.

TASTE FOR MURDER

As Reséndiz continued to criss cross America, his taste for murder grew. On March 23, 1997, he bludgeoned nineteen-year-old Jesse Howell to death and left his body beside the railroad tracks at Ocala, Florida. On the same day, Reséndiz raped, strangled, and suffocated Howell's sixteen-year-old fiancée Wendy Von Huben, then buried her in a shallow grave.

On July 5, 1997, Roberto Charles a transient drifter was beaten to death in a rail yard at Colton, California. Reséndiz was regarded as the prime suspect. On August 29, he approached twenty-one-year-old Christopher Maier and his girlfriend Holly Dunn Pendleton near the railroad tracks in Lexington, Kentucky. Wielding what looked like an ice-pick, Reséndiz demanded money. They had no cash, so Reséndiz grabbed Maier's backpack and used the straps to tie his arms behind his back. Pendleton could have run, but decided to stay with her boyfriend. Reséndiz took off her belt and bound her with it, pushing the couple into a ditch and gagging them, then he beat Maier's head in with a rock.

After killing her boyfriend he pulled down the terrified Pendelton's jeans and raped her, beating her unconscious after he had finished, and leaving her for dead. Miraculously, Pendleton eventually recovered, suffering a broken jaw, a smashed eye socket, an inch-deep stab wound to her neck as well as many other cuts and bruises. Having very nearly died, Holly Dunn Pendleton remains the only known survivor of an attack by the Railroad Killer.

On October 4, 1998, Reséndiz continued his killing spree. Climbing through the window of eighty-seven-year-old Leafie Mason's house, just fifty yards from the Kansas City Southern Rail Line at Hughes Spring, Texas, he beat the old lady to death with a tyre iron.

CLOSING IN

In the early hours of December 17, 1998, Reséndiz broke into the opulent home of thirty-nine-year-old paediatric neurologist Dr Claudia Benton in West University Place, Houston, Texas, just down the street from the railroad track, intent on robbery. Inside, he found her asleep in bed. He raped her, then stabbed her thirty-nine times with a butcher's knife and beat her to death with a two-foot bronze statue. He grabbed any cash and jewellery he could find and fled in the victim's Jeep Cherokee.

Later when the Jeep was recovered in San Antonio, Reséndiz's fingerprints were found on the steering column. He already had an extensive criminal rap sheet dating back some twenty years, and was wanted for burglary, but at the time he murdered Claudia Benton, the Railroad Killer was still unidentified.

When his fingerprints were found on the victim's car, the police at last could connect the identity of the Railroad Killer with Reséndiz. But the killer was quick and continued to elude capture, simply jumping on the next freight car to make his getaway.

On May 2, 1999, Norman J. "Skip" Sirnic, the forty-six-year-old pastor of the United Church of Christ in Weimar, Texas, and his forty-seven-year-old wife Karen were bludgeoned to death with a sledgehammer while they slept. Karen had also been sexually assaulted. Their parsonage was adjacent to the railroad. Their red Mazda was found in San Antonio three weeks later and more fingerprints tied the murders to Reséndiz and the Railroad Killer case.

A month later, on June 2, 1999, the US Border Patrol apprehended Reséndiz near El Paso attempting to cross the border illegally. Although a wanted man, due to a computer glitch he was simply deported back to Mexico.

Two days later he was back in the US, killing again.

On June 4, 1999, twenty-six-year-old Houston schoolteacher Noemi Dominguez was raped and bludgeoned to death with a pickaxe in her apartment near the railroad tracks. Taking the pickaxe with him, the killer drove the ninety miles to Fayette County. There in a farmhouse at Schulenburg, Texas, he killed seventy-three-year-old Josephine Konvicka while she slept. He left the pickaxe embedded in her head and DNA linked the crime to the Dominguez murder.

On June 15, 1999, Reséndiz arrived in Gorham, Illinois. He slept rough in the trees behind eighty-year-old George Morber's trailer, a hundred yards from the railroad tracks. As soon as Reséndiz saw the retired prison warder drive off, he climbed through the window. When Morber returned, surprising the intruder, Reséndiz tied him up and killed him with a shotgun blast to the back of the head.

When Morber's daughter, fifty-one-year-old Carolyn Frederick, dropped by to clean up her father's trailer, Reséndiz bludgeoned her to death with the shotgun so violently that the barrel broke. Fingerprints found at the crime scene identified Reséndiz as the killer.

THE DEVIL RULED MY LIFE
By then Reséndiz was on the FBI's Top Ten Most Wanted Fugitives list. Two hundred agents were assigned to the case and more than a thousand sightings were phoned in

by the public. The FBI's reward of $50,000 was upped to $125,000 when local jurisdictions chipped in.

Agents brought Reséndiz's common-law wife Julietta Reyes from Mexico when she volunteered to do anything she could to get Reséndiz to surrender. She also handed over ninety-three pieces of stolen jewellery he had mailed to her.

Meanwhile enterprising young Texas Ranger Sergeant Drew Carter contacted Reséndiz's sister Manuela who lived in Albuquerque. She feared that her brother might be killed in a shoot out with the FBI, or go on to kill again, and agreed to help. Another relative got a message to Reséndiz who was hiding out in Ciudad Juarez across the border from El Paso.

At 9:00 a.m. on July 13, 1999, he surrendered on the international bridge connecting the two cities, fearing the bounty hunters who were already on his trail. Mexico was no safe haven as he had also committed at least seven murders there.

Four murder charges had been filed against him in Texas, others in Kentucky, and Illinois. But Reséndiz only faced trial for one – the murder of Claudia Benton.

On June 21, 2006, a Houston judge issued a death sentence for Reséndiz to be executed for killing Claudia Benton. The death sentence did not worry Reséndiz. He had no doubt that he could not die as he was half man, half angel, saying, "I don't believe in death ... as a person, I'm eternal. I'm going to be alive forever." Statements such as these led psychiatrists to voice the opinion that Reséndiz had become completely delusional.

On June 27, 2006, he was given a lethal injection in Texas State Penitentiary, Huntsville, Texas. Claudia Benton's husband, George, witnessing the execution said Reséndiz was "evil contained in human form." Reséndiz's final words were: "I know I allowed the Devil to rule my life … I deserve what I am getting."

14

PAUL DUROUSSEAU
The Cabbie Killer

A merican serial killer Paul Durousseau strangled seven young women in Florida and Georgia between 1997 and 2003. All his victims were young, single, African American women. He was also suspected of the murder of several local women when he was stationed in Germany with the US Army in the 1990s.

SMELL OF DEATH

On January 1, 2003, family members of nineteen-year-old Nikia Shanell Kilpatrick visited her apartment in Jacksonville, Florida. They were worried because none of them had seen her over the holiday period. When they arrived at the house, they saw Nikia's two-year-old son at the window. Inside the apartment they found her younger son, who was just eleven months old, crawling on the floor. The air was filled with the smell of death.

They found Nikia's decomposing body in the bedroom. She had been tied up, sexually abused, and strangled with a cord around her neck. The medical examiner found that Nikia had been killed two days earlier and was six-months pregnant at the time of her death. Although they were malnourished, the children had survived the trauma by eating dried food from the kitchen.

While the police found some important evidence at the crime scene, nothing pointed immediately to a suspect. But they were certain of one thing. The perpetrator was practised in the art of killing. This was not his first murder.

OBVIOUS PARALLELS

On January 10, 2003, twenty-year-old nursing assistant Shawanda Denise McCallister was found dead in her Jacksonville apartment. Just like Nikia Kilpatrick, she had been bound, sexually abused, and strangled with a cord. She was also pregnant at the time of her death and investigators drew the obvious parallels to Nikia's killing.

They were also able to link the two deaths to a third case. Less than a month before, on December 19, 2002, the police had found the dead body of eighteen-year-old Nicole L. Williams in a ditch, wrapped in a light blue blanket thought to have come from a Jacksonville hotel.

In a method almost identical to the killings of Nikia and Shawanda, Nicole had been bound, sexually assaulted, and strangled. DNA taken from the three women's bodies showed that the same killer was responsible for all three deaths.

There was more horror to come. On February 5, construction workers found the body of seventeen-year-old Jovanna Tyrica Jefferson in a ditch on a vacant lot. She had been missing since January 2003. When the police arrived, they also found the remains of nineteen-year-old mother-of-two Surita Ann Cohen who had been missing since February 4. Once more, they had been bound and sexually abused before they were killed by strangulation.

The killing spree had lasted two months, and the police now had five dead strangled young women on their hands. But in the last two cases there was a vital clue which they picked up. On the night they disappeared, both Jovanna and Surita had been seen with a cab driver named Paul Durousseau.

VIOLENCE AND RAPE

Born in 1970 in Beaumont, Texas, Durousseau had a long police record dating back to December 1991 when he was first arrested in California for carrying a concealed handgun. A second concealed firearm offence occurred the following month. He joined the US Army. While stationed in Germany, he fell in love with a twenty-one-year-old service woman he had met in a nightclub. They married in Las Vegas, Nevada, in 1995.

Stationed at Fort Benning, Georgia, two years later, Durousseau was arrested and charged with kidnap and rape, but was acquitted. A month later the naked body of a twenty-six-year-old woman named Tracy Habersham was found in a ditch. She had been raped and strangled with a cord. At that time Durousseau was not a suspect. Later, though, DNA would connect him to the case and he confessed.

Durousseau was then found in possession of stolen goods, court-martialled and dishonourably discharged from the Army. Although this put a strain on his marriage, Durousseau and his wife moved to Jacksonville, Florida, her home town, where they had two daughters.

The couple were struggling with their finances and Durousseau's frequent lewd adulterous behaviour with other women in the neighbourhood often led to arguments followed by domestic violence. In August 2001, he was jailed for six weeks for physically abusing his wife, after having served a month with two years probation of another sentence for the rape of a Jacksonville woman in June 2001. The following year he was charged with burglary, but was acquitted.

Despite his lengthening criminal record, he was still able

to find temporary work. In January 2003, he began driving for Gator City Taxi, a local cab company. For Durousseau, picking up young women in his cab was an opportunity that was too good to be true.

A MAN CALLED "D"

Soon after he started at Gator City Taxi, seventeen-year-old Jovanna Jefferson was seen getting into a taxi driven by a man called "D". When she did not return home, her aunt called her cell phone. It was answered by a cab driver who said she would be home soon. She never returned. Jovanna's mother went to Gator City Taxi and discovered that "D" was Paul Durousseau.

He had split from his wife, but visited her new house to see his daughters. There he was arrested for a violation of his probation for the earlier rape case. While he was in jail, the police built a case against him using the matching DNA samples and other forensic evidence linking him to the crime scenes, along with cab and cell-phone records.

On June 17, 2003, Durousseau was charged with five counts of first-degree murder for the deaths of Nikia Kilpatrick, Shawanda McCallister, Nicole Williams, Jovanna Jefferson, and Surita Cohen. He also faced two counts of child abuse against Nikia's two small children, who had been left alone in the apartment for up to two days with the decomposing remains of their mother.

Charges for the 1997 Fort Benning murder of Tracy

Habersham followed and, on August 26, he was charged with the 1999 murder of twenty-four-year-old Tyresa Mack. She had been strangled with a cord in her Eastside Jacksonville apartment. Again the DNA samples matched. Durousseau had been seen leaving her apartment carrying a television.

At the trial, Durousseau took the stand and admitted having sex with Tyresa Mack, Nikia Kilpatrick and Shawanda McCallister before their deaths but said he wasn't the one who killed them. He admitted to lying to detectives when he initially denied knowing any of them and spent about ninety minutes on the stand, answering questions about his relationships with the dead women.

He said he met Mack in April 1999 and that, for three months, he saw her frequently. The last time he saw her was on July 26, the day she was killed, and she was alive when he left. When he heard about her death, he did not contact police because he didn't have any fresh information to give them.

Convicted of the murder of Tyresa Mack, on December 13, 2007, he was sentenced to death by lethal injection. The other murder charges were dropped, though they could be reinstated if he was not executed.

BREAKING NEWS UPDATE – DEC 10, 2021
JACKSONVILLE, FLA.
Jacksonville Florida Local News Headlines / WJXT

Channel 4. Published: December 10, 2021, 4:31 PM

Paul Durousseau, a convicted murderer who is also suspected in the deaths of five other women, was resentenced Friday to life in prison. In 2007, Durousseau was convicted of first-degree murder and sentenced to death for the 1999 murder of 24-year-old Tyresa Mack, one of six murders he was accused of committing from 1997 to 2003 in Jacksonville and Georgia. Only the case involving Mack went to trial. Durousseau was a taxi driver at the time of the suspected killings, which were spread out in Jacksonville for years until his arrest in 2003. After the first conviction, the jury's verdict was 10-2 for the death penalty. But state law has since been changed to require a unanimous verdict, including in some cases retroactively. The high court rejected arguments for a new trial. This week was Durousseau's new sentencing, with a newly selected jury. That jury on Friday arrived at a 10-2 majority recommendation, but it was not unanimous. Durousseau was then subsequently sentenced to life in prison.

15

WAYNE BERTRAM WILLIAMS
The Atlanta Child Killer

In the summer of 1979, a spate of slaying of black children and young people began in Atlanta, Georgia. Charles T. Sanders, a white supremacist affiliated with the Ku Klux Klan and one-time suspect, was secretly recorded praising the killer for "wiping out a thousand future generations of n***ers". However, suspicion of blame for the Atlanta Child Killings was gradually shifted onto African American small time music promoter Wayne Bertram Williams.

SUMMER OF DEATH

In the early hours of July 21, 1979, fourteen-year-old Edward Hope Smith left the skating rink where he had spent the evening with his girlfriend to go home to one of Atlanta's rundown housing projects. A few days later, fourteen-year-old Alfred Evans left home to go and see a karate movie in downtown Atlanta. Both of them were found dead on July 28 in a wooded area in the southwest of the city. One had been shot, the other probably strangled. On the strength of a phone call, the police dismissed the killings as "drug related."

On September 4, 1979, fourteen-year-old Milton Harvey, who had escaped from the projects when his parents moved to a middle-class neighbourhood, borrowed a bicycle and took a cheque to the bank for his mother. The bike was found a week later abandoned on a deserted dirt track. His badly decomposed body was found miles away on a rubbish dump just outside the city limits.

A few weeks later, nine-year-old Yusuf Bell disappeared. Police dismissed the testimony of a witness who said she had seen Yusuf getting into a car with a man she believed to be the former husband of Yusuf's mother Camile. The boy's body was found on November 8, stuffed into a hole in the concrete floor of an abandoned elementary school. He had been strangled. Suddenly the community took notice of this cluster of killings.

On March 10, 1980, twelve-year-old Angel Lenair was

found tied to a tree. She had been strangled with an electrical cord around her neck and a pair of panties – not her own – were shoved down her throat. There was evidence of sexual abuse.

The following day ten-year-old Jeffrey Mathis did not return from an errand he was running for his mother. Again he had been seen getting into a blue car. Then on May 18, fourteen-year-old Eric Middlebrooks got a phone call at about 10:00 p.m. He grabbed his tools and told his foster mother that he was going out to fix his bike. His body was found a few blocks away the following morning. He had been bludgeoned to death. The police assumed he had been the unwitting witness to a robbery.

Things got worse. On June 22, seven-year-old LaTonya Wilson was abducted from her home. But this was just the beginning of what became known as the "Summer of Death".

THE DEAD AND THE DISAPPEARED

On June 23, 1980, ten-year-old Aaron Wyche went missing. His body was found under a bridge on a six-lane highway. He had died from asphyxia, though the medical examiner said this was because of the way he had landed when he fell from the parapet. But Aaron was afraid of heights and would not have climbed onto the bridge voluntarily.

Then on July 6, 1980, nine-year-old Anthony Carter disappeared while playing hide and seek. His body was found behind a warehouse less than a mile from home. He had been stabbed to death. On July 30, eleven-year-old Earl Terrell disappeared after leaving a swimming pool. A man called his aunt and told her that he had taken Earl to Alabama and it would cost her $200 to get him back. He did not call again.

The police suspected a child pornography ring had been operating across the street from the pool. John David Wilcoxen was arrested after thousands of indecent photographs were found in his possession. A witness said that Earl Terrell had visited Wilcoxen's house several times.

On August 20, thirteen-year-old Clifford Jones, who had come to Atlanta to visit his grandmother, went missing, his body was later found in a dumpster. He had been strangled and the shorts and underwear he was wearing were not his. Evidence suggested that the manager of a local laundromat was responsible. He admitted knowing Clifford. Three young witnesses said they had seen him beat and strangle a black boy, and dump him with the trash. Others had also seen him dump a large object swathed in plastic in the dumpster. Nothing was done.

There were other suspects. Twelve-year-old Charles Stephens went missing on October 9, 1980. His body was found on a hillside the following morning. He had died from suffocation. A drug dealer said that he had seen the boy, dead, on the backseat of a client's car. The client threatened him with a gun, saying he would kill him if he said anything. The dealer said the man was a paedophile.

As LaTonya Wilson and Earl Terrell had been abducted and possibly transported over the state line – a federal offence – the FBI got involved. Pressure from a parents' group also forced the local police finally to set up a task force. They began a list of the dead and the disappeared which grew to contain more than sixty names, though many similar cases didn't make it onto the list.

Twenty-two-year-old Faye Yearby was found tied to a tree like Angel Lenair in January 1981. She had been stabbed to death, but she was left off the list as she was considered too old. Ten-year-old Darron Glass, who disappeared on September 14, 1980, was also left off because he had run away several times before.

CONNECTING THE VICTIMS

Investigator Chet Dettlinger, compiler of *The List*, spotted that a number of the victims knew each other and the places where the victims were last seen, or where their bodies had been dumped, were confined to specific areas. This area gradually expanded along certain highways.

The body of LaTonya Wilson was found in mid-October, not far from her home. It was too badly decomposed to determine the cause of death. City patrols were stepped up and a curfew was imposed for Halloween in case the killer targeted trick-or-treaters.

Nine-year-old Aaron Jackson, a friend of Aaron Wyche, was found dead under a bridge in November 1980. He had been smothered like Charles Stephens. Aaron Jackson was also friends with sixteen-year-old Patrick "Pat Man" Rogers, a singer who had a crush on his sister. Connected to at least seventeen other victims, Rogers disappeared on November 10. Like Darron Glass, he was thought to have run away. Rogers' body was found on December 21, 1980, face down in the Chattahoochee River. He had died from a blow to his head. Before he left, Rogers had told his mother that he had found someone to manage his singing career. The man's name was Wayne Williams.

Fourteen-year-old Lubie Geter disappeared in January 1981 and was found the following month. He was wearing only his underwear and the medical examiner believed he had been strangled. He had connections to the suspect in the Terrell case and another paedophile.

Geter's friend, fifteen-year-old Terry Pue, disappeared soon after. An anonymous caller told the police where they could find his body. He had been strangled. The caller said there was another body nearby. Those remains were not found until years later and were too badly decomposed to be identified, but they were thought to be those of Darron Glass.

Eleven-year-old Patrick Baltazar disappeared on February 6, 1981. Shortly before, the task force had received a phone call from him, saying the killer was coming after him. They failed to respond. His body was found in a park. He had been strangled and the rope thought to have been the murder weapon was found nearby.

On March 6, 1981, the body of thirteen-year-old Curtis Walker was found. He had been strangled. His uncle, who he lived with in the projects, was also murdered. Curtis made the list. His uncle did not. The same day, the remains of ten-year-old Jeffrey Mathis were found. He had been missing for almost a year.

Fifteen-year-old Joseph "Jo-Jo" Bell went missing on March 2, 1981. Two days later, a work colleague at Cap'n Peg's seafood restaurant said that Jo-Jo called him, saying he was "almost dead" and begging for his help. His mother then received a call from a woman, saying she had Jo-Jo. The mother contacted the task force who, again, did not respond. His body was found on April 19, 1981, in the South River. Cause of death: probably asphyxia.

Eleven days after Jo-Jo went missing, a friend named Timothy Hill also disappeared. Together they had visited the home of paedophile Thomas Terrell. The body of thirteen-year-old Timothy Hill was found in the Chattahoochee River on March 30, 1981. Cause of death: asphyxia. He had connections to Alfred Evans, Jeffrey Mathis, Patrick Baltazar, and Anthony Carter.

RIVER OF FLOATING CORPSES
By then, the river had become the killer's preferred

dumping ground and the victims were becoming progressively older. Soon vigilante groups were roaming the projects looking for suspects.

On March 20, 1981, twenty-one-year-old Eddie "Bubba" Duncan, a boy with physical and learning difficulties, went missing. He had connections to Patrick Rogers. On April 8, 1981, his body was found in the Chattahoochee River. Cause of death: probable asphyxia. He made the list, though earlier he would have been considered too old.

Twenty-year-old Larry Rogers – no relation to Patrick Rogers – made the list in April 1981 when his body was found in an abandoned apartment. He also had learning difficulties and had been strangled. He, too, had connections to Wayne Williams who had protected Larry's younger brother after he had got into a fight, giving him refuge in a flat near where Larry was found dead.

Twenty-three-year-old ex-convict Michael McIntosh lived across the street from Cap'n Peg's seafood restaurant. He disappeared on March 25, 1981, after telling a store owner that he had been beaten up by two black men. He, too, frequented Thomas Terrell's house. His body was found in the Chattahoochee River in April. Cause of death: probable asphyxia.

Ex-convict John Porter was twenty-eight when he went missing. He had mental problems and had been caught fondling a two-year-old boy. His body was found on the sidewalk of an empty lot in April 1981. He had been stabbed six times. At first, he did not make the list until he was linked to Wayne Williams by forensic evidence.

Twenty-one-year-old ex-con Jimmy Payne had also disappeared the same month. He was depressed and had tried to hang himself. His body was found floating in the Chattahoochee River a month after he had last been seen alive. The corpse had been in the water for a week and the cause of death could not be determined.

William Barrett, aka Billy Star, a seventeen-year-old juvenile delinquent, went missing in May. His body was found close to home. He had been strangled and stabbed. The medical examiner said the stabbing happened after he was strangled. He had connections to Lubie Geter and a convicted paedophile they both knew.

When twenty-seven-year-old ex-con Nathaniel Carter dropped out of sight, he was living in the same apartment block as LaTonya Wilson. A known acquaintance of Michael McIntosh, he was a gay prostitute, drug dealer, and an alcoholic. Due to his irregular lifestyle, it is not known exactly when he disappeared.

Then, in the early hours of May 22, 1981, the police were staking out the James Jackson Parkway Bridge across the Chattahoochee River, where a number of bodies had been found, when they heard a loud splash. A white 1970 Chevrolet station wagon on the bridge above was stopped. The driver was Wayne Williams.

Asked what he was doing Williams, a small-time music

promoter, said he was on his way to audition a singer named Cheryl Johnson. But neither the address nor the phone number he gave for her checked out. Two days later the naked body of Nathaniel Carter was fished out of the Chattahoochee River, downstream. Cause of death: probably asphyxia.

DUBIOUS FORENSICS

Wayne Williams was charged with the murder of Nathaniel Carter and Jimmy Payne, but none of the Atlanta Child Murders. Until the last moment, the prosecution withheld information that four witnesses had said they had seen Carter alive after May 22. They were not called. The prosecution case depended on forensic evidence supplied by the FBI which they alleged, connected Williams to ten of the murders – mention of the other cases was allowed in court to show a pattern in the killings. Fibres from the bodies matched carpet fibres found in Williams' home and his car. Although these carpets were ubiquitous, the defence did not have the money to contest the dubious forensics given by the FBI labs.

Witnesses testified that Williams had been seen with a number of the victims. He was shown to be a habitual liar and did himself no favours when he lost his temper while being cross-examined. He was convicted and given two life sentences. The Atlanta police then announced that twenty-two of the twenty-nine cases on the list had been solved. Many people, including Georgia state supreme court justices, former prosecutors and victims' family members, found the conviction unsafe. Nevertheless, Williams remains in jail.

Williams was never tried for any of the Atlanta Child Murders, but after he became a suspect, the killings stopped. Even so, Wayne Williams has always maintained his innocence. His attorneys argue that the authorities at the time concealed incriminating evidence of a Ku Klux Klan conspiracy, and that the carpet fibres which "proved" Williams' guilt would not be credible now under contemporary scientific examination. He has requested two retrials which have both been rejected, and police continue to attribute twenty-two deaths to him.

Williams is serving his two life sentences at Telfair State Prison, Helena, Georgia. On November 20, 2019, he was denied parole with the next eligible parole date being November 2027 when Wayne Williams will be sixty-nine years old.

PART 2

EUROPEAN SERIAL KILLERS

1

COLIN IRELAND
The Gay Slayer
UNITED KINGDOM

On March 9, 1993, a telephone call was put through to the newsroom of *The Sun* newspaper in London. In a gruff voice, the caller gave an address in the southwest of the city. He said: "I've murdered a man. I'm calling you because I'm worried about his dogs. I want them to be let out. It would be cruel for them to be stuck there."

Clearly, he was more worried about the dogs than the victim. "I tied him up and I killed him and I cleaned up the flat afterwards," the caller said. "I did it. It was my New Year resolution to kill a human being. Is that of any interest to you? He was a homosexual and into kinky sex."

TAUNTING THE POLICE

The newspaper alerted the police who went to the address given. Forcing open the door, they found the two dogs. Their owner, forty-nine-year-old Peter Walker, was found naked and spread-eagled on his four-poster bed, his wrists and ankles tied tightly to each post. There was a plastic bag over his head.

Walker, a theatre director, had been openly gay for some twenty years. As the victim could not have put the bag over his own head after tying his hands, detectives deduced that another person must have done it.

On May 28, 1993, the body of thirty-seven-year-old librarian Christopher Dunn was found tied and gagged at his home in northwest London. He was naked except for a leather bondage harness and had a plastic bag over his head. His testicles appeared to have been scorched. Later it was discovered that £200 had been taken from his bank account. Clearly, Dunn had been tortured to reveal the PIN number of his debit card.

Two more deaths occurred in similar circumstances. On June 4, thirty-five-year-old HIV-positive American executive Perry Bradley was found at his home in west London, gagged, bound, and strangled – £100 was missing from his wallet and £200 had been taken from his bank account. Three days later, thirty-three-year-old residential home supervisor Andrew Collier was found tied to his bed in northeast London. The body of his strangled cat lay on his naked body with its mouth around Collier's penis.

The killer had taunted the police with a series of telephone calls. Before Collier's body was discovered, he said that he had read the FBI Crime Classification Manual, and had decided to become a serial killer: "I know what it takes to become one. You have to kill one over four to qualify, don't you? I have already killed three. It started as an exercise, I wanted to see if it could be done, to see if I could really get away with it … Have you found Christopher Dunn yet? I killed him too. I haven't seen anything in the papers."

FAIRY LIQUIDATOR

A few days later, the same caller explained why he had killed Collier's cat. "I don't want anybody to get any wrong ideas about me. I am not an animal lover," he said.

Confessing to the murder of Perry Bradley, he said: "I did the American. You've got some good leads on my identity from clues at the scene."

Police inquiries soon established that at least three of the victims were regulars at The Coleherne Arms, a gay pub near Earls Court underground station and close to Bradley's flat.

Forty-one-year-old Maltese-born chef Emmanuel Spiteri was at the Coleherne on the night of June 12. Three days later, police received another phone call.

"Have you found the body in southeast London yet, and the fire?" the caller said.

Forcing open the door of Spiteri's apartment, they found him naked and bound. He had been strangled. An attempt had been made to set fire to a pile of furniture, but the flames had died out before the whole flat went up.

The police set out to trace Spiteri's movements. After leaving the Coleherne, he would have taken the tube to Charing Cross main-line station where he would have changed to an overground train to take him to his home in the southeast. The police quickly spotted Spiteri on the CCTV tapes several times. Following him was a heavily built man, over six feet tall, apparently in his thirties.

The pictures, together with a computerized photofit and an artist's impression, were widely circulated, but no one came forward to say they knew the man.

By July 21, the police were no further forward in their investigation. But, on the same day, a tall, burly man walked into a lawyer's office in Southend-on-Sea, thirty miles from London, and said he needed legal representation. His name was Colin Ireland, but the press had already dubbed him the "Fairy Liquidator" after the popular brand of washing-up liquid.

SEXUALLY AMBIVALENT
Born in 1954, Ireland began a life of petty crime as a

youngster. His rap sheet included thirty arrests and nineteen convictions. He served a short spell in the British Army, but claimed to be a veteran of the French Foreign Legion. He spent two years in prison for robbery. After being married briefly for a second time, he became a drifter. Boasting of the survival techniques he had learned in the Army, he would spend nights alone in the marshes of Kent, eating rabbits and birds he had snared.

Having hired the lawyer, they travelled back to London and together they went to the police. Ireland admitted he had been with Spiteri, but insisted he had left when another man arrived. But the police were able to match his fingerprints to one found in Andrew Collier's home. Confronting Ireland with this evidence, they expected a full confession. However, Ireland remained obstinately silent.

Meanwhile psychologist Paul Britton,who had already assisted police on a number of occasions, was asked to draw up a profile of the killer. He described the offender as sexually ambivalent.

"The victims must have seen something in him. Unless they were convinced he was homosexual, they wouldn't have invited him home or allowed themselves to be tied up," he said. "He won't like the fact that they regard him as one of their own."

Britton felt that the precision and economy of the killings, and the "command and control" style of communication he had used with the police and media, suggested some military training. He said that the killer had created a dramatic tableau at each murder scene: "One, it gave him pleasure; and, two, it set you a puzzle."

When told that the police had a suspect – Ireland – in custody, Britton drew up a plan for his questioning.

"Every soldier knows to give nothing away under interrogation," he said. "However, he isn't truly a trained soldier. He doesn't have the personal resources to sustain himself indefinitely. It is extremely difficult to maintain a silence, and he doesn't yet know how difficult. He's going to learn."

But, after two days of intensive questioning, Ireland still admitted nothing and was remanded in prison. "He will still be hearing the questions you ask him," said Britton. "He has to set the record straight. That's when he'll confess."

After three weeks on remand, Ireland asked to speak to the police, adding, "but not those bastards who interviewed me. They really got under my skin."

In a detailed statement given over two days, he admitted all five murders. He was tried at London's Old Bailey in December 1993, found guilty and given five life sentences with the recommendation that he never be released. He died in prison in HMP Wakefield, Yorkshire, in 2012. He was fifty-seven.

2

DONALD NEILSON
The Black Panther
UNITED KINGDOM

After a series of murders, Donald Neilson kidnapped a teenage heiress, turning himself into the most wanted criminal in Britain. Throughout his criminal career, he dressed in black and wore a black hood, which earned him the nickname The Black Panther.

Born Donald Nappey in 1936, he was teased both at school and during National Service in Kenya, Aden, and Cyprus. He loved the army, but his wife persuaded him to give up life in the services and return to their home in Bradford. When their daughter was born in 1960, he changed his name to Neilson so that she would not suffer the bullying he had endured.

He worked as a jobbing builder, but failed to make ends meet. Financial failure as a taxi driver and a security guard led him to become embittered and overbearing. His wife and daughter suffered. A photograph album found in their home showed them in combat gear, camped out under camouflage netting and throwing soft-drink cans as make-believe grenades.

BRACE AND BIT

To supplement his income, Neilson took to burglary. Known as the "Brace and Bit Robber", he would drill a hole in the window frame of a house and flip the catch. It is thought that he committed some four hundred burglaries this way, but this did not bring him the money he needed. So he took to robbing sub-Post Offices as they were less well defended than main branches. He robbed nineteen in all.

On February 16, 1972, he broke into a sub-Post Office in Heywood, Lancashire. The owner Leslie Richardson woke to be confronted by a hooded man carrying a shotgun. In the ensuing struggle the shotgun went off, blasting a hole in the ceiling. Richardson pulled off the hood and got a good look at the robber before he made off.

Two years later, he broke into a sub-Post Office in Harrogate, North Yorkshire. He shot the sub-postmaster

Donald Skepper in front of his wife and son. Neilson fled empty handed and Mr Skepper died of his wounds. The police made the connection with the incident in Heywood, but the photofits developed from the survivors' testimony did not match.

By the time Neilson struck again in Accrington, Lancashire, the police had interviewed over thirty thousand people in the hunt for the man the media were now calling The Black Panther. This time sub-postmaster Derek Astin woke to find a hooded man in his bedroom. They fought and the shotgun went off. Mr Astin died of his wounds in hospital. The *modus operandi* matched the attacks in Heywood and Harrogate. So did the spent cartridges the perpetrator had left behind.

When Neilson struck again two months later, he chose a different method of entry. Armed with a bottle of ammonia attached to a torch, he knocked on the back door of the sub-Post Office in Langley, Worcestershire, at 7:00 p.m. while the owner Sidney Grayland and his wife Margaret were stocktaking.

When Mr Grayland answered, Neilson planned to blind him with the ammonia, but only succeeded in squirting himself in the face. He ripped off his hood just as Mr Grayland's wife entered. Neilson attacked her, fracturing her skull and shot her husband dead, while leaving his wife critically injured. Again the spent cartridge matched those from the previous attacks. Neilson had made off with just £800 in cash and postal orders.

RANSOM DEMAND

He decided to up his game. He read in the *Daily Express* that seventeen-year-old Lesley Whittle had inherited £82,500 – worth some £700,000 today – from her father who had run a successful coach company based at Highley and nearby Kidderminster. On January 14, 1975, Neilson broke into her home in Highley, Shropshire, abducting her from her bedroom, allowing her only to put on a dressing gown and slippers.

When Lesley did not appear for breakfast the next morning, her mother went to investigate and discovered a ransom note demanding £50,000 in used notes punched on a strip of Dymotape. It told the family not to go to the police, but to take the ransom with them to a call box in Kidderminster that evening and await a call.

However, Lesley's older brother Ronald disobeyed and contacted the police and the news leaked to the media. Now that the kidnap was in the public domain, the police figured that the kidnapper would fear being entrapped and call off the ransom drop. The phone in the call box rang. No one answered.

That night Neilson attempted to raid a security depot in Dudley, West Midlands, where he intended to leave another ransom note. However, he was stopped by security guard Gerald Smith, who he shot six times. Fleeing the scene,

Neilson left behind a Morris 1300 car he had stolen. The spent cartridges matched those from The Black Panther attacks, but the police did not immediately connect the incident to the Whittle kidnapping and overlooked the car.

NAKED AND STRANGLED

The following night, Ronald Whittle answered the phone to hear a recording of Lesley's voice telling him to go to a phone box in Kidsgrove, Staffordshire. He drove there, followed by several unmarked police cars. He found another Dymotape message telling him to go to Bathpool Park in Staffordshire and wait for a torch signal. But he got there late and no signal came.

Earlier a courting couple had driven into the park and were puzzled by a torch signal that was flashed at them. Then a police car turned up. Neilson fled, convinced that it was a trap. There were recriminations between West Mercia Police, who were investigating the case, and the Staffordshire constabulary, whose car it was.

Detective Chief Superintendent Bob Booth, who was leading the inquiry, wanted to search the park, but he was over-ruled by Scotland Yard whose detectives had taken over the case.

A week later, the West Midlands Police came across the stolen Morris 1300. Inside the car was a cassette tape and four envelopes that contained detailed instructions for the ransom drop. They called West Mercia Police.

DCS Booth then ordered a search of Bathpool Park. His team found another Dymotape message which read: "Drop the suitcase in the hole." Nearby was a drainage shaft. Inside, the police found a ledge with a sleeping bag on it.

Then to their horror, they found the naked body of Lesley Whittle hanging from a metal hawser. It had strangled her. The drainage shaft was just a few yards from where Ronald Whittle had stopped, intending to deliver the ransom. They had found the hostage, but they were no closer to finding the culprit.

Still short of money, Neilson returned to robbing sub-Post Offices.

CATCHING THE PANTHER

One night in December 1975, PCs Tony White and Stuart Mackenzie were in a Panda car near Mansfield, North Nottinghamshire, when they saw a man dressed in black and carrying a holdall, acting suspiciously outside a sub-Post Office.

When they called him over to question him, he pulled a shotgun out of the holdall and ordered PC White to get in the back of the car. Keeping the gun trained on PC Mackenzie, the gunman ordered him to drive to Blidworth, six miles away. He told them not to look at him or he would kill them both, and ordered White to find some rope to tie them up.

In his confusion about which way to go, White noticed that the gunman was distracted. He seized the gun, while Mackenzie stamped on the brake, bringing the car to a halt outside The Junction Chip Shop in Rainworth. In the ensuing struggle, the gun went off, grazing White's hand, but otherwise doing no harm. Two men came running from the queue in the chip shop and helped restrain the gunman.

Once he was handcuffed to the railings by a bus stop, a search of his bag revealed two Panther masks.

CONFRONTED WITH EVIDENCE

In custody, Neilson refused to answer any questions. But his fingerprints matched one found on a notebook in the drainage shaft with the body of Lesley Whittle. Searching his house in Bradford, police found guns, ammunition and a model of a black panther.

Confronted with the evidence, Neilson finally cracked and made a full confession. However, he maintained that he had not killed Lesley, saying she must have slipped off the ledge and died, or even thrown herself off, killing herself. But when she was found, she was emaciated. He had left her there on her own to starve.

In July 1976, Donald Neilson went on trial at Oxford Crown Court and was given five life sentences. Neilson's wife Irene was sentenced to a year for cashing stolen postal orders. Her husband appeared as a surprise witness at her appeal, but his testimony failed to convince the court that he had coerced her into wrongdoing.

On December 17, 2011, Neilson was taken from Norwich Prison to Norwich University Hospital with breathing difficulties. He was pronounced dead the next day.

3

PETER SUTCLIFFE
The Yorkshire Ripper
UNITED KINGDOM

More than a hundred years after the Jack the Ripper murders, Peter Sutcliffe, the Yorkshire Ripper, picked up where Jack had left off. By the time he was caught, twenty women had been savagely attacked, thirteen brutally murdered and a whole community was virtually under siege. In a reign of terror spanning nearly six years, he managed to elude the biggest police squad that has ever been assembled to catch one man. It started on October 30, 1975, when a Leeds milkman saw a shapeless bundle on a recreation ground and went to investigate.

FRENZIED ATTACKS

A woman was sprawled on the ground with her jacket and blouse torn open, and her bra pushed up. Her trousers had been pulled down below her knees and in her chest and stomach there were fourteen stab wounds.

What he didn't see, however, was the massive wound on the back of her head that had caused her death. Two vicious blows delivered by a heavy, hammer-like implement smashed her skull. The stab wounds had been inflicted in a frenzied attack on the corpse.

The body belonged to a twenty-eight-year-old mother of three, Wilma McCann. She had died just a hundred yards from her home. Although her clothes had been interfered with, her panties were still in place and she had not been raped. Her purse was missing, so the police treated her murder as a by-product of robbery.

This was reviewed after a second killing, this time in Chapeltown, the red-light district of Leeds, three months later. Not all the women who worked there were professional prostitutes. Forty-two-year-old Emily Jackson was an enthusiastic amateur who had sex with other men for fun.

On January 20, 1976, Jackson and her husband went to the Gaiety pub on the Roundhay Road. She left her husband in the lounge and went hunting for business. Later she was seen getting into a Land Rover in the car park. At closing time, her husband drank up and took a taxi home, thinking his wife had found a client who wanted her for the night.

Emily Jackson's body was found the next morning under a coat on open ground. Like Wilma McCann, her breasts were exposed and her panties left on. Again, she had been killed by two massive blows to the head with a heavy hammer. Her neck, breasts and stomach had been stabbed over fifty times in a furious attack after she died. Her back had been gouged with a Phillips screwdriver and the impression of a heavy, ribbed Wellington boot was stamped on her right thigh.

The post mortem indicated that Emily Jackson had had sex before the attack, not necessarily with the murderer. Once again, there seemed to be no real motive. And the killer had left only one real clue: he had size-seven shoes.

RIPPER PARALLELS

Over a year later, on February 5, 1977, twenty-eight-year-old part-time prostitute Irene Richardson left her tawdry rooming house in Chapeltown half-an-hour before midnight. The following morning, a jogger in Soldier's Field, a public playing-field just a short car ride from Chapeltown, saw a body on the ground. It was Irene Richardson. She lay face down. Three massive blows had shattered her skull. Her skirt and tights had been torn off. Again, her neck and torso were studded with knife wounds. The post mortem indicated that she had not had sex and had died only half-an-hour after leaving her lodgings.

After the murder of Irene Richardson, the police linked the three cases. They were plainly the work of a serial killer and the parallel with the Jack the Ripper murders sprang into the media's imagination. The murderer of Wilma McCann, Emily Jackson and Irene Richardson soon became known as the Yorkshire Ripper.

The streetwalkers of Chapeltown moved away and some began plying their trade in nearby Bradford. But the next victim, Patricia "Tina" Atkinson, was a Bradford girl. She lived near the red-light district in Oak Lane. On April 23, 1977, she went to her local pub, The Carlisle, for a drink with her friends, leaving just before closing time. When she was not seen the next day, people assumed she was at home, sleeping it off.

The following evening, friends dropped round and found the door to her flat unlocked. Inside, they found her dead. Four hammer blows had smashed into the back of her head. She had been flung on the bed and her clothes pulled off. She had been stabbed in the stomach seven times and the left side of her body had been slashed to ribbons. There was a size-seven Wellington boot print on the sheet.

VOICE OF GOD
The footprint belonged to Peter Sutcliffe who thought he

was on a moral crusade to rid the streets of prostitutes. The eldest of six children, he had been born in Bingley, six miles north of Bradford. He was small and weedy. Bullied at school, he clung to his mother's skirts.

Although he showed no interest in girls, he spent hours preening himself in the bathroom. He later took up body building. Leaving school at fifteen, he took a job as a gravedigger at a cemetery in Bingley. At his trial Sutcliffe claimed that he had heard the voice of God during his three years working there. It told him to kill prostitutes.

Sutcliffe's first proper girlfriend, Sonia, was a sixteen-year-old schoolgirl when he met her in the Royal Standard, his local pub. She suffered the same introversion as Sutcliffe and would only speak to members of his family when it was absolutely unavoidable.

A devout Catholic, Peter was devastated when it was discovered that his mother was having an affair with a neighbour, a local policeman. His father arranged for the children, including Peter and bride-to-be Sonia, to be present at a Bingley hotel for a humiliating confrontation. His mother arrived in the bar believing she was meeting her boyfriend, only to be greeted by her husband and children.

He forced her to show the family the new night-dress she had bought for the occasion. This was particularly painful for Peter who had discovered earlier that Sonia also had a secret boyfriend.

Later that year, 1969, Sutcliffe carried out his first known attack. He hit a Bradford prostitute over the head with a stone in a sock following a row over a £10 note. Psychiatrists later said that the discovery of his mother's affair triggered his psychosis.

UNMISTAKABLE RIPPER TRADEMARKS

After an eight-year courtship, Peter and Sonia married. They spent the first three years of their married life living with Sonia's parents, then they moved to a large detached house in Heaton, a middle-class suburb of Bradford.

On June 25, 1977, Sutcliffe dropped his wife off at the Sherrington Nursing Home where she worked nights. With his neighbours Ronnie and Peter Barker, he went on a pub crawl around Bradford. It was well after midnight when he dropped the Barker brothers at their front door.

But instead of parking his white Ford Corsair outside his house, Sutcliffe drove to Leeds. At around 2:00 a.m., he saw a lone girl wearing a gingham skirt on Chapeltown Road. He parked his car, got out and began to follow her down the quiet side street.

The girl's body was found lying by a wall the next morning by a group of children on their way into the adventure playground in Reginald Terrace. She had been struck on the back of the head, then dragged twenty yards and hit twice more. She was also stabbed once in the back and repeatedly through the chest. The Ripper trademarks were unmistakable.

However, the victim was not a prostitute. Jayne McDonald was sixteen, had just left school and was working in the shoe department of a local supermarket. On the night of her death, she had been out with friends in Leeds and was on her way back to her parents' home, which was just a few hundred yards from where her body was found.

The murder of a teenage girl gave the investigation new impetus. By September, the police had interviewed almost seven hundred residents in the area and taken 3,500 statements, many of them from prostitutes who worked in the area.

Two weeks after the killing of Jayne McDonald, the Ripper savagely attacked Maureen Long on some waste ground near her home in Bradford. By some miracle she survived, but the description of her assailant was too hazy to help the inquiry.

The 304 full-time police officers now investigating the case had soon interviewed 175,000 people, taken 12,500 statements and checked 10,000 vehicles. The problem was that they had no idea of what type of man they were looking for.

Certainly no one would have suspected long-distance lorry driver Peter Sutcliffe. The thirty-one-year-old was a polite and mild-mannered neighbour, a hard-working and trusted employee, a good son and a loyal husband.

Nothing about him suggested that he was a serial killer.

SMASHING HER SKULL

Those who knew Sutcliffe would also have been surprised if they had seen him out picking up prostitutes. But that's what he did, regularly. On October 1, 1977, Jean Jordan climbed into Sutcliffe's new red Ford Corsair near her home in Moss Side, Manchester.

She took £5 in advance and directed him to some open land two miles away. They were a few yards away from the car when Sutcliffe killed Jean Jordan, smashing her skull eleven times with a hammer. He dragged her body into some bushes, but another car arrived and he made a quick getaway.

As he drove back to Bradford, Sutcliffe realized that he had left a vital clue on the body. The £5 note he had given Jean Jordan was brand new. It had come directly from his wage packet and could tie him to the dead girl.

For eight long days, he waited nervously. In that time, there was nothing in the press about the body being found. So he risked returning to Moss Side to find the note. Despite a frantic search, he could not find Jean Jordan's handbag. In frustration, he started attacking her body with a broken pane of glass.

He even tried to cut off the head to remove his smashed skull signature. But the glass was not sharp enough to sever the spine. In the end, he gave up, kicked the body several times and drove home.

The following day, an allotment owner found Jean Jordan's naked body. The damage to her head made her unrecognizable and she was eventually identified from a fingerprint on a lemonade bottle she had handled before leaving home for the last time.

The police also found the £5 note. They set about tracing it. In three months they interviewed five thousand men. One of them was Peter Sutcliffe, but they missed him and let him go about his gruesome business.

VANISHING TWIN

Sutcliffe's next victim was eighteen-year-old Helen Rytka, who shared a miserable room in Huddersfield with her twin sister Rita. The two of them worked as a pair in the red-light district around Great Northern Street. Stories about the Yorkshire Ripper murders scared them, so they had devised a system which they thought would keep them safe. They based themselves outside a public lavatory.

When one of them was picked up, the other took the number of the client's car. They each gave their client precisely twenty minutes and then returned to the toilet at a set time. But their system went horribly wrong.

On the snowy night of January 31, 1978, Helen arrived back at the rendezvous five minutes early. At 9:25 p.m. a bearded man in a red Ford Corsair offered her the chance of a quick £5. She thought she could perform her services quickly and make it back to the rendezvous before Rita returned.

Helen took her client to a nearby timber yard. There Sutcliffe had sexual intercourse with her in the back of the car. As she got out to return to the front seat, Sutcliffe swung at her with his hammer. He missed and hit the door of the car. His second blow struck her on the head. Then he hit her five more times.

Sutcliffe dragged Helen's body into a woodpile and hid it there. Her bra and black polo-neck sweater were pushed up above her breasts. Her socks were left on, but the rest of her clothes were scattered over a wide area. Her black lace panties were found the next day by a lorry driver, pinned to the shed door.

Back at the lavatory, Rita was desperately worried, but fear of the police prevented her from reporting her sister's disappearance for three days. A police sniffer dog found the hidden body. There were three gaping wounds in the chest where she had been stabbed repeatedly.

HAMMERED AND HIDDEN

A few weeks later, a passerby spotted an arm sticking out from under an overturned sofa on wasteland in Bradford's red-light district. He thought it was a tailor's dummy but the putrid aroma sent him rushing to a telephone.

The body was that of twenty-two-year-old Yvonne

Pearson. She was a high-class hooker who serviced rich businessmen and had been killed two months earlier, ten days before Helen Rytka. The killing bore all the hallmarks of a Ripper attack – a hammer had been used to smash her skull. Her bra and jumper were pulled up exposing her breasts, and her chest had been jumped on until her ribs cracked. Her black flared slacks had been pulled down. Horsehair from the sofa was stuffed in her mouth.

Although he had hidden her body, the killer seemed concerned that it had not been found and returned to make it more visible. He tucked a copy of the *Daily Mirror*, from four weeks after her death, under her arm.

Two months after Yvonne Pearson's body was found, the Yorkshire Ripper attacked forty-one-year-old Vera Millward. The Spanish-born mother of seven children, Vera resorted to prostitution in Manchester's Moss Side to help her support her family. On the night of May 16, she went out to get painkillers from the hospital for her chronic stomach pains. She died in a well-lit part of the grounds of Manchester Royal Infirmary. Sutcliffe hit her three times on the head with a hammer and then slashed her across the stomach. Her body was discovered by a gardener the next morning on a rubbish pile in the corner of the car park.

Three months after Vera Millward's death, the police visited Sutcliffe again because his car registration number had cropped up during special checks in Leeds and

Bradford. They returned to question him about the tyres on his car. They were looking for treads that matched the tracks at the scene of Irene Richardson's murder, twenty-one months earlier. As before, Sutcliffe was helpful and gave them no reason to suspect him.

WEARSIDE JACK

Suddenly the Ripper's killing spree stopped. For eleven months he dropped out of sight. But Sutcliffe could not contain his desire to murder. On the night of April 4, 1979, he drove to Halifax. Around midnight, he got out of his car and accosted nineteen-year-old Josephine Whitaker as she walked across Savile Park playing fields. As they moved away from the street lamps, he smashed the back of her head with a hammer and dragged her body into the shadows. It was found the next morning.

Like Jayne McDonald, Josephine Whitaker was not a prostitute. She lived at home with her family and worked as a clerk in the headquarters of the Halifax Building Society. By then no woman felt safe on the streets after dark.

On the morning of June 17, 1979, two months after Josephine Whitaker's death, the police received a buff-coloured envelope. It contained a cassette tape with a 257-word message in a broad Geordie accent. Addressed to Assistant Chief Constable George Oldfield the words taunted the police boss: "I'm Jack. I see you are still having no luck catching me. I have the greatest respect for you George, but Lord! You are no nearer catching me now than four years ago when I started. I reckon your boys are letting you down, George. They can't be much good, can they?"

A huge publicity campaign was mounted. The public could dial in and listen to the "Geordie Ripper Tape," in the hope that someone might recognize the voice. Within a few days, more than 50,000 people had called.

Language experts confirmed the accent as genuine Wearside, and pinned it down to Castletown, a small tightly knit suburb of Sunderland. Eleven detectives were installed in a Sunderland hotel and a hundred officers combed the town. Only four thousand people lived in Castletown, but the police could not find their man.

In the end the "Wearside Jack" tape turned out to be a hoax perpetrated by one John Samuel Humble who also sent several fake taunting letters to the police pretending to be the Ripper. It is thought that Humble's actions misled the investigation and helped sustain the Ripper attacks on women for eighteen months. Eventually more than twenty-five years later, DNA from one of Humble's envelopes was traced back to him, and in 2006 he was sentenced to eight years for perverting the course of justice.

In July 1979, Detective-Constable Laptew visited Sutcliffe again. His car had been spotted in the red-light district of Bradford on thirty-six separate occasions. This time Laptew felt suspicious of Sutcliffe but, because all eyes were focused on the Geordie tape, his report was not followed up and Sutcliffe was allowed to claim his eleventh victim.

THREE MORE STRUCK DOWN

On Saturday, September 1, 1979, Sutcliffe cruised the streets around Little Horton, a residential area of Bradford. At about 1:00 a.m. he saw Barbara Leach, a student, moving away from a group of friends outside the Mannville Arms. Just two-hundred yards from the pub, he attacked Barbara Leach and dragged her body into a backyard. He stabbed her eight times, stuffed her body into a dustbin and slung an old carpet over it. The corpse was found the following afternoon.

Two high-ranking officers from Scotland Yard were sent to Bradford but got nowhere. A task force from Manchester reviewed the £5 note inquiry in the Jean Jordan murder case. They narrowed down the field to two hundred and seventy suspects, but could get no further.

Like everyone else in Yorkshire, Sutcliffe spoke to family and friends about the Ripper. He would make a point of picking up Sonia from work to protect her and told a workmate: "Whoever is doing all these murders has a lot to answer for." Once his colleagues at the depot made a bet that he was the Ripper – but Sutcliffe just laughed and said nothing.

The Ripper took another break of nearly a year. Then on August 18, 1980, he struck for the twelfth time. The victim was Marguerite Walls, a forty-seven-year-old civil servant. She was working late at the Department of Education and Science in Leeds and left the office at 10:00 p.m. to walk home.

Her body was found two days later, under a mound of grass clippings in the garden of a magistrate's house. She had been bludgeoned and strangled, but her body had not been mutilated so the police did not realize that she was one of the Ripper's victims.

Three months later, Sutcliffe had just finished eating a chicken dinner in his car when he saw Jacqueline Hill, a language student at the University of Leeds, get off the bus outside the Kentucky Fried Chicken outlet. His fingers were still greasy when he viciously struck her down.

He dragged her body to waste ground behind the shops and attacked it savagely. Death had struck Jacqueline so suddenly that one of her eyes had remained open. Sutcliffe stabbed it repeatedly with a rusty Phillips screwdriver which he had sharpened into a fine point.

STUMBLING ON THE RIPPER

The Home Office then appointed a special Ripper Squad to solve the case, but it got no further than the West Yorkshire force. What they needed was a lucky break.

On January 2, 1981, Sergeant Robert Ring and Police

Constable Robert Hydes started their evening shift by cruising along Melbourne Avenue in Sheffield's red-light district. They saw Olivia Reivers climbing into a Rover V8 3500 and decided to investigate.

The driver – a bearded man – identified himself as Peter Williams. He said he wanted no trouble. Then he scrambled out of the car and asked if he could relieve himself. He went over to the bushes lining the street and, while pretending to take a pee, dropped a ball-peen hammer and sharp knife which he kept in a special pocket of his car coat. The police did not notice this as Olivia Reivers was remonstrating loudly they were ruining her livelihood. Little did she know that Ring and Hydes had just saved her life by unwittingly stumbling on the Yorkshire Ripper.

By the time the man had strolled back to his car, the police had discovered that the number plates were false. He was taken to the police station where he admitted his name was Peter William Sutcliffe.

During his interview, Sutcliffe said his main worry was that the police would tell his wife that he had been picked up with a prostitute. Otherwise, he was calm and apparently forthcoming. He readily admitted that he had stolen the number plates from a scrapyard in Dewsbury. The police even let him go to the lavatory alone, where he hid a second knife in the cistern.

There was no real reason to suspect Sutcliffe, but his details were forwarded to the West Yorkshire Police before he was released. He was locked up for the night. The next morning Sutcliffe was taken, unprotesting, to Dewsbury police station.

There he was quite chatty. In passing, he mentioned that he had been interviewed by the Ripper Squad about the £5 note and that he had also visited Bradford's red-light district.

Dewsbury police called the Ripper Squad in Leeds. Detective Sergeant Des O'Boyle discovered that Sutcliffe's name had come up several times in the course of the investigation. He drove to Dewsbury. When he called his boss, Detective Inspector John Boyle, in Leeds that evening, he told Boyle that Sutcliffe was blood group B – the rare blood group the police knew the Ripper had. Sutcliffe was locked in his cell for a second night.

Meanwhile, Sergeant Ring heard one of his colleagues casually mention that the man he had arrested was being interviewed by detectives from the Ripper Squad. Ring went back to Melbourne Avenue. Hidden in the bushes there, he found Sutcliffe's ball-peen hammer and knife.

MURDERER OR MAD MAN

Sonia Sutcliffe was questioned and the house was searched. Then Boyle told Sutcliffe that the hammer and knife had been found in Sheffield. Sutcliffe, who had been talkative up to this point, fell silent.

"I think you're in trouble, serious trouble," said Boyle.

Sutcliffe finally spoke.

"I think you are leading up to the Yorkshire Ripper," he said.

Boyle nodded.

"Well," Sutcliffe said, "that's me."

Sixteen weeks later, Sutcliffe stood trial at the Old Bailey. The Crown Prosecution, defence counsel and Attorney General Sir Michael Havers agreed that Sutcliffe was mentally ill, suffering from paranoid schizophrenia. But the judge would have none of this. He told both counsels that the jury would listen to the evidence and decide whether Sutcliffe was a murderer or a mad man.

Sutcliffe pleaded guilty to manslaughter, saying that the voice of God had sent him on a mission to kill prostitutes. The jury would not accept this and found him guilty of thirteen murders. The judge recommended he should serve at least thirty years when handing down twenty concurrent life sentences which Sutcliffe began at HM Prison Parkhurst on May 22, 1981.

During his imprisonment Sutcliffe was the victim of multiple assaults by other inmates. He required thirty stitches in a facial wound in 1983 after being attacked with a broken coffee jar. In 1997 he lost the vision in his left eye after being stabbed in the eye with a pen, and then in 2007 an attempt to blind his right eye with a cutlery knife ended up stabbing his cheek. In 2010, the UK Secretary of State for Justice, Jack Straw, confirmed that he would never be released.

Suffering from a number of health problems, including obesity and diabetes, on November 13, 2020, at age 74, the Yorkshire Ripper died in prison custody from Covid-19-related complications following a suspected heart attack two weeks previously.

4

ROBERT BLACK
Smelly Bob
UNITED KINGDOM

Robert Black was orphaned twice over. His mother Jessie Hunter Black gave birth to him on April 21, 1947. She refused to put his father's name on the birth certificate. Within a few days, she gave him up for fostering. Emigrating to Australia with her new husband, she never had any contact with him again.

He was taken in by foster parents Jack and Margaret Tulip who lived in Kinlochleven, near Glencoe in the West Highlands. Jack Tulip died when Robert was five and he had no memory of him. Margaret, who used to pull down

Robert's trousers and pants to spank him with a belt, died when he was eleven.

At school, he was known as "Smelly Robbie Tulip," a bully and a loner who used to associate with younger kids who he could dominate. He was aggressive, foulmouthed, and violent.

THE ABUSER AND THE ABUSED

From the age of eight, he used to push things up his anus. He said he would have preferred to have been a girl and have a vagina rather than a penis, though he had no desire to be homosexual. The vagina was an early obsession.

When he was five, he recalled undressing with a little girl so they could examine each other's genitalia. During Highland Dance classes he would lie on the floor so he could look up girls' skirts and remembered taking the nappy off a baby so he could look at her vulva.

Sent to a children's home near Falkirk, he and two other boys took a girl into a field, removed her panties and tried to rape her. Unable to penetrate her, they contented themselves by playing with her vagina.

As a result, Black was sent to an all-boys home where he was sexually abused by a male member of staff. At school, he excelled at swimming and football, but was denied a professional career due to his poor eyesight.

At the age of fifteen, he left the home and got a job as a delivery boy, later saying he had molested thirty or forty girls on his rounds. At the age of seventeen, he asked a seven-year-old girl if she would like to see some kittens. He took her to a derelict building where he choked her until she was unconscious. Then he took her panties off and put his finger up her vagina.

Afterwards, he masturbated over her inert body. She was later found wandering the streets, crying and bleeding. In court he was admonished and put on probation, but punished no further as this was presumed to be an isolated incident.

CHILD PORNOGRAPHY

To give him a new start, Social Services moved him to Grangemouth where he met Pamela Hodgson. They got engaged, but she broke it off after a couple of months. Years later, when he was finally caught, he told officers: "Tell Pamela she's not responsible for this."

He claimed he did not molest any girls while he was with Pamela, but soon after they broke up he sexually abused the nine-year-old granddaughter of his landlady and was ordered to leave the house. After losing his job, he returned to Kinlochleven where he molested the seven-year-old daughter of a couple who rented him a room. Found guilty of indecent assault, he was sent to borstal.

On his release, he moved to London where he indulged his fantasies with child pornography. He took a job as a swimming pool attendant so he could ogle young girls and, at night, would swim lengths of the pool with a broom-handle up his backside. When a young girl said that he had touched her inappropriately, he was sacked.

In 1972, a couple rented him a room in their house. Their children called him "Smelly Bob". He took a job with a firm called Poster Dispatch and Storage, delivering posters around England and Scotland. In the back of the van he would keep objects that he would insert in his rear end while fantasizing about touching young girls. He would also dress in girls' clothes – particularly swimsuits – while masturbating. And he fantasized obsessively about assaulting a seven-year-old girl, leaving her for dead.

ABDUCTION AND MURDER

On the afternoon of July 30, 1982, eleven-year-old Susan Maxwell, who lived outside Cornhill-on-Tweed on the English side of the England-Scotland border, went to play tennis with a friend two miles away in Coldstream in Scotland. On the way home, she disappeared.

On August 13, her body was found outside Uttoxeter in England's Midlands, two hundred and fifty miles away. It was a hot summer and her body was so badly decomposed she had to be identified from dental records. Her panties had been removed and lay folded behind her head, and her yellow shorts had been replaced.

On the evening of July 8, 1983, five-year-old Caroline Hogg went out to play in the park in Portobello on the outskirts of Edinburgh. It was a small community where everyone knew each other. She had been told not to talk to strangers and was forbidden to go beyond the park to the promenade or the local fairground called Fun City.

When she did not return home, her family went out to look for her. People told them that they had seen her holding hands with a scruffy man at Fun City. A search was organized, but it proved fruitless. Her body was found near Twycross in Leicestershire three-hundred miles from home, but just twenty-four miles from where Susan Maxwell had been found. Again her body was badly decomposed but, this time, it was naked.

Soon the inquiry was overwhelmed with index cards, so for the first time since the Yorkshire Ripper enquiry a computer system was used. But it was only introduced on the Caroline Hogg case. Susan Maxwell's investigation remained manual.

Nearly three years passed until March 26, 1986, when ten-year-old Sarah Harper ran an errand for her mother in Leeds, Yorkshire. At 8:00 p.m., she went to buy a loaf of bread at the corner shop just over a hundred yards from her home. On the way back, she disappeared. The family searched for her, then called the police.

On April 19, her body was found floating in the River Trent. Her vagina and anus had been "violently explored". There were other horrific injuries and it was determined that she had been dumped in the river while she was still alive. She was found within twenty-six miles of the bodies of the other two girls. Her case too was added to the computer system, but to no avail.

Four more years passed. Then on July 14, 1990, six-year-old Mandy Wilson was walking to a friend's house in the village of Stow in the Scottish Borders when a man grabbed her and bundled her into a van. A witness took down the registration number and called the police. When they arrived, the van drove by again. An officer ran out into the road and stopped the van. The driver identified himself as Robert Black.

CHILLING CALCULATION

Behind the seat, Mandy Wilson was found in a sleeping bag. There was an Elastoplast bandage over her mouth and her hands were tied behind her back. Black had already sexually assaulted her.

He claimed he had "a rush of blood" when he abducted her, but he had little choice in pleading guilty when the case came to trial. The judge said there was no "rush of blood" – the abduction was "carried out with chilling, cold calculation" and sentenced him to life imprisonment. He would not be let out until it was considered safe to do so.

The investigations into the murders of Susan Maxwell, Caroline Hogg, and Sarah Harper continued. The police put together a case against him using work logs, petrol receipts, and a *modus operandi* linking the murders to

Mandy Wilson's abduction. This was circumstantial. There were no witnesses and no forensic evidence. Nevertheless the case was taken to court.

After three days of deliberation, the jury brought in a guilty verdict. Black was given three life sentences and was to serve a minimum term of thirty-five years on each conviction.

Black was also convicted of the attempted kidnapping of fifteen-year-old Teresa Thornhill in Nottingham in 1988. He was also suspected of the abduction and murder of ten young girls in Britain which bore the same MO, as well as some in Ireland, France, Germany, and the Netherlands. He died in jail in 2016, aged 69, and his ashes were scattered in the sea.

5

PETER TOBIN
Bible John?
UNITED KINGDOM

In May 2007, sixty-year-old Peter Tobin was found guilty of the rape and murder of twenty-three-year-old Polish student Ángelika Kluk and sentenced to life imprisonment with a minimum tariff of twenty-one years. Tobin was a known sex offender and it was suspected that he had been responsible for other offences, including rape and murder. Police forces across Great Britain began opening their Cold Cases files and began searching the houses where Tobin had lived.

UNBURYING THE BODIES

The following month, the police searched Tobin's old home at 11 Robertson Avenue in Bathgate, West Lothian, in connection with the disappearance of fifteen-year-old schoolgirl Vicky Hamilton who was last seen less than a mile away on February 10, 1991, waiting for a bus home to Redding near Falkirk. Tobin left Bathgate soon after Vicky went missing.

Vicky's DNA had been found at the house. The body was not found, but on July 21, 2007, Tobin was charged in connection with Vicky Hamilton's disappearance. The police went on to search 50 Irvine Drive in Margate, Kent, a property Tobin had occupied after he left Bathgate.

They dug up the garden looking for the body of Dinah McNicol, an eighteen-year-old sixth former who lived in Tillingham, Essex. She had been hitchhiking home from a music festival in Hampshire with a boyfriend who got out at Junction 8 of the M25 near Reigate. She stayed in the car and was never seen again.

A body was found in the back garden at 50 Irvine Drive. But it was not Dinah's. DNA tests proved that it was Vicky Hamilton's body the police had unearthed. Her dismembered corpse was in plastic bin bags that yielded Tobin's fingerprints. There were traces of what appeared to be semen. The DNA matched Tobin's. A knife then found in the loft at Robertson Avenue carried a tiny fragment of skin. This yielded a partial DNA match to Vicky.

The police continued digging up the garden at 50 Irvine Drive and found the body of Dinah in a shallow grave just yards away from Vicky's. Both bodies contained traces of amitriphtyline. This would have made the girls drowsy and dizzy, and unable to defend themselves against rape. Dinah's trousers and panties had been pulled down below her buttocks indicating a sexual assault had been attempted. Again Tobin's fingerprints were found on the bin bags he had used to wrap the body and on the tape he used to seal them. Tobin was charged with the murder of both young women.

PREYING ON WOMEN

Born in Johnstone, Renfrewshire, on August 27, 1946, Tobin had a history of violent crime that stretched back over forty years. He spent time in a young offender institution before serving jail terms for burglary, forgery, and conspiracy. He also spent his adult life preying on vulnerable women, inflicting pain and humiliation – not just to innocent strangers, but also those unfortunate enough to become one of his three wives. Former wives and girlfriends described him as a monster who sought to take total control of their lives, isolating them from their friends and family while mocking them in front of his.

His first wife, clerk-typist Margaret Mackintosh, was seventeen when she married him in Brighton in 1969. Some forty years later she still bore the scars of a knife attack that he made on her. Tobin had stabbed her in the area of her vagina, leaving her bleeding heavily. The knife, he said, was "metal tampax." If it had not been for the prompt action of a neighbour, she would have died. When she tried to leave him, he decapitated the puppy that he had bought for her. After a year she ran off and they divorced in 1971.

Tobin met his second wife, Sylvia Jefferies, in 1973. She said that she lived in a constant state of fear. "He'd whack me so hard it would send me flying across the room," she said. In 1976, she left with their son.

His third wife was Cathy Wilson, who at sixteen, was more than twenty years his junior. After two years of marriage, she found she had become a prisoner in her own home. Tobin would not allow her to go outside. "He was violent on almost a daily basis," she said. "If he said something and I dared to speak back or answer him in a way he thought disrespectful he would blow up."

Realizing that she had to escape, she waited until Tobin went out with a friend one night. "He'd taken my car keys, house keys, money, bank books and my driving licence with him but I had a stash of grocery money he didn't know about," she said. "It was only £25 but it paid for a bus ticket to Brighton. I was terrified he would find us and drag us back. I was literally sitting in the station crying with fear until the bus left."

LAYING FALSE TRAILS

On Friday, February 8, 1991, Vicky Hamilton had left home to spend the weekend with her older sister in Livingston, West Lothian. Fifteen-year-old Vicky had just had a pregnancy test. She travelled back to Redding on the Sunday evening and had to change buses at Bathgate, where she vanished. The bus stop was right around the corner from Tobin's house.

When Vicky Hamilton was reported missing, police scoured the neighbourhood. But they did not interview Tobin. He had only recently moved into the district and kept himself to himself. It has not been established what he did with Vicky Hamilton after he raped and killed her.

The knife he had used to cut up his young victim was hidden in the loft. Meanwhile Tobin was laying false trails for the police. Eleven days after Vicky had gone missing, Tobin went to Edinburgh, where he dropped Vicky's purse. It contained an identity card and a piece of paper with the word "Samaritans" on it. A passer-by handed it in to the police, distracting their attention from Bathgate, though later it would count against him. DNA belonging to his son was found on it.

Tobin then moved to Margate in Kent. He arrived at 50 Irvine Drive with his secret cargo – the dismembered body of Vicky Hamilton, destined for a shallow grave in the back garden. Soon she would be joined by another corpse.

On Saturday, August 3, 1991, Dinah McNicol met

David Tremett at the Torpedo Town Festival in Liphook, Hampshire. On Monday, they set off to hitchhike back to their homes. At a service station near the M25, they were picked up by a scruffy man in a green hatchback. Though Tremett, who sat in the back, thought the man was a little odd, he chatted away to Dinah in the front.

The driver stopped to let Tremett out at the turn-off for Redhill where he lived. Worried about leaving Dinah alone with a strange man, he suggested she came with him. But she was eager to get home to Tillingham and said she would be okay.

Dinah's father had been expecting her on August 5, but she did not arrive home. Then money began to disappear from her bank account. It was withdrawn in sums of up to £250 from ATM machines along the south coast between Havant in Hampshire and Margate. Nine months later, the disappearance of Dinah McNicol featured on the TV police bulletin programme *Crimewatch*.

POTENT COCKTAIL

Despite their acrimonious divorce, Cathy Wilson still allowed Tobin to have access to their son Daniel. On August 4, 1993, when the five-year-old went to stay with his father, he walked into Tobin's room in a flat he was renting in Havant and found two fourteen-year-old girls, one of them unconscious. The two girls had called to visit the woman next door, who was not in. They knocked on

Tobin's door and asked if they could wait there.

Tobin plied them with cider and vodka. One of them passed out; the other was sick. When she tried to wake her friend, Tobin threatened her with a knife and said he would kill her if she kept on crying. He forced her at knife point to take a potent cocktail of pills and wine. When Daniel came in, the girl begged him to get help, but Tobin ushered him out. Once the girl was unconscious, Tobin raped and sodomized her.

Afraid that a search of the flats might already be underway, Tobin called Cathy, telling her to come and collect Daniel. Once they were gone, Tobin turned on the gas, opened the window and escaped down a drainpipe. But his attempt to gas the victims failed. One of the girls awoke to find her panties round her ankles. Her friend was lying naked next to her. She fled and raised the alarm.

Tobin went to stay with the Jesus Fellowship at the King's House Centre, near Southam. A few days after he left, one of the Fellowship was watching *Crimewatch* and recognized Tobin. He was arrested soon after in Brighton.

At Winchester Crown Court Tobin pleaded guilty to the rape of one of the girls and the indecent assault of the other. He was sentenced to fourteen years and released on licence after seven. Almost immediately, he breached the terms of the licence when he moved home without informing the police of his new address. He was returned to prison for another three years and put on the Sex Offenders Register.

KILLING ÁNGELIKA KLUK

After his release, Tobin returned to his native Scotland, to live in Paisley. There he met twenty-four-year-old Cheryl McLachlan and invited her to watch a football match back at his flat. She had visited him there before. This time, though, he was agitated, and he attacked her with a kitchen knife. She got away and went to the police. But when they arrived at Tobin's flat, he was already gone. A warrant was issued for his arrest, but they failed to trace him.

Tobin then adopted the name Pat McLaughlin and again found refuge with a religious community – this time at St Patrick's RC Church in Anderston. Under the "open doors policy", they took him on as an odd-job man. There he befriended Ángelika Kluk.

A devout Catholic, she was from the small town of Skoczów in Poland. In Glasgow she found a flat in the Anderston district, just five minutes walk from St Patrick's. After mass one day, she introduced herself to Father Gerry Nugent who ran the "open doors policy" for the needy.

A few weeks later, her landlord asked her to leave. Father Nugent invited her to stay in one of the rooms in the chapel house. They became close. They would exchange a hug before they retired to their separate beds. Then came a kiss on the cheek. Soon their beds were separate no longer.

She got a job as a nanny to a wealthy Russian family. There she met Martin MacAskill, the forty-year-old owner of a chauffeuring business. They soon became lovers. As MacAskill was married, they made love in the chapel house. Then his wife found out about it and MacAskill and his wife went to Majorca in an attempt to patch up their twelve-year marriage.

On September 24, 2006, just a few days before Ángelika was due to return to Poland, she was helping Tobin paint a shed that they had built in the garage. She needed the company. Father Nugent was barely on speaking terms with her now, and she had not seen MacAskill for ten days. By then Tobin had been working at St Patrick's for about two months and had been dreaming of having sex with Ángelika ever since he had arrived.

He clubbed her on the back of the head. He bound and gagged her. Then he raped her. When Ángelika tried to fend him off, he grabbed a knife and stabbed her nineteen times. He wrapped her body in a plastic sheet and shoved it down a hatch under a rug outside the confessional box.

THE MISSING AND THE DEAD

Martin MacAskill, who had returned to Scotland, started phoning Ángelika's mobile. When he could not contact Ángelika, he called her sister Aneta who was also in Glasgow. Together they searched Ángelika's room at St Patrick's. Nothing was missing, except her mobile phone. MacAskill called the police. Two constables arrived to search the premises and took statements from everyone there, including the handyman.

Early the following morning, Tobin collected his meagre possessions and left. He lay low in the centre of Glasgow and, that night, took a bus to Edinburgh. The police issued a photograph of him as the last person to have seen Ángelika alive.

In a renewed search of the church and its surrounds, they found a table-leg with Ángelika's blood on it and several blood-soaked towels. In the bin, they found a pair of jeans with the left knee covered with more of Ángelika's blood. Then one of the forensics team stumbled across the hatch in front of the confessional. Opening it, they found her body, still bound and gagged. And in a bin-liner on top of her body, they found a bloodstained kitchen knife.

Tobin checked himself into the National Neurological and Neurosurgery Hospital in Queen Square, London, under a false name, complaining of chest pains. The doctors could find nothing wrong with him and soon suspected that both the symptoms and the name were fictitious. The police arrived the next morning.

Despite the forensic evidence, Tobin pleaded not guilty when he appeared in the High Court in Edinburgh the following March. During the six-week trial, Tobin denied raping and murdering Ángelika Kluk. He was convicted and sentenced to life, with a minimum term of twenty-one years.

Tobin went on trial for the murder of Vicky Hamilton

in November 2008, the jury took less than two-and-a-half hours to find him guilty. He was again sentenced to life with a tariff of at least thirty years.

At his trial for the murder of Dinah McNicol in December 2009, Tobin instructed his counsel not to offer any defence. However, he pleaded not guilty, so the prosecution had to take the time and trouble of proving its case. Given the evidence, this was not too difficult. The jury took just thirteen minutes to deliver a unanimous verdict of guilty. Handing down a third life sentence, the judge said he should never be released.

When he was convicted of the murder of Vicky Hamilton, Tobin boasted to a prison psychiatrist that he had killed forty-eight women. The psychiatrist provoked Tobin by saying: "Prove it."

Some experts such as criminology professor David Wilson believe that Tobin was "Bible John", the nickname given to the serial killer who murdered three women in Glasgow in the 1960s. Bible John has never been caught and is still unidentified. However the significant similarities between the methodology of the two killers has led to speculation that Bible John and Peter Tobin are one and the same man.

THE BIBLE JOHN KILLINGS

Bible John's first victim was twenty-five-year-old nurse Patricia Docker. On the evening of February 22, 1968, she decided that she needed a night out. Her husband, a corporal in the RAF, was stationed in England, and she was staying with her parents with her young son. It was a Thursday night and they were happy to babysit.

She got dressed up for the occasion and fixed her hair. It seems she went to a number of ballrooms that evening. She was seen at the Majestic Ballroom in Hope Street, then moved on to the Barrowland Ballroom in Gallowgate, but she never got home.

At dawn the following morning, a cabinet maker on his way to work found the naked body of a dead woman in a quiet lane behind Carmichael Place, a few yards from Patricia's parents' house in Langside Place. She had been strangled with her own tights. None of her other clothing could be found.

The police determined that she had been dead for several hours and they came to believe that she had been strangled elsewhere and dumped there. When Patricia Docker did not return home, the police came to the obvious conclusion and Patricia's parents had the terrible task of identifying the body.

Glasgow had had recent experience of serial killers. Ian Brady, convicted of the Moors Murders in 1966, had been born there. Ten years before Patricia Docker was killed, Peter Manuel had been hanged. A sociopath and burglar, he had killed at least eight people. So when Patricia's naked body was found dumped in the street, Glaswegians feared the worst.

A year-and-a-half later, thirty-two-year-old Jemima McDonald fancied a Saturday night out. On the evening of August 16, 1969, she dropped off her three kids with her sister Margaret for the night. Then Jemima headed for the Barrowlands. High bouffant hair-styles were still in fashion in Glasgow in 1969 and she travelled across town with a scarf over her hair. When she arrived at the ballroom she went into the ladies where she took out her rollers and finished off her makeup.

She spent much of the evening dancing with a tall slim man in his late twenties or early thirties. He wore a blue suit, his red hair was cut short and his appearance was neat. Early the next morning, she was seen leaving the ballroom with him.

The next day, Jemima did not come to pick up her kids as expected. Margaret grew worried. Later that day she overheard street children talking about a body they had discovered in a derelict building in MacKeith Street nearby. Margaret got the kids to direct her to the building where she found her sister's battered body.

Jemima was fully clothed, but there were similarities to the Patricia Docker case. Both women had been strangled with their own pantyhose. Both had been found near their home. Jemima's handbag was missing and screams were heard that night. The police released a sketch of the tall man she had been seen leaving the Barrowlands with. For the first time in a Scottish murder investigation, Jemima's family offered a reward of £100. No one collected it.

BACK AT THE BARROWLANDS

Despite the publicity the murders were getting, people were not put off going to the Barrowlands. Twenty-nine-year-old Helen Puttock was hell bent on going there on the night of October 30, 1969. Her husband, a soldier, who was going to stay at home with their two young boys, begged his wife to be careful. But Helen was not worried. She would not be alone. She was going with her sister Jean and was sure they would be safe together.

At the Barrowlands, they met two young men named John. One said he came from Castlemilk. Helen spent most of the evening dancing with the other John. He was tall, slim and had red hair. When they left the Barrowlands, Castlemilk John and the two women took a cab. During the journey, he said he had been raised in a strict religious household and was able to quote long passages of the Bible – giving rise to the sinister nickname Bible John. Peter Tobin was also a Roman Catholic with a strong religious background.

John spoke of how his father regarded dance halls as "dens of iniquity", condemning the women who frequented them as evil. He also referred to Moses and said: "I don't drink at Hogmanay. I pray."

Bible John seemed upset by Jean's presence. He wanted

to be alone with Helen. Ignoring Jean for much of the ride, he did not even say goodbye when they dropped her off. The next morning Helen's fully-clothed body was found in the street by a man walking his dog. Again she had been strangled with her own nylons and her handbag was missing.

Jean gave the police an accurate description of the man they wanted to question. The suspect was around six feet tall and of medium build. He had blue-grey eyes and light reddish hair, which he kept cut short.

An artist's impression of the suspect was circulated. Jean was called to the police station over 250 times to see suspects, but none of them turned out to be the man she and her sister had shared a taxi with. Helen's husband made an appeal to his wife's killer to turn himself in and offered his life savings as a reward for information leading to his arrest.

PRIME SUSPECTS

Over fifty-thousand statements were taken and over a hundred policemen worked on the case. Younger officers in plain clothes mingled with the dancers in the Barrowlands. His short hair lead the police to believe that he might be a member of the armed forces – or even a policeman. A Dutch psychic called in by a local newspaper drew a map, but a search of the area drew a blank.

Although only three murders have been officially

ascribed to Bible John, he may have committed others. In 1977 another young woman who spent her last night in the Glasgow dancehall was found strangled and without her handbag. This sparked a renewed round of interest in Bible John. In 1983, a wealthy Glasgow man hired a private detective to find a childhood friend who he thought resembled Bible John. The man was found living in the Netherlands and was cleared.

Another man who had been cleared was John McInnes, a suspect in the investigation in the 1960s. He bore a close resemblance to the sketch of the suspect, but Jean had failed to identify him. Nevertheless, he continued to be a prime suspect until, in 1980, he committed suicide.

In the 1960s, DNA fingerprinting was as yet undreamt of. But in 1996, DNA from the semen left on Helen Puttock's tights was compared to a sample taken from one of John McInnes's siblings. The match was inconclusive. Nevertheless the police requested the exhumation of John McInnes's body from a graveyard in Stonehouse, Lanarkshire.

The resulting publicity led to the harassment of McInnes's family. But when the tests were completed it was found that his DNA did not match the semen on Helen Puttock's tights. Nor did his teeth match a bite-mark on her wrist. Jean said that she always knew that McInnes was not the killer and she had repeatedly told Strathclyde Police they had the wrong man. John McInnes was re-buried and finally left to rest in peace.

THE REAL BIBLE JOHN

But the investigation was still not over. In October 2000, Professor Ian Stephen, a leading criminal psychologist who is said to have inspired ITV's *Cracker*, passed the name of a new suspect on to the Lothian and Borders Police, asking them to forward it to Strathclyde. He said he obtained the new lead from an expatriate Scot living in the US who suspected a member of his extended family was Bible John. The suspect was the son of a policeman. He was married in the Glasgow area and lived in Lanarkshire with his wife and two children, until he moved to England in 1970.

In December 2004, DNA taken from a Glasgow crime scene two years earlier was an eighty per cent match to the semen found on Helen's tights. Samples were still being collected from a number of suspects in their fifties and sixties. In October the following year Strathclyde Police set up a new Unresolved Case Unit to re-examine the evidence in the Bible John Killings.

However Joe Jackson, a detective involved in the original Bible John investigation who went on to become head of Glasgow's CID, dismissed the evidence. As DNA fingerprinting was not developed until 1984, he said it was unlikely that the samples from the 1960s were collected or stored properly. Besides the semen stain on her tights may not necessarily have come from the killer.

Jackson is convinced that Peter Tobin is the real Bible John, saying "I saw his photo after the church killing and thought, this is as near Bible John as you're going to get."

FEELING TOTAL TERROR

Tobin was in his early twenties, living in Glasgow at the time and a regular at city dance halls. He met his first wife, Margaret Mackintosh, then seventeen, at a Glasgow dance hall in 1968. Soon he was raping, beating and strangling her. Tobin left Scotland in 1969, the year the killings stopped.

After Tobin's conviction, detectives issued pictures of him as a younger man who does bear a striking similarity to the artist's impression of Bible John drawn up at the time. When the picture of the young Tobin was shown on *Crimewatch* in 2010, sixty-three-year-old Julia Taylor came forward. She said that he had approached her in the Barrowlands forty years before and had pestered her to go to a party with him in Castlemilk.

"When I kept refusing to go to the party, his whole face and attitude changed," she said. "He turned from being charming to being really odd and frightening. He said, 'You better get off the dance floor because I am not dancing with you any more.'" Julia remembered walking off the floor to get her coat as Tobin circled around watching her.

"It was chilling," she said. "I saw a bouncer and I was

going to tell him to check the man out but I was scared. I just ran out and never stopped. I looked back and he was watching me, glaring at me. I was scared stiff and I have never forgotten that feeling of total terror."

ALIAS BIBLE JOHN

Tobin's first wife Margaret Mackintosh remembered visiting his parents in Paisley, just a few miles outside Glasgow. Before they were married, he took her to Earlbank Avenue, two hundred yards from where Helen Puttock was found.

Back then Tobin dressed, like Bible John, in a conservative black suit. Under normal circumstances both were polite, even chivalrous. Both Tobin and Bible John sexually assaulted and strangled their victims, using their clothing as gags or ligatures.

Professor David Wilson, an expert on serial killers, pointed out that Bible John was not the type of murderer who would quit while he was still at large and Tobin was uncharacteristically old to have started killing at the age of forty-four, if Vicky Hamilton was his first victim.

Among the collection of women's jewellery found in Tobin's former home was a cap badge from the Royal Electrical and Mechanical Engineers, the regiment Helen Puttock's husband belonged to.

There are many other murders that Tobin is thought to have been responsible for. He was a regular visitor to the Norfolk coast and, after his conviction, the Norfolk Constabulary began to re-examine the case of April Fabb who disappeared on April 8, 1969.

The thirteen-year-old was cycling the mile-and-a-half from Metton near Cromer to Roughton to deliver a packet of cigarettes to her brother-in-law. Her blue and white bicycle was found by the side of the road, but she was nowhere to be seen. It is thought that Tobin was in the area at the time. In 2010, a well nearby was excavated but did not produce any fresh leads.

Eighteen-year-old Jackie Ansell Lamb was hitchhiking from London to Manchester on March 8, 1970, when she went missing. A woman answering her description was seen getting into a car at Keele motorway services on the M6 between 4:00 and 5:00 p.m. A farmer found her body in a wood near Knutsford, Cheshire, six days later. She had been sexually assaulted and strangled. Tobin used the M6 on his numerous trips between Scotland and southern England.

TOBIN'S UNKNOWN KILLINGS

On March 10, 1970, eighteen-year-old insurance clerk Susan Long was killed after leaving the Gala Ballroom in Norwich for home in Aylsham nine miles away. On the way she was raped and strangled. Her body was found the next morning in a lovers' lane dumped in the street near to her home, in a way that was strikingly similar to the murder victims of Bible John.

In October 1970, twenty-four-year-old teacher Barbara Mayo went missing after leaving her home in London to go hitchhiking. Her half-naked body was found six days later by walkers in a wood at Hardwick Hall, a National Trust stately home near Chesterfield, Derbyshire, less than a mile from the M1 motorway, another national route between England and Scotland that Tobin may have used. She had been raped, punched around the head and strangled with a length of flex.

The Norwich police also re-investigated the case of a headless woman's body found at the side of the road in Cockley Cley, near Swaffham, in 1974. She was wearing a frilly, pink Marks and Spencer's nightdress and was bound in a way similar to Dinah McNicol (Tobin's second victim). The body was wrapped in brown plastic sheeting bearing the initials NCR. The Scottish company National Cash Register only made six sheets of this between 1962 and 1968. Tobin was in Glasgow at the time. He had used plastic sheeting to wrap the bodies of Vicky Hamilton and Ángelika Kluk.

A few days after the discovery of the headless corpse, twenty-one-year-old Pamela Exall went missing from the Dinglea Campsite in Snettisham, twenty miles from Cockley Cley.

Thirteen-year-old Genette Tate, fourteen-year-old Suzanne Lawrence and twenty-two-year-old Jessie Earl were all killed in a two-year period following 1978 after Tobin's second marriage broke up. Genette was abducted from her paper round. As in the case of April Fabb, her bicycle was found but no trace of her body has ever come to light. Her father said she bore a distinct resemblance to Dinah McNicol.

Less than a year later, in July 1979, Suzanne Lawrence left her sister's home in Harold Hill to make her way home to nearby Romford. She never arrived. Driving between the south coast and Norfolk, Tobin would have travelled through Harold Hill.

Art student Jessie Earl went missing from her bedsit in Eastbourne in 1980. Her body was found on Beachy Head nine years later. Her wrists had been tied with her bra, as Vicky Hamilton's had been. During Operation Anagram the police visited her parents' home to see if they could collect some DNA evidence that might link her to Tobin who was living just twenty-five miles away in Brighton when she went missing. He moved back to Glasgow soon after. Following his known killings he regularly put a distance between himself and the scene of the crime.

SINS OF THE PAST

Tobin has also been linked to a string of unsolved deaths across the UK. Fourteen-year-old Patsy Morris disappeared in London in 1980. Her body was discovered hidden in undergrowth on Hounslow Heath in mid-summer. Her father, George Morris, believes that she might have been one of Peter Tobin's victims. "As soon as I read about the other girl's body being found in his backyard, something inside me clicked," he said.

George Morris had read about the 1981 discovery of sixteen-year-old Pamela Hastie's body in Rannoch Woods in Johnstone, Renfrewshire, the town where Tobin had been born. She had been raped and strangled. A local man served twenty-one years for her murder, but the case against him was quashed in 2007 and the police began investigating Tobin for the offence.

Ten years earlier the naked body of thirty-seven-year-old mother-of-two Dorothea Meechan had been found in Renfrew. Her clothes and handbag were missing and beside the body was a note that said: *"Mr Polis, I have killed that woman in cold blood. Bible John."*

Richard "The Snake" Coubrough spent thirty-four years in jail for strangling her. He was freed in 2005, but the case was still in front of the Court of Criminal Appeal when he died. The police also investigated Peter Tobin for the murder.

The bodies of nine-year-old Nicola Fellows and her playmate ten-year-old Karen Hadaway were found in Wild Park on the outskirts of Brighton in October 1986. Both had been raped and strangled. Twenty-year-old Russell Bishop was charged but a jury took just two hours to find him not guilty. Tobin was living in Brighton at the time.

In 1988, eighteen-year-old Louise Kay had been out clubbing in Eastbourne on the night she disappeared. She drove a girlfriend home in her dad's Ford Fiesta, dropping her off at 4:30 a.m. She said she intended to drive back to her parents' house, which was just outside the town. However, neither Louise nor the car have been seen since. Tobin was working in a hotel in Eastbourne at the time of her disappearance.

The half-naked body of sixteen-year-old prostitute Natalie Pearman was found at Ringland Hills near Norwich in November 1992. She was found strangled after disappearing from the red-light district of Norwich. The case was briefly linked to Steve Wright, who was convicted of the murder of five prostitutes in Ipswich in 2006. Her killer has never been found. Again Tobin frequented the area.

On December 23, 1992, fourteen-year-old Johanna Young left home to go to the local fish-and-chip shop in Watton. Her semi-naked body was found on Boxing Day in a water-logged pit near Wayland Wood, just eight miles from where the headless woman had been found in 1974. She had a fractured skull, but had still been alive when her assailant dumped her and she drowned.

When Sussex police heard of Tobin's frantic knife attack on Ángelika Kluk in 2006, they began investigating any connection he might have had to the death of thirty-five-year-old mother-of-three Jennifer Kiely who had been stabbed sixteen times. Her body was found in a beach shelter in Eastbourne where the killer had tried to burn it.

While the police have not been able to establish that Tobin was responsible for any of these murders, Professor Wilson and Joe Jackson remain convinced that he was Bible John.

As of 2021 Peter Tobin was still denying it. "People just think I am Bible John but I'm not. It wasn't me. Nothing to do with me. I didn't kill them," seventy-five-year old Tobin reportedly said to his cellmate in HMP Edinburgh, according to the *Daily Record*. The cellmate went on: "He told me things about some of the murders he's committed … and bodies they've been looking for but haven't found. Maybe he wants to get stuff off his chest before he dies but it's stomach-churning."

6

DONATO BILANCIA
The Monster of Liguria
ITALY

In the late 1990s, there was a series of murders in
Liguria, the north-western coastal region of Italy whose
capital is Genoa. They were linked by the murder weapon
– a .38 Smith & Wesson pistol using the same wadcutter
ammunition designed for shooting paper targets.
However, there was no consistency in the *modus operandi*.
Some murders seemed to have been motivated by theft.
Others had a sexual motive. The rest seemed to be purely
random.

After six months the inveterate gambler Donato Bilancia

was arrested. Suspicion fell on him after an identikit picture of the killer had been circulated. It was based on the description given by a victim who had survived by playing dead. Bilancia had also bought a second-hand Mercedes but had not completed the transfer of ownership. Fines for traffic violations continued to be sent to the old owner who spotted that the offences had taken place near the murders and at around the same time.

When arrested, Bilancia confessed everything – including a couple of murders that the police had not linked to the other killings. His frank confession and his cooperation with forensic psychiatrists gave an insight into the behaviour and mind set of a serial killer.

SEX PEST

Born in 1951, Bilancia was frequently beaten for minor transgressions of the rules laid down by his father. He wet the bed, a common trait among latent serial killers. His parents put the mattress out on the balcony to dry where it could be seen by neighbours, a further humiliation as two girls around his age lived in the apartment opposite. Visiting his cousins, his father would pull down his pants to show them his undeveloped penis. "This was the event that crucified me for the rest of my life," he said.

For revenge, he began stealing money from his parents which, when he grew older, he spent on gambling and prostitutes. He then embarked on a life of crime. In 1974, he was arrested for carrying an unlicensed gun. He spent eighteen months in a psychiatric ward and prison for robbery, followed by another six months for burglaries in France. After that, there was a custodial sentence for armed robbery. And in 1985, illegal gambling was added to his rap sheet.

Bilancia's mental state seems to have been further unbalanced when his older brother committed suicide, throwing himself and his four-year-old son under a train. He was then reported by a prostitute for sexual aggression and unlawful imprisonment, and an assistant in a lingerie shop accused him of being a sex pest. Then in 1996, he was seen at an anti-Mafia trial.

CARNAGE BEGINS

The murders began on October 15, 1997, when he was forty-seven – a late start for a serial killer. He had lost heavily gambling in what he believed was a rigged game. Bilancia waited outside the apartment of the owner of the gambling den Giorgio Centanaro. When Centanaro came home at about 2:00 a.m., Bilancia forced his way in with a gun which in the end he decided not to use because of the noise. Instead he forced Centanaro to strip to his underwear, bound him with tape and suffocated him with a pillow, kicking him in the testicles to check he was dead.

"I left the body in front of the apartment door," he said. "I wanted everyone to know he'd been murdered."

Next Bilancia went after Maurizio Parenti, Centanaro's partner who had hooked Bilancia in to the game. Tricking his way into Parenti's house one night, he pulled a gun, handcuffed Parenti and put tape over his mouth. Then Bilancia emptied Parenti's safe, taking thirteen million lira (about £5,600) and five Rolex watches. After that, he beat Parenti with the butt of the gun and shot him dead. Carla Scotti, Parenti's new wife of just three weeks, was also in the apartment. Bilancia bound her arms and legs, and shot her as well.

He took the watches he had stolen to Bruno Solari and his wife Maria Luigia Pitto, retired jewellers, but they wanted nothing to do with stolen goods. "I had to shoot them both because they could have identified me," Bilancia said. Then he helped himself to their jewellery.

Entering the office of money-changer Luciano Marro, Bilancia ordered him at gunpoint to empty the safe, then shot him numerous times. Out of pure revenge, he next sought out fifty-two-year-old night-watchman Giangiorgio Canu who had testified against him some years before and killed him.

RED-LIGHT SHOOTINGS

Two months later, Bilancia picked up Albanian prostitute Bodejana Almerina, alias Stela Truja, in Foce, Genoa's red-light district, and offered her a large amount of money to come home with him for sex. Instead he took her into the hills outside the city. In an isolated spot, he made her strip naked and told her to get out of the car. When she refused, he savagely dragged her out of the car and shot her in the head.

His next victim was Russian prostitute Ljudmila Zubskova. Again he took her to an isolated spot, made her get on her knees and shot her in the head. Then he shot money-changer Enzo Gorni and emptied his safe of thirty million lira.

Next he picked up twenty-four-year-old transsexual Julio Castro, alias Lorena, and drove him to a nearby villa. In the garden, Bilancia parked with the passenger door against a tree, so Lorena could not get out. He was forcing Lorena to give him oral sex when two cars turned up driven by security guards Massimo Gualillo and Candido Randò. Bilancia shot them both.

Meanwhile, Lorena escaped and hid in the bushes. Bilancia found him and shot him twice in the abdomen. When he heard moaning from the security men, he reloaded his gun and shot them again. Then he fired another three shots at Lorena, hit him in the face with the gun butt and left him for dead. Lorena survived though and gave a description of his assailant to the police.

A few days later, Evelyn Esohe Endoghaye, alias Tessy Adobo, a twenty-seven-year-old Nigerian prostitute, was murdered. Again Bilancia took her to an isolated area, but this time he had sex with her first. He dragged her out of the car by the hair. When she tried to escape, he shot her in the knee. She fell to the ground and he shot her twice in the head.

I WANTED TO KILL A WOMAN
On April 3, 1998, he visited the apartment of Luisa Ciminello, another prostitute, with the intention of killing her. But when he drew the gun she burst into tears and begged for mercy, saying she had a two-year-old child. Bilancia found he could not pull the trigger and left Ciminello alive.

On Easter Day, April 12, Bilancia got on a train to Venice where he spotted thirty-two-year-old nurse Elisabetta Zoppetti sitting in first-class. When she went to the toilet, he followed her. When she started screaming, he shot her in the head. Then he went through her handbag and stole her ticket as he had not bothered to buy one.

"I got on the train because I wanted to kill a woman, even if I did not touch her," he said. "I didn't want to have sex with her. I just wanted to kill her as part of my criminal plan."

Two days later he picked up a young Slav prostitute named Mema Valbona, alias Kristina Kwalla, and reverted to his previous *modus operandi*. He offered her money to come home with him, took her to an isolated area, had sex, then dragged her out of the car and shot her in the head.

On April 18, he lost a lot of money at the casino in San

Remo along the coast from Genoa. On the train, he saw a young woman named Maria Ángela Rubino.

"I remember that I felt a sudden, irresistible urge to kill her," he said.

When she went to the toilet, he followed her and forced his way in, then shot her in the head. But her black underwear excited him, so he masturbated over her dead body.

Two days later, he filled up his car at a petrol station. He had no money with him, so he shot the fifty-one-year-old attendant Giuseppe Mileto, and helped himself to the day's takings – approximately two million lira, then went back to the casino.

After his arrest Bilanica confessed to everything, but refused to appear in court. Three forensic psychiatrists testified, finding him sane at the time of the crimes. He was given thirteen life sentences with three years' solitary confinement.

7

DÁMASO RODRÍGUEZ MARTÍN

The Warlock

CANARY ISLANDS, SPAIN

A ctive on the island of Tenerife in the 1980s, Dámaso Rodríguez Martín is considered the Canary Islands' most infamous killer.

Born in 1944, Dámaso was one of five brothers. The family lived at Las Montañas – "The Mountains" – in the village of El Batán, a district of the city of San Cristóbal de La Laguna at the northern end of Tenerife. Even though the family was poor, his parents Martín Rodríguez Silveria and Celestina Martín Perdomo were determined to give him a decent education. It did no good. At the age of seventeen he was arrested for theft and spent a year in jail.

On his release in 1963, he joined the Spanish Legion, the Spanish equivalent of the French Foreign Legion, whose former leader Francisco Franco was then dictator of Spain. The Legion was stationed in the small Spanish colonial territories left in North Africa after the independence of Morocco. Rodríguez was sent to the Western Sahara whose decolonization Morocco was demanding.

After his discharge from the Legion in 1966, Rodríguez returned to Tenerife where he married Mercedes Martín Rodríguez the following year. They settled in Las Mercedes, another district of San Cristóbal de La Laguna. Their first child was born in 1973, their second in 1975.

Rodríguez was a voyeur. On November 11, 1981, he saw a couple making love in a car in the district of El Moquinal. He killed the young man and raped his girlfriend with her boyfriend's body dead in the car beside them. He drove her and the body out to Llano de los Viejos, a forested area outside the town, where he abandoned them.

It did not take the police long to discover that the perpetrator was Dámaso Rodríguez. He was sentenced to fifty-five years in jail for murder, rape, theft of a firearm and unlawful possession of weapons.

After nearly ten years in jail, he escaped on January 17, 1991, and fled to the Anaga, a mountainous region to the west of San Cristóbal de La Laguna. He had a plan to murder his wife who had cut herself off from him while he was in jail. However, when he visited her at home, he found her with family and friends.

A week later, on January 23, the body of German tourist Karl Flick was found on the forest road leading to the village of El Solís. The next day, at 3:15 p.m., in a remote area of the Roque de El Moquinal, the Civil Guard recovered the body of his wife, Marta Küpper, who had been raped and strangled. They appeared to have been begging for their lives.

On February 19, a family moving into a house in the area found that the door had been forced open. They called the police. When a sergeant commander in the Civil Guard tried to enter the house, he was met with shotgun fire from inside where Rodríguez had been hiding. A gunfight broke out. Outgunned Rodríguez tried to kill himself, lodging the barrel of the shotgun under his chin and pulling the trigger with his toe. But the gun was too long and his first suicide bid failed. There was more gunfire, but a second attempt at suicide succeeded. A magic symbol etched into the wall of the house in Anaga earned him the nickname of *El Brujo* – The Warlock or Witch Doctor.

8

MARC DUTROUX
The Paedophile Rapist
BELGIUM

B elgian child molester Marc Dutroux liked to kidnap young girls and keep them as his sex slaves. He was finally caught and incarcerated after two young girls who he had repeatedly raped were released from his cellar in Marcinelle, Belgium, in 1996. It was only then that the bodies of two eight-year-old girls were found buried in the garden of another house belonging to Dutroux. They had starved to death in the cellar where he had sexually abused them. The two eight-year-olds were Julie Lejeune and Melissa Russo.

NAKED AND CHAINED

The two girls had been kidnapped together by Dutroux from Grâce-Hollogne in Belgium on June 24, 1995. Not only did he sexually abuse the two defenceless children, he produced pornographic videos of the abuse which it is thought he circulated to a paedophile ring.

While Dutroux admitted raping the two girls, he refused to take responsibility for their deaths. They had died while he was in jail for four months for stealing a car. He claimed that, before he went to prison, he had told his accomplice Bern Weinstein to feed them. Dutroux claimed he was so annoyed at Weinstein's failure, he had given him barbiturates and buried him alive alongside the girls at Sars-La-Buissiere, where his body was later found.

Another of Dutroux's accomplices, Michel Lelièvre admitted kidnapping seventeen-year-old An Marchal and nineteen-year-old Eefje Lambrecks on August 22, 1995, when the two girls were on a camping trip to the Belgian port of Ostend. Their bodies were found under a shed next to another house owned by Dutroux.

At one time, there had been four girls at the house in Marcinelle – Julie and Melissa in the dungeon; An and Eefje chained up upstairs. Eefje had made several escape attempts. Eventually, he found the two teenagers so troublesome, he drugged them and buried them alive.

Four girls and Weinstein were already dead when twelve-year-old Sabine Dardenne was kidnapped on her way to school in Tournai on May 28, 1996. She was abducted from her bike when a rusty camper van pulled up beside her. She tried to fight off her abductor, but she was small for her age and he was a full-grown man. He forced some pills in her mouth, trussed her up in a blanket and shoved her in a trunk.

When she was released she found herself in a room with a man who told her to undress and get into one of the bunk beds. Once she was naked he put a chain around her neck. The following day, he told her that her parents had been asked for a ransom. If they did not pay up, the kidnappers intended to kill her. Meanwhile he took pictures of her naked in her chains, then sexually abused her.

She complained about being kept naked all the time. Eventually he gave her back her underwear and her jeans. But regularly, she was forced to undress again for more photo sessions and sexual abuse.

Then she was told that her parents had refused to pay the ransom. As a result, the boss of the supposed kidnap gang had ordered that she be killed. Her captor pretended to be her saviour and said he would hide her in the tiny, airless cellar which was three feet wide and nine feet long.

She was put down there in a cage with a stinking mattress. Occasionally, he would go away for days on end, leaving her alone down there. Otherwise there would be more nude photographs taken and "other things".

Eventually he forced her to sleep with him in chains

and raped her. This was painful and left her bleeding. She feared that she was going to die from loss of blood in her underground prison.

LUCRATIVE SEX TRADE SIDELINE

Her captor Marc Dutroux was already a convicted paedophile. Born in Ixelles, Belgium, in 1956, Dutroux married at the age of nineteen and fathered two children. The marriage ended in divorce in 1983 after he began an affair with Michelle Martin. In 1986, Dutroux and Martin were arrested for the abduction and rape of five young girls. Dutroux was sentenced to thirteen years. Martin got five. They married while in prison in 1989 and would eventually have three children together when they were both released after just three years for good behaviour.

Unemployed Dutroux turned to mugging, drug dealing and stealing cars that were smuggled into Eastern Europe. But his most lucrative sideline was the sex trade. He made and sold pornography, and sold young girls into prostitution across Europe. By 1996, he owned seven houses in Belgium. Most of them stood vacant and were perfect hiding places for the kidnapped girls.

The police knew of his activities through informants. In 1995, Dutroux's own mother wrote to prosecutors telling them that her son had been keeping young girls in one of his empty houses. No one did anything about it.

As her captivity dragged on, Sabine fell into despair.

It was summer time and she wanted to go out in the sunshine. He shoved two chairs together and told her she could "sunbathe" – naked, of course – right there in the front room.

She kept saying she was lonely and wanted a friend. Dutroux brought her one. Sabine was taken upstairs where she found another girl naked and chained to the bed. Fourteen-year-old Laetitia Delhez asked Sabine how long she had been there. It had been seventy-seven days. Soon she joined Sabine in the cellar. But she brought important news. She had seen Sabine's picture on posters that had been put up all over the country. Sabine had not been forgotten as she had feared.

RAPED AND ABUSED

Laetitia had been snatched in the town of Bertrix on the French-Belgian border. She had been walking home from the swimming pool when an old van pulled up alongside her. Dutroux had grabbed her and bundled her through the side door in the same way Sabine had been taken. From Laetitia's description, it seemed that the driver was the same man Sabine had seen.

Two years older than Sabine, Laetitia had already had her first period, so Dutroux forced her to take contraceptive pills. After he had raped and abused Laetitia, Dutroux suddenly stopped coming. A couple of days later the girls figured he must have gone away again.

In fact, on August 13, 1996, Dutroux, his wife, and the driver Michel Lelièvre had been arrested. There had been a witness to the abduction of Laetitia Delhez who noted down part of the licence-plate number of the van which was registered to Dutroux. A search was made of the house by an officer of the child protection squad, but the door to the cellar was so skilfully concealed he found nothing.

Two days later, Laetitia and Sabine heard bricks being chipped from the walls. The two girls were terrified. Then they heard Dutroux's voice saying "it's me". There were other men with him. Fearing the worst, Sabine refused to come out. But Laetitia then recognized one of the men. He was a policeman from Bertrix. As they left, both Sabine and Laetitia gave Dutroux a kiss on the cheek.

After eighty days in the dank cellar, Sabine was taken out into the sunshine and fresh air. It was only at the station that Sabine discovered the police had long ago given up any hope of finding her alive. It was Laetitia the police were looking for when they visited Dutroux's house.

PAEDOPHILE PORN
When Dutroux's various houses were searched, the police found over three hundred pornographic videos featuring children. Six thousand hair samples taken from the dungeon were analyzed to see if Dutroux had kept other victims there. It was only after that the four bodies were found in the back garden.

During the investigation businessman Jean-Michel Nihoul was arrested. He had organized an orgy at a Belgian château attended by police officers, several government officials and a former European commissioner. His mistress Marleen De Cockere was charged with criminal conspiracy concerning Dutroux's activities. Seven other people were arrested in connection with the paedophile ring and nine police officers in Charleroi were detained for questioning over possible negligence in the investigation.

Demands were made to tighten parole conditions for convicted paedophiles. There was also a call for the restoration of the death penalty which had been banned in Belgium just months before Sabine and Laetitia were found.

The outrage boiled over when the investigating judge in the case, Jean-Marc Connerotte, was dismissed for having attended a fund-raising dinner to help the search for missing children. The Belgian Supreme Court decided that this might taint his objectivity in the Dutroux case. In protest 300,000 people took to the streets of Brussels, dressed in white as a symbol of innocence.

It was the largest demonstration in Belgium since World War II. There was talk that the government was involved in a cover-up and strikes broke out across the country. The prime minister promised to speed up judicial reforms and the King of Belgium had to speak out on the Dutroux case.

DUTROUX ON THE RUN

The parliamentary committee investigating the matter published a report saying that failures in the investigation of the paedophile ring meant that the four girls who were dead could have been saved. A complete reorganization of the Belgian police force was called for after the police made another blunder. Dutroux made an escape when he travelled to Neufchâteau to consult files to be used in his forthcoming trial. There, he knocked out one of his police guards, and punched another to the ground and took his gun. Then he stole a car and went on the run with the local gendarmerie on his tail.

Sabine heard helicopters circling above her school. Another pupil asked her if she was frightened when they heard that Dutroux had escaped. But Dutroux would have had to have been exceptionally stupid to come within a mile of her. Police officers patrolled the school corridors and bodyguards were sent to her home.

But Dutroux was soon recaptured. He had taken refuge in a wood, but had given himself up to a forest warden. Nevertheless, the state police chief, the minister of justice and the minister of the interior were forced to resign.

Convicted for assault and theft, Dutroux was sentenced to five years. But his trial for kidnapping and murder was delayed when a magazine in Luxembourg printed the names of fifty alleged paedophiles said to have come from the files of the investigation.

Dutroux managed to stall things further by claiming that the Belgian state was violating his human rights. He demanded to be released from solitary confinement. This outraged the Belgian people again, considering what he had put his victims through. The state argued that Dutroux was receiving special treatment for his own protection.

CRIMINAL MASTERMIND

Then a Belgian TV channel aired an unauthorized interview with Dutroux. In it, he admitted imprisoning Julie, Melissa, An and Eefje, in effect confessing his guilt. The authenticity and admissibility of this evidence then had to be evaluated. This meant his trial for the substantive charges of murder and kidnap was postponed repeatedly. It was over seven years before the case came to court.

The trial eventually began on March 1, 2004. There were four defendants – Dutroux, his now ex-wife Martin, Lelièvre and Nihoul. In court Dutroux insisted he was merely a pawn of the criminal mastermind Nihoul who ran the paedophile ring. He claimed the girls he kidnapped were sold on to Nihoul who provided them to other paedophiles. To muddy the water further Dutroux claimed that two police officers helped in the kidnapping of An Marchal and Eefje Lambrecks.

The investigating judge Jacques Langlois then alleged that it was Michelle Martin who had left Julie and Melissa to starve, not Weinstein. She had been afraid to go down into the cellar to feed them in case they attacked her, although she claimed she had no idea how or why they had died.

Jean-Marc Connerotte then testified that Dutroux had constructed the dungeon and its ventilation system so well that it would have been difficult to detect the girls' presence even with sniffer dogs. He also testified that his investigation had been hampered by people in government.

Contracts had been taken out against investigating magistrates. He needed armed guards and bullet-proof vehicles to protect him from powerful individuals who did not want the truth to come out. And he blamed the incompetence of the police in Charleroi for the deaths of Julie Lejeune and Melissa Russo.

The failure of the Belgian authorities was demonstrated again when a key to Dutroux's handcuffs were found in his cell, smuggled in, apparently, in a bag of salt. Those running the prison were then accused of trying to facilitate his escape.

LOOKING HIM IN THE EYES

The final showdown came on April 19, 2004, when Sabine Dardenne, then aged twenty, took the stand. She told of the ordeal Dutroux had subjected her to, both physically and mentally, and rejected out of hand an apology he gave in court. When Sabine looked him in the eyes, he was forced to lower his gaze.

On the second day of her testimony, Dutroux accused her of asking him to kidnap another victim so that she could have a friend. He also claimed that he had protected her from the paedophile ring.

"So, if I understand you, I should be thankful?" she asked.

Laetitia Delhez also testified. Then the two of them accompanied the court on a visit to the house and the dungeon where they had been held. Back in the courtroom, Dutroux admitted the kidnapping and rape charges, again expressing his "sincere regret". But he denied murdering the girls found buried in the garden, blaming Martin, Lelièvre and Nihoul.

At the end of the three-month trial, the task for the jury was not an easy one. The eight women and four men were sent to a fortified army barracks in Arlon, where the judge asked them to evaluate 243 questions. They had to review around 400,000 pages of evidence, including the testimony of over five hundred witnesses. It took them three days to return with a verdict.

VAST NATIONAL NETWORK

Dutroux was found guilty of kidnapping and raping all six girls, and murdering An Marchel, Eefje Lambrecks, and Bernard Weinstein. Lelièvre was found guilty of kidnapping, but acquitted of murder. Martin was convicted of kidnapping and rape. The jury could not agree a verdict in Nihoul's case and were sent back to re-evaluate the 243 questions.

The evidence showed that he was involved in supplying prostitutes, but the court accepted he had had nothing to do with the paedophilia. He was eventually acquitted of involvement in the abductions of the girls, but was convicted of human trafficking and drugs charges.

On June 22, 2004, Dutroux was sentenced to life and put at "the government's disposition". That meant, if he was, by some fluke, paroled again in the future, the government could return him to prison. Lelièvre got twenty-five years; Martin thirty; Nihoul five. But the question left unanswered was: Was there really a vast national network of paedophiles at work in Belgium as Dutroux claimed?

Sabine Dardenne has said that she has never completely overcome the guilt she felt over Laetitia, who she believed was abducted because she asked Dutroux for the company of a friend. But the request was the innocent plea of a twelve-year-old. Laetitia did not blame her. Indeed, if Laetitia had not been kidnapped, Sabine would probably not have survived her ordeal and Dutroux would have been free to abduct, abuse, and murder other girls.

9

NESTOR PIROTTE
The Crazy Killer
BELGIUM

Before Marc Dutroux came along, Nestor Pirotte was Belgium's most feared serial killer. He dodged the death sentence twice and repeatedly escaped to kill again.

Born in 1933, he was the son of the gamekeeper at the Château de Beau Chêne and a seamstress and notorious beauty named Florence Delvaux who dressed in aristocratic clothes she made herself and doted on her son. They lived in the gatehouse of the huge estate. From an early age Pirotte boasted of being the son of the neighbouring squire. His mother did not deny it.

ARISTOCRATIC DELUSIONS

He played with the children of the château and became steeped in aristocratic ways. During his military service, he boasted of his aristocratic origins to seduce women and yearned to make these delusions of grandeur more substantial. Needing money, he stole from his comrades and the mess funds. At the age of twenty he was given a three-month suspended prison sentence.

He wanted to buy himself a scooter so he could travel around the local balls in some sort of style – for the 1950s at least. Learning that one of his great-aunts had sold her herd of cows, he approached her for cash. She refused. Equipped with an iron bar, he hid behind the stables. When she passed by, he beat her head in. Searching her house, he only came up with a few hundred Belgian francs, worth less than £20 in today's money. His great-aunt had already invested the money she had received to buy new cows.

The authorities had no trouble apprehending Pirotte. A gendarme had seen him a few days earlier observing his great-aunt's movements and warned him: "Nestor, you will be arrested if any crime occurs in this region."

He was tried in a military court, where his father Léon collapsed in tears. His mother though, appeared "cold and haughty" throughout. One of the guards said: "She was dressed like a duchess going to a gala evening."

In October 1955, he was sentenced to death. Although the death penalty was still officially on the statute book, his sentence was automatically commuted to life imprisonment. Pirotte then decided to play the insanity card. He bragged about deviant sex and overdosed on barbiturates. The psychiatrists who examined him figured he was trying to manipulate them. But after repeated bouts of hysteria, he was transferred to a new psychiatric facility at Tournai, which was showcased and visited regularly by French magistrates and politicians as they were building a similar establishment at Fresnes. His charm, wit and storytelling ability hypnotized them. Even the director was won over.

EXCEEDINGLY DEVIOUS

After fourteen years, Pirotte was released. But he still fancied himself as a wealthy aristocrat. He masqueraded as the Comte de Meeûs, the Comte de Larivoisière and the Comte de Leidekerque. But it was as the Comte de Ribeaucourt that he made an appointment at the branch of the BBL bank in Genval on May 14, 1968, to negotiate a loan. During the interview, he shot the bank manager in the head. Making off with the money, he had time to buy a gold watch before he was arrested a week later.

In prison, he tried to escape using a rope to scale a six-metre wall. Caught, he threw himself off, pretending he was making a suicide attempt and was sent back to the psychiatric facility at Tournai.

After ten years, he was released again and went to work

in a radio and television shop in Verviers. He bought a luxury car, got involved in dubious business deals and charmed women with tales of his aristocratic heritage. But soon he ran out of money. He bought a .38 revolver and came up with story about locating a stash of gold bars. After his attempt to extort money out of his mistress Madeleine and her two employees failed, their dead bodies were found in the restaurant "La Vieille France" in Spa on December 11, 1980, along with that of a dog. The restaurant's owner's son was also missing. His body was found the following month. The name of the last customer on the slate at the restaurant was "Nestor".

With all the witnesses dead, the police had trouble building a case against him. However, Pirotte was soon arrested in Brussels for violating the conditions of his parole and was sent back to jail. But Pirotte was exceedingly devious and a hard man to hold in custody, and on the night of August 2, 1981, he escaped again. The news sent the public into a panic.

In an attempt to make himself look more aristocratic he curled his hair and dyed it red. Calling himself the Comte de Meeûs d'Argenteuil, he told an antique dealer that he wanted to sell some furniture and convinced the man to follow him through a wood to a make-believe castle, intending to rob him. But the antique dealer had not brought the money he had promised. Furious, Pirotte shot him in the chest.

His plea of not guilty due to insanity was thrown out by the court. Again he was sentenced to death, which was automatically commuted to life imprisonment. Renewed attempts to escape failed and he died behind bars on July 29, 2000. None of his family had visited him for twenty years. Indeed, they were so ashamed that they moved away. The only person to follow his coffin was a woman who he had known in his youth. His grave in the cemetery of Ham-sur-Heure is marked only by a wooden cross with no name on it.

10

ANATOLY ONOPRIENKO
The Terminator
UKRAINE

Admitting to fifty-two murders, Anatoly Onoprienko told a reporter from the BBC that he wanted to hold the world record for serial killing. As it was, he only just matched the body count of Andrei Chikatilo, the Rostov Ripper, who was convicted of fifty-two murders and had been tried for fifty-three and claimed at least three more. Then there was Mikhail Popkov who admitted fifty-nine murders. And that is just in the former Soviet Union. There are serial killers in Asia and Latin America who have killed many more.

MAN ON A MISSION

Onoprienko was born in the Ukraine in 1959. His mother died when he was a young child and his father put him in an orphanage, though kept his older brother. Feeling rejected, he thought they could have looked after him too.

At the age of seventeen, he became a sailor and met his future wife and they had a son. On his sea voyages his murderous fantasies took shape. Later, he claimed he hadn't become a murderer by his own free will.

"I've been chosen to fulfil a mission. In a way, I feel related with Messir, the hero from the Russian author Bulgakov's book," he said. "He was evil, and so am I. I did what I had to do: kill people. I don't owe any more explanation to my victims, their families and the police."

He also claimed he once spoke to Hitler who advised him to start a new world war. Otherwise he was told to kill by inner voices which either came from God or space aliens – or even a famous American magician.

"I have been taken over by a higher force, something telepathic or cosmic, which drove me," he said. "For instance, I wanted to kill my brother's first wife, because I hated her. I really wanted to kill her, but I couldn't because I had not received the order."

He also claimed he was being experimented on like a rabbit in a laboratory to prove that man could kill and live with his crimes: "To show that I can cope, that I can stand anything, forget everything."

THE HUNTER

Onoprienko first killed at the age of thirty – late for a serial killer. And his first murders were not committed alone. His accomplice was Sergei Rogozin who he met at a local gym where they worked out. They turned to burglary to eke out their meagre incomes. They carried weapons, they said, for self defence.

One night the two intruders were discovered by the home owner. To avoid arrest, they killed the entire family – two adults and eight children. Onoprienko and Rogozin then split up their partnership, but Onoprienko went on killing on his own.

Soon after, he saw a husband and wife standing by their car on the motorway. "I just shot them," he said. "It's not that it gave me pleasure, but I felt this urge. From then on, it was almost like some game from outer space."

Two more were killed soon afterwards. He liked to stop cars and shoot the drivers.

"To me it was like hunting. Hunting people," he said later. "I would be sitting, bored, with nothing to do. And then suddenly this idea would get into my head. I would do everything to get it out of my mind, but I couldn't. It was stronger than me. So I would get in the car or catch a train and go out to kill."

A few months later he shot and killed five people, including an eleven-year-old boy, who were sleeping in a car. He then burned their bodies. "I was approaching the car only to rob it," he said. "I was a completely different person then. Had I known there had been five people, I would have left."

He said he had derived no pleasure from the act of the killing.

"Corpses are ugly," he said. "They stink and send out bad vibes. After I killed the family in the car, I sat in the car with their bodies for two hours not knowing what to do with them. The smell was unbearable."

Then the killings stopped, in the Ukraine at least. Onoprienko travelled illegally around several European countries, working occasionally as a manual labourer but mainly living off the proceeds of petty crime and robbery. He was deported from Austria and Germany.

POINT BLANK

Back in the Ukraine in 1995, he began a three-month killing spree. He would enter an isolated home, round up all the residents and shoot them at point blank range, steal what he could carry and set the house on fire to cover his tracks. Any potential witness or passer-by would also be murdered.

The first occurred on December 12, 1995, when he killed a thirty-seven-year-old forestry teacher, his wife and two infant sons, one of whom was just three months old. He left with the couple's wedding rings, a golden cross on a chain, earrings, and a bundle of worn clothes, then set the house on fire.

Onoprienko then set about terrorizing the village of Bratkovychi. On New Year's Eve, a middle-age man, his wife and her two nineteen-year-old twin daughters were killed. He chopped off the wife's finger to steal her engagement ring. One of the sisters was so afraid that she had bitten her hand through to the bone. The house was then set ablaze and two men on the street were also killed.

On January 5, 1996, he shot two businessmen who were sitting in their car which had broken down. Further down the road he killed a pedestrian and a patrolman. The following day, he killed three more in a halted car. Afterwards he spotted a woman carrying two shopping bags full of groceries. He shot her twice and stole her groceries, along with her coat, boots and ring.

Back in Bratkovychi on January 17, he killed a family of five, including a six-year-old boy and burned their house down. Then he killed two witnesses – a twenty-seven-year-old woman railway worker and a fifty-six-year-old railway passenger.

On January 30, he shot a thirty-two-year-old driver and a twenty-eight-year-old nurse and her two sons. He killed a family of four on February 19, shooting the father and son, and bludgeoning the mother and daughter to death with a hammer. He'd found the seven-year-old girl cowering in her bed, praying.

"Seconds before I smashed her head, I ordered her to

show me where they kept their money," he said. "She looked at me with an angry, defiant stare and said, 'No, I won't.' That strength was incredible. But I felt nothing."

Another family of four perished on February 27. The mother and father were shot, their two daughters, aged seven and eight, were hacked to death with an axe. Afterwards a neighbour, a businessman, was shot and hacked to death outside his house.

Then at Busk, not far from Bratkovychi, a family of five were shot and burned. One child was ripped open from its stomach to its throat. By this time, two-thousand police investigators, both federal and local, were assigned to the case and a division of the National Guard, with rocket launchers and armoured vehicles, were called in to protect the villages.

GOD WILL PUNISH YOU

On April 7, 1996, Easter Sunday, the local police station in Yavoriv in the Western Ukraine got a call from Pyotr Onoprienko who said that his cousin Anatoly from Zhitomirskaya had come to stay, but Pyotr had to ask him to leave after his wife found he had brought with him an arsenal of weapons. As he left, Anatoly told Pyotr: "God will punish you and your family on Easter."

The officer who received the call was intrigued. He had recently read a police report that a Russian-made twelve-gauge Tos-34 shotgun had been reported stolen in the Zhitomirskaya area. It was the type used in the Bratkovychi killings. He quickly assembled a task force of twenty patrolmen and detectives.

Anatoly Onoprienko had moved in with his girlfriend, a hairdresser named Anna Kazak, and her two children in nearby Ivana Khristitelya Street. The police surrounded the building. Fortunately, Anna and the children were out at church. Onoprienko was expecting them home soon, so when a knock came at the door, he opened it.

The police asked to see his ID. He went to the closet and tried to grab a pistol, but the police subdued him. The handgun had been stolen from a murder scene in Odessa. Searching the flat, the police found 120 other items that had been stolen from murder scenes, including the Tos-34 shotgun. And when Anna returned home, they found she was wearing the engagement ring savagely stolen in Bratkovychi by Onoprienko.

THE TERMINATOR

In the police station, Onoprienko refused to talk to anyone below the rank of general. However, a skilled interrogator told him they could hardly call in a general unless he could convince them that he had something to say. He admitted stealing the shotgun, then eight of the murders.

When the general turned up, he confessed to fifty-two murders in all. It also transpired that he had spent time in a hospital in Kyiv, suffering from schizophrenia. Identified only as Citizen O, his therapists had suspected that he was a killer. Nevertheless, he was judged fit to stand trial.

It took two-and-a-half years before he went to trial as, under Ukrainian law, the defendant has the right first to study all the evidence. This ran to a hundred volumes of gruesome photographs of mutilated bodies, crime scenes and stolen items.

In court in November 1998, he was confined to a cage to protect him from outraged onlookers who wanted to tear him to pieces. One woman shouted out that shooting was too good for him – "He needs to die a slow and agonizing death."

Onoprienko admitted the charges against him, but had little else to say, apart from: "This is your law, I consider myself a hostage." The press dubbed him "The Terminator".

He claimed, of course, that there were conspiracies by higher powers against him. They were experimenting on him and were out to murder humanity.

"I love all people and I loved those I killed," he said. "I looked those children I murdered in the eyes and knew that it had to be done. For you it's fifty-two murders, but for me that's the norm."

He showed no contrition. "I have never regretted anything and I don't regret anything now," he said.

SATAN'S SERVANT

He was sentenced to death by shooting, but on joining the Council of Europe, Ukraine had promised to ban capital punishment. Leonid Kuchma, president of the Ukraine, considered a moratorium but, in the end, was forced to commute the sentence to life in prison.

"I started preparing for prison life a long time ago – I fasted, did yoga, I am not afraid of death," Onoprienko told a newspaper reporter. "Death for me is nothing. Naturally, I would prefer the death penalty. I have absolutely no interest in relations with people. I have betrayed them."

Then he revealed that he did have feelings, in a way.

"The first time I killed, I shot down a deer in the woods," he said. "I was in my early twenties and I recall feeling very upset when I saw it dead. I couldn't explain why I had done it, and I felt sorry for it. I never had that feeling again."

Again he warned that the authorities should kill him – he was Satan's servant.

"If I am ever let out, I will start killing again, but this time it will be worse, ten times worse. The urge is there. Seize this chance because I am being groomed to serve Satan. After what I have learnt out there, I have no competitors in my field. And if I am not killed, I will escape from this jail and the first thing I'll do is find Kuchma and hang him from a tree by his testicles."

Protesting his innocence, Onoprienko's one-time accomplice, Sergei Rogozin was sentenced to thirteen years, commuted to twelve on appeal. Onoprienko died of a heart attack in jail in 2013, aged fifty-four, leaving open the question that other murders may have occurred in the six-year lull between 1989 and 1995.

PART 3

ASIAN SERIAL KILLERS

1

NIKOLAI DZHUMAGALIEV
Metal Fang
KAZAKHSTAN

K nown as "Metal Fang" for the white metal dentures he had been given to replace his missing front teeth as a result of a fistfight, Dzhumagaliev was a necrophiliac, cannibal killer, who murdered and ate at least nine people. Drinking their blood and dismembering his victims, he saved bite-sized portions to cook and eat later.

Born in 1952 in Uzynagash, Kazakhstan, then part of the Soviet Union, he studied to be a railway worker before being conscripted into the Red Army at the age of eighteen. Having completed his national service, he aimed to become a chauffeur or to go to university. He failed on both counts. Instead he travelled around the Soviet Union working variously as sailor, forwarding agent, electrician, and bulldozer operator. In 1977, he returned to Uzynagash to take a job as a firefighter.

Unlike many serial killers, Dzhumagaliev had a fairly normal sex life – to start with. "I began my sex life in 1970, when I was eighteen years old and I constantly had several girls," he said. "They loved me, but I don't know why. In 1977 I contracted syphilis from Tatiana P. Then in May 1978, I contracted trichomoniasis from a girl named Lyuba. At the same time I cohabited with Tatiana Y."

DESPERATE FOR FEMALE FLESH

But things were not right. Dzhumagaliev considered himself a descendent of Genghis Khan, but, as an Asian, he felt alienated from white women for their pride and licentiousness, which are unacceptable in patriarchal Islam. "From them, from women, come all misfortunes – prison, crimes," he said.

Long before his first murder he was desperate to eat female flesh, but he kept his desires suppressed even as his hatred of women grew. Dzhumagaliev was not a spontaneous killer. He spent two years planning his first murder, all the time dreaming of dismembered female bodies: "Hands, legs, torsos float so slowly ... I took the side of animals and with people I did only what they do with animals."

He chose a Seventh Day Adventist as his first victim. "I have always loved hunting. I often went to hunt, but this was my first time hunting a woman," he said. "When I went to the Uzynagash-Maybulak highway, I saw the young woman. She walked alone. Everything inside me pounded and I rushed after her. Hearing my steps, she turned around, but I caught up with her and, grabbing her by the neck, dragged her towards the dump.

"She began to resist, and then I cut her throat with a knife. Then I drank her blood. At that moment, a bus appeared from the direction of the Fabrichniy village. I lay down on the ground and hid next to the murdered woman. While I was lying there, my hands were frozen. When the bus passed, I warmed my hands on the woman's body and, having undressed her, began to cut her up.

"I cut out the chest along with strips of fat from the corpse, cut out the calves, separated the pelvis and thighs. Then I put all these parts in a backpack and brought them home. I melted some of the fat, and salted some of it and ate it like lard. Once, having minced the flesh in a meat grinder, I made dumplings. All the meat I always ate only myself and did not treat anyone. Fried the heart and kidneys twice. I also fried the meat. But it was tough and it took a long time to cook it on its own fat.

"I ate this woman's meat for about a month. The first time I ate human flesh by force, and then I got used to it."

The rest of the corpse was found on January 25, 1979, at a dump near the village of Fabrichniy, which was not far from his home in Uzynagash. A criminal case was opened, but the investigation led nowhere.

The murders continued. On the night of April 21, Dzhumagaliev killed seventy-year-old Anna Marinova who was returning home after evening prayers in Fabrichniy. At 2:00 a.m. on June 21, another elderly woman and her daughter, Alina and Lida Ivanova, were sleeping in their house in Uzynagash when Dzhumagaliev broke in and killed them. His next victim was twenty-three-year-old Valentina Prochazka.

SQUEEZING HER NECK

Dzhumagaliev relished retelling the encounter with Valentina. "On June 27, 1979, my partner Tatiana Y. told me that a girl named Valentina stole her personal belongings," he said. "Tatiana reported this to the police. I scolded Tatiana for telling the cops and ordered her to bring this thief to my house that evening. Then I went to my friends to drink vodka. When I returned to my room in the evening, I saw a young and pretty girl. Tatiana Y. herself was in temporary accommodation with my sister Zoya. The girl and I sat for a while, and then I undressed her and we had sex. And everything happened with her consent.

"Then I thought that my girlfriend might enter the room

and suggested that Valentina go to the barn. I picked her up from the bed and carried her in my arms to the shed located in the yard. In the barn we had sex again, but I was not satisfied. And then I had a desire to strangle the girl. Squeezing her neck with both hands, I began to choke her.

"At that moment I wanted her again. Then I took my knife and carefully cut her throat. I began to suck her blood and got excited again. Having had sex with her again, I realized that she had already died. Having dismembered her body at the joints, I put the meat in a barrel, and what was left was buried in the garden."

On August 21, 1979, Dzhumagaliev was arrested, but not for these five murders. He had shot dead one of his fellow firefighters while drunk. He was diagnosed with schizophrenia. Formally sentenced to four-and-a-half years in jail, he was released after one.

DRAINING HER BLOOD

On November 8, 1980, Dzhumagaliev was in a house in Fabrichniy having sex with twenty-six-year-old Tatiana Garriova. They were drunk and fell asleep. At night he woke up and thought: "Why am I sorry for the infidels?" He cut her throat and began to drink her blood.

"In the book *Black Mist* I read that if you cut a person's throat and look intently, you can see how the soul leaves the body," he said. "I looked, and looked, but never saw it."

He murdered Valya Soyka, age twenty-two, on December 13, and in the morning of December 18, he murdered twenty-seven-year-old Zoya Slivka. He had been partying all night with friends and girlfriends when he took Zoya into the next room.

"I had sexual intercourse with her and decided to make an experiment – again to see whether the soul flew out or not," he said. "I read in the book that, if you drink blood, you can make a prophecy – and that the most delicious is human meat. She was asleep. I hit her, draining her blood into basin."

Then he took several sips of blood and cut off a piece of flesh from the neck. He began to butcher the corpse, cutting off the head and arms, but did not have time to go further.

He was naked when friends came in and saw what he was doing. Shocked, they reported him to the police. Four officers arrived to find a maniac sitting on the bed, butchering his victim's corpse and smearing his naked body with her blood. He fled and hid out in the mountains. Searching his house, the police found a barrel of salted human meat.

Dzhumagaliev soon got tired of hiding in the mountains and took refuge with a relative, who gave him some clothes and tried unsuccessfully to hide him from the police. He was arrested the next day.

EATING FEMALE MEAT

At his trial, which began on December 3, 1981, he told the woman judge: "I killed women for several reasons. Firstly, I satisfied my sexual desire for them in this way. Secondly, I felt an irresistible attraction to the female body so I tried to know it completely. Therefore, I ate female meat. Thirdly, in the book *Black Mist*, which I read several years ago, it is written that the women of the ancient Germans drank blood to become divine. I also wanted to be divine and so drank their blood. And I managed to divine. I predicted my whole life from 1980 to 1988, and until 2000 I saw vaguely.

"This is my revenge on women for violating the laws of nature. A man should be higher than a woman in everything, but in life everything goes wrong. I wanted to strike fear into all the women in the area. I killed for a reason: having killed Tatiana G., I sacrificed her on the anniversary of the death of my grandmother, and Valya on December 13, 1980 – as a sacrifice for the hundredth anniversary of the birth of my grandfather. I did not kill for any one reason, I always killed for complex reasons."

Having already been diagnosed as a schizophrenic, Dzhumagaliev was not sent to prison. He spent eight years in a psychiatric hospital. In 1989, while being transferred to another hospital, he escaped. He spent two years on the run.

In the spring of 1991 he was in the Fergana Valley in

Uzbekistan. He had grown tired of being a fugitive, so he committed a petty theft, hoping to get caught and take a rest in prison. But he was recognized and returned to the hospital in Tashkent.

In January 1994, Dzhumagaliev was discharged and sent under observation to his native Uzynagash, where he was shunned, particularly by women. He went on the run again. There were rumours that he left a trail of dismembered bodies wherever he went.

Recaptured he was sent to a secure hospital where he spent his time repairing watches and audiovisual equipment. Once he petitioned for the death penalty, but this was considered another symptom of his mental condition. In September 2014, Dzhumagaliev was convicted of a tenth murder, which he had committed in 1990. There seems little prospect of him ever being released.

2

MIKHAIL POPKOV
The Werewolf
EASTERN RUSSIA

Mikhail Popkov was, perhaps, Russia's most prolific serial killer. He was known as The Werewolf in the press because he struck at night, and he mutilated the corpses of his victims by stabbing them up to 170 times, leaving the body looking as if a werewolf had ripped it apart.

Outwardly, he appeared to be the perfect husband and father, working days as a policeman, but leading the secret life of a serial killer at night, copulating with the bodies after he killed them. Popkov admitted the rape and murder of more than eighty women, though there may have been many more.

After he had been sentenced to life imprisonment for twenty-two murders in 2015, Popkov claimed to have stopped killing in the year 2000 when one of his victims gave him syphilis rendering him impotent. Then, in 2017, he admitted that he continued killing for another ten years and confessed to the murder of another sixty women in the Irkutsk Oblast of central Siberia.

After quitting the police force, Popkov travelled regularly between his hometown of Angarsk to Vladivostok on Russia's Pacific coast, a journey of over two thousand miles, and homicide officers feel that he may have killed along the way. They believed that he was gradually confessing his crimes in stages to delay his transfer from the relative comfort of the regular prison to a tough penal colony to serve out the rest of his life sentence.

PSYCHIC REVENGE

Popkov began killing in 1992 when he found two used condoms in the trash at his home and suspected his wife Elena, who was also a police officer, of cheating on him. Although it seems that the condoms had actually been left by a houseguest, one of Elena's work colleagues later admitted that he had a brief affair with her.

A few weeks after this discovery, Popkov found the need to kill "spontaneously", as he told investigators. "I just felt I wanted to kill a woman I was giving a lift to in my car," he said.

In 2015, he had claimed his aim was to "cleanse" his hometown of prostitution. Even if his victims were not prostitutes, he felt that women who went out by themselves at night to drink alcohol in bars needed to be punished. The theory was that Popkov was taking some sort of psychic revenge on an alcoholic mother who abused him as a child.

"My victims were women who walked the streets at night alone, without men, and not sober, who behaved thoughtlessly, carelessly, not afraid to engage in a conversation with me, sit in the car, and then go for a drive in search of adventure, for the sake of entertainment, ready to drink alcohol and have sexual intercourse with me," he said. After he had sex with them, he decided whether or not to murder them.

"In this way, not all women became victims, but women of certain negative behaviour, and I had a desire to teach and punish them," he said. "So that others would not behave in such a way and so that they would be afraid."

The women were reassured by his police uniform and felt safe getting into a police car late at night.

"I was in uniform. I decided to stop and give a woman a ride, I frequently did that before," he said. "The woman began talking to me, I offered to give her a lift, she agreed … That same morning, I drove the head of the criminal investigation to the murder scene."

Popkov not only got a thrill from killing his victims, he was able to double his pleasure by reliving every perverted detail of the crime when he got involved in the investigation.

LEADING A DOUBLE LIFE

He was lucky not to have been caught much earlier as one of his victims survived and identified him. On January 26, 1998, a fifteen-year-old known as Svetlana M said a police car had stopped and offered her a lift. The officer took her into woodland where he forced her to strip naked. He then smashed her head against a tree. She lost consciousness.

The next day she was found alive near the village of Baykalsk, some seventy miles from where she had been picked up. Somehow she survived the night in the sub-zero temperatures of a Siberian winter without any clothing. When she awoke in hospital, she was able to identify the officer who had tried to kill her.

However, Popkov's wife provided him with a false alibi, which was believed as she was a police officer. Neither his wife nor their daughter could believe that he was a killer, saying he was a perfect husband and father.

"I had a double life," he said. "In one life I was an ordinary person ... In my other life I committed murders, which I carefully concealed from everyone, realizing that what I was doing was a criminal offence."

His colleagues in the police force also found it hard to believe that Popkov was a killer. Nor did he exhibit any signs of mental instability.

"I was in the service, in the police, having positive feedback on my work," he said. "I never thought of myself as mentally unhealthy. During my police service, I regularly passed medical commissions and was recognized as fit."

But another clue had been overlooked. Some of the murder weapons were taken from the store of those confiscated by the police. After the murder, he would wipe off his fingerprints, then throw them away near the crime scene. Otherwise he would use anything to hand.

"The choice of weapons for killing was always casual," he said. "I never prepared beforehand to commit a murder, I could use any object that was in the car – a knife, an axe, a bat."

Nevertheless he could be fastidious. "I never used rope for strangulation," he said, "and I did not have a firearm either. I did not cut out the hearts of the victims."

This was not true. One of his victims had her heart gouged from her body. Others were mutilated or dismembered. A young medical student was beheaded. Her body was found in a rubbish container in Angarsk, her head dumped elsewhere.

And he took chances. One of his victims was a teacher at his own daughter's music school.

"Her corpse was found in the forest along with the

body of another woman," he said. "My daughter asked me to give her money because the school was collecting to organize funerals. I gave it to her."

CLOSED COFFINS

Another near miss came in 2000 when he returned to the scene of the crime. After he had left thirty-five-year-old Maria Lyzhina and thirty-seven-year-old Liliya Pashkovskaya for dead, he found that the chain he wore round his neck was missing and went back to retrieve it.

"I realized that I lost it in a forest glade when I killed two women," he said. "I realized that I would absolutely be identified by the lost chain, and experienced the greatest stress. I realized that I should return to the scene of the crime, if the police or the prosecutor's office had not been there yet."

When he returned to the scene he found the chain right away, but spotted that one of the women was still breathing.

"I was shocked by the fact that she was still alive, so I finished off her with a shovel," he said.

The two women had worked together in a shop. On June 2, they went to see Maria's sister. At midnight they headed home. It was a warm summer night, and instead of taking a taxi they decided to walk. Three days later, their bodies were found in the forest near Veresovka village. The killer had left their children motherless. Maria had a fourteen-year-old daughter, and Liliya had a twelve-year-old daughter and three-year-old son.

While it is the custom in Russia for coffins to be left open, the two women's coffins were closed because they were so badly mutilated.

TANYA AND YULIA

Popkov committed another double murder in 1998. The bodies of twenty-year-old Tatiana "Tanya" Martynova and nineteen-year-old Yulia Kuprikova were found in a suburb of Angarsk. Tanya's sister Viktoria Chagaeva had given her a ticket for a concert. Tanya was married with a small child and her twenty-four-year-old husband Igor begged her not to go as there was a killer on the prowl. Ignoring his pleas, she made the mistake of stopping for a quick drink with a few friends after the show. Then the two girls accepted a lift from a policeman.

"On the morning of October 29, Igor called me saying Tanya had not come back home," said Viktoria. "I got truly scared. It was the first time, she had ever done this before. There were no mobile phones at that time, we could only call Yulia's parents thinking Tanya must have stayed overnight there for some reason. But Yulia's parents said she had not come home either."

They went to the police, but were told that they must wait three days before the two young women could be listed as missing.

"It was 1:00 a.m. when Tanya's husband Igor and I came to the police," said Viktoria. "We did not tell our mother yet. Igor was absolutely devastated and only repeated: 'She was killed, she was killed.' I was shocked too, but I simply could not believe it and replied: 'What are you talking about?'"

That night a shepherd found their naked bodies near Meget, a village close to Angarsk. The bodies were found next to each other. Both had been raped after they were dead, then mutilated.

"My elder brother Oleg went to the morgue to identify Tanya," said Viktoria. "He had just flown from Moscow. He felt sick when he saw the body, she was so mutilated. He was almost green when he came out of there. He just could not say a word. I did not dare to go in and look."

Tanya's mutilation was to her body and the back of the head, so the coffin could be left open with her face showing. However, Yulia's coffin had to be closed as her face was so badly disfigured.

"Many people attended Tanya's funeral," said Viktoria. "It felt as if the whole town was there. Our poor mother lost her consciousness several times, she needed a lot of medicine to cope. Igor was in almost the same condition."

HORROR STRUCK

Indeed, their mother never recovered from the loss of her daughter. "She felt as if she had died with Tanya, life became useless for her," said Viktoria. "She lived only because she was visiting various mediums one by one, looking for the killer and wasting her money. Nobody gave her any serious information but she kept doing it. She died in 2007 aged sixty-six from a heart attack. I think her heart could not cope with the pain any longer."

When Popkov was arrested in 2012, Viktoria realized that she knew him. They had both competed in a biathlon at a local sports ground.

"I was struck with horror when I saw the picture of this maniac in the paper and online," she said. "My sister's killer was looking into my eyes. I immediately felt as if I'd met him. Looking at him, I could hardly breathe. Some minutes later I looked at him another time and thought – oh my God, I know him!" She was so shocked, she took a knife and cut his face in the newspaper.

"I remember him as a tall slim man, he was always alone, with a slippery and shifty glance," she said. "I think such people just must not live. This beast took the life of my sister, who had so many happy years in front of her. I cried a lot that day, but it is time to be quiet and just wait. He will be punished by law and criminals in jail will punish him too. I am sure he will pay for all the murders one day."

BORN IN THE WRONG CENTURY

That a fellow officer committed these terrible crimes under

their noses perturbed the police. A former police colleague said: "When I read about him in the press I literally choked, because I used to work with him and thought I knew him. He was an absolutely normal man. He liked biathlon; once on duty he shot a rapist during an arrest. There was an investigation and he was not punished, the chiefs considered he had taken fair action."

Another ex-colleague said: "I used to work closely with him for five years. He knew lots of jokes and stories, and could be the soul of the party."

Popkov was captured on June 23, 2012, when 3,500 policemen and former policemen were asked to provide DNA samples. His matched the sperm found on some of the victims.

"I couldn't predict DNA tests," he told a reporter from *Komsomolskaya Pravda* in a jailhouse interview. "I was born in the wrong century."

When Popkov pleaded guilty to the two dozen murder charges, the judge asked him how many murders he had committed in total. In reply, Popkov just shrugged. "I can't say exactly," he said. "I didn't write them down."

3

GAO CHENGYONG
The Chinese Jack the Ripper
CHINA

The Chinese Jack the Ripper, Gao Chengyong, killed and mutilated eleven women between 1988 and 2002 and then inexplicably stopped. Fourteen years later the fifty-two-year-old killer was arrested in the grocery store he ran with his wife in Baiyin City in Gansu province, northwest China.

Nine of the murders had taken place in Baiyin itself, and two outside the city in Baotou, Inner Mongolia. According to the Ministry of Public Security, the suspect confessed to all eleven murders. He targeted young women wearing red clothing and long hair. Usually his victims lived alone.

He followed them home, where he would kill them. If he found the victim attractive then he would rape them otherwise he would just cut their throat. Sometimes he would rape them after he had killed them. He also cut off parts of their sexual organs as trophies and mutilated the corpse with multiple stabbings in frenzied attacks similar to the original Jack the Ripper in London's east end.

In 2004, cold-case investigators tied all eleven murders to a single perpetrator. The police said: "The suspect has a sexual perversion and hates women. He's reclusive and unsociable, but patient."

BRUTALLY MUTILATED

Gao's first victim was a twenty-three-year-old woman who worked at the Baiyin Non-Ferrous Metal Company. She was found dead in her home with twenty-six wounds on her body on May 26, 1988. Gao said she had caught him during a break-in.

In 1994, he killed a nineteen-year-old woman at the power supply bureau in Baiyin, stabbing her forty-three times. The killer then cleaned himself up in a washroom in the staff dormitory. Four years later he killed an eight-year-old in the same dormitory, stuffing her body in a cabinet. Gao said that he cold-bloodedly drank a cup of tea before leaving.

That year, Gao killed four women, throwing their

severed body parts in the Yellow River. One victim was a woman that he had picked up at a dancehall. The police suspected local gangsters, but that line of enquiry got nowhere.

As the killings went on, the mutilations became more brutal. In 1998, the hands, ears, and breasts of his sixth victim, Cui Jinping, had been cut off and taken. He had stabbed her twenty-two times before cutting her throat. Her mother found her ripped apart body, but despite extensive searches, the missing parts were never found.

On May 22, 2001, a victim managed to get to a phone and call the police, saying she was being murdered. They heard her final gasps, but nothing more. The scene of the crime was just a block from the police station. If they had known where she was, the police may have arrived in time.

By 2004 police had finally linked the eleven murders to one killer and were taking DNA samples from the population of Baiyin City, but have no success in finding a match. This was because Gao did not officially live there. He remained registered in Qingcheng, a town seventy-five miles away where he had grown up. So he managed to avoid the fingerprint checks required by Chinese citizens applying for the national identity card needed to travel.

Gao was only caught in 2016 because his uncle was arrested for bribery and his DNA was taken. Its similarity to the killer's was noticed. The police then screened the DNA of his uncle's male relatives. Gao's was a perfect match and he was confirmed after twelve years of searching as "The Chinese Jack the Ripper."

CALM CONFESSIONS

When the police arrived to arrest him on August 26, 2016, they asked him if he knew why he was being arrested. He confessed to all eleven murders that had started twenty-eight years before, giving details only the killer could have known. Asked if he ever felt regret or remorse for the victims and their families, he very calmly shook his head.

He had given up killing in 2002, he said, because he had gone to work as a construction worker outside town to earn money to put his sons through college. Besides he was getting old and was not strong enough to go on killing.

Apparently Gao had once dreamt of being a pilot, but had been frustrated for "political reasons". His wife of thirty years, wailed when she heard of his arrest. She said that he would leave her for days at a time. It was then that he was killing.

After eighteen years, Cui Jinping's brother Cui Xiangping said that the family had given up hope that her murder would ever be solved. Their mother could not stop crying after hearing the news of Gao's arrest.

In a two-day trial in July 2017 in Baiyin, Gao bowed to his victims' families three times in apology after pleading guilty. He said he could not afford to give them compensation, but was willing to donate his organs. Gao Chengyong was executed on January 3, 2019.

4

YASUTOSHI KAMATA
The Osaka Ripper
JAPAN

Born in 1940 in the city of Ozu in the south of Japan, Yasutoshi Kamata married a local woman, but when he found she was unfaithful he moved to the Nishinari-ku district of Osaka in 1960 where he made a living selling stolen goods. He did not start killing until 1985.

MONSTER WITH 22 FACES
His first victim was forty-six-year-old housewife Fusae Azuma who he met in a local bar. She was a married woman with three children and, after drinks and a meal,

he took her back to one of the numerous apartments he had. When she resisted his sexual advances, he strangled her and dumped her body in a wooded area outside Kobe.

The following month he killed nineteen-year-old student Midori Chinen. She had disappeared on her way to work at a home for the mentally handicapped. He took her to a sushi restaurant, then to an apartment. When she asked him for 10,000 yen, he grew angry and strangled her.

Then he spread out vinyl sheets on the floor and cut up her body using a saw and a kitchen knife. He put her remains in a cardboard box and drove them in a rental car out into the countryside where he dumped them. They were found the next day.

Three months later Kamata sent a letter to the police chief, taunting him. It was signed "The Monster with 22 Faces". This was a reference to an earlier extortion case where a gang calling itself "The Monster with 21 Faces" demanded money from food manufacturers by threatening to contaminate their produce. The perpetrators were never caught but they were thought to be part of the local Yakuza.

TOO SMALL TO CHOP UP

Kamata's letter named the sushi restaurant where he had taken Midori Chinen and which body parts he had removed. When the police checked, they found that she had been seen there with a middle-aged man. As this was information only the killer could have known, the police concluded that the letter was genuine.

When an investigator came to a snack bar that Kamata frequented, he left town. But he was back in Osaka on January 22, 1987, when he kidnapped nine-year-old Kumiko Tsujikado. He intended to sexually assault her, but when she screamed he strangled her and dumped her body in the mountains. She was too small to chop up, he said, and was just the right size to fit in a cardboard box without being dismembered. Pretending she was still alive, he repeatedly called her school demanding a ransom of thirty-million yen. Her body was found on May 4, 1987.

There was then a six year break. Kamata had been convicted of a series of thefts and was in jail until March 1993. However soon after he was released he was back in action.

In July 1993, he paid forty-five-year-old snack-bar employee Kazue Suda to come back to his apartment, where he strangled her. Again he dismembered her body and dumped the remains in the mountains. They were not found until the following April and were so badly decayed that they had to be identified from dental records.

At the end of March 1994, Kamata paid thirty-eight-year-old waitress Kimiko Nakano to come back to his apartment where, again, he strangled her. Her dismembered body was discarded in a forest and he sold her clothes. Her remains were discovered on April 3, the day before those of Kazue Suda were found.

WORKPLACE KNIVES

The murders ended in April 1995, when Kamata was arrested for stealing clothes from a warehouse. He was a suspect in the murder of Midori Chinen as he was known to be in the area around the sushi restaurant where she had last been seen. His rental car had also been spotted in the vicinity on the day of her disappearance. When his fingerprints were taken, it was found that they matched those on the letter from "The Monster with 22 Faces".

It was then found that he was acquainted with Kazue Suda and Kimiko Nakano, and had access to knives at his workplace similar to those sharp implements used to cut up the bodies. He admitted killing Midori Chinen and was charged with her murder. Soon after he admitted two other murders, including that of Fusae Azuma which, until then, the police had not connected with the other cases. Her body was finally located ten years after Kamata had dumped it in the woods.

During the investigation, Kamata admitted all the murders except for that of Kumiko Tsujikado. The killer, he said, had been a friend of his. He had merely disposed of the body. Although his voice was very similar to that of the ransom caller, an expert witness for the defence argued that it was not identical and Kamata was acquitted on that charge.

In court, Kamata denied all the murders, again saying that they had been committed by some supposed friend. He had only helped dispose of the bodies, but the police had beaten him into signing a confession. Nevertheless, he was convicted for the first two murders and sentenced to death.

An appeal confirmed the convictions and the death sentence was upheld by the Supreme Court. A campaign to end capital punishment left him sitting on death row for seventeen years. But in 2016, the minister of justice signed the death warrant and he was hanged.

5

TSUTOMU MIYAZAKI
The Japanese Vampire
JAPAN

Also known as the Otaku Murderer for his love of anime and manga, Tsutomu Miyazaki was born in 1962. He was born prematurely which left him with a rare birth defect. His hands were gnarled and the bones in his wrists fused so he could not rotate his hands without turning the whole of his forearms. As a result he was shunned at school.

His father owned the local newspaper *Akikawa Miyazaki* and was involved in politics. His mother, too, was very busy and had little time for him. He was largely brought up by his beloved grandfather. When he died, Miyazaki ate some of his ashes.

As a loner, Miyazaki spent much of his time reading comics and watching anime and horror movies. His grades at school declined and he did not get into university. Instead he studied to be a photo-technician at college and went to work in a print works.

OBSESSED WITH LITTLE GIRLS

Miyazaki avoided women his own age, perhaps because he was physically immature. "His penis is no thicker than a pencil and no longer than a toothpick," a classmate remarked. Yet his sex drive was strong. At college, he took his still and video cameras to the tennis courts to take crotch shots of female players. He also became tired of adult porn magazines. "They black out the most important part," he complained. So he turned to child porn as Japanese obscenity laws banned the depiction of pubic hair, but not sex organs.

He also identified with little girls. "I felt all alone," Miyazaki explained later. "And whenever I saw a little girl playing on her own, it was almost like seeing myself." He was obsessed with them.

Moving back into the family home, he shared a room with his older sister. But his two younger sisters shunned him. One of them caught him watching her when she was taking a shower. When she yelled at him, he attacked her and smashed her head against the side of the bathtub. When his mother learned of the incident and suggested that he spend more time working and less time watching videos, he attacked her too.

On August 22, 1988, three months after the death of his grandfather and one day after his own twenty-sixth birthday, Miyazaki abducted four-year-old Mari Konno who had been playing in front of a friend's house. He lured her into his black Nissan Langley and drove her out to a wooded area where he murdered her and molested her dead body which he later dumped, taking her clothes with him.

A few days after Mari disappeared, her mother received a postcard which said: "There are devils about." The police dismissed it as the work of a crank.

Later he returned to collect Mari's decomposed corpse. He removed her hands and feet which he kept in his closet. He burned the rest of her remains in a furnace and put her skeleton in a box on the front doorstep of her family home, along with ten teeth, photographs of Mari's clothes and underwear, and a note that read: "Mari. Cremated. Bones. Investigate. Prove."

NOW I'LL TELL

The police noticed that the photos had been taken with a Mamiya 6x7 camera, the type used by printers. The box was the double-walled corrugated variety often used to ship camera lenses. The typeface on the notes came from a phototypesetter and the paper came from an industrial copier.

However, it was initially determined that the teeth did not come from Mari, a finding that was overturned later. This gave the Konno family some hope that Mari may still be alive.

Miyazaki saw the announcement and wrote a three page letter which he sent to the newspaper *Asahi Shimbun* along with a photograph of Mari. The letter was headed "Crime Confession".

"I put the cardboard box with Mari's remains in it in front of her home," it began. "I did everything. From the start of the Mari incident to the finish. I saw the police press conference where they said the remains were not Mari's. On camera, her mother said the report gave her new hope that Mari might still be alive. I knew then that I had to write this confession so Mari's mother would not continue to hope in vain. I say again: the remains are Mari's."

It was signed "Yuko Imada", a pun on the Japanese for "Now I'll tell".

As Mari's ashes were buried, her father Shiego Konno said: "Her hands and feet didn't seem to be with the remains. When she gets to heaven, she won't be able to walk or eat. Please return the rest of her remains."

The Konnos returned home after the funeral to find another "Confession from Yuko Imada". This one chronicled the changes Miyazaki had observed in Mari's dead body. It read: "Before I knew it, the child's corpse had gone rigid. I wanted to cross her hands over her breast but they wouldn't budge ... Pretty soon, the body gets red spots all over it ... Big red spots. Like the Japanese flag. Or like you'd covered her whole body with red *hanko* seals ... After a while, the body is covered with stretch marks. It was so rigid before, but now it feels like its full of water. And it smells. How it smells. Like nothing you've ever smelled in this whole wide world."

COMIC-BOOK DEATHS

Six weeks later, he saw seven-year-old Masami Yoshizawa walking down a rural road and picked her up. He drove her to the same place he had murdered Mari. He killed her, stripped her before rigor mortis set in and had sex with her corpse, then dumped her body, going off with her clothes.

Murdering little girls did not bother Miyazaki at all. He displayed a complete disregard for life. "I've killed cats," he said later. "Threw one in the river. Did another in with boiling water." He also throttled his own dog to death with a strand of wire. The little girls he killed were to him no more than comic-book characters dying evil comic-book deaths.

Four-year-old Erika Namba was returning from a friend's house when Miyazaki lured her into his car. He drove her out to a nature reserve where he forced her to take her clothes off and photographed her naked in the backseat. When a car drove by, Erika began to sob and Miyazaki strangled her. He wrapped her body in a sheet and disposed of her clothes in the woods.

After he drove off, he skidded and the front wheels of his car got stuck in a ditch. He switched on the hazard lights and carried Erika's body out into the woods, and returned with the sheet to find two men standing by his car. Casually he opened the boot and put the sheet away. The two men helped him get the car back onto the road and he drove away without thanking them.

The police found Erika's corpse the next day, its hands and feet bound with nylon cord. The two men who had helped Miyazaki with his car on the night of the murder came forward, but misidentified it as a Toyota Corolla II.

Erika's family also received one of Miyazaki's evil notes. This one read: "Erika. Cold. Cough. Throat. Rest. Death." The families also received phone calls from a caller who did not speak. If they did not answer the phone, it would ring for twenty minutes.

POSSESSED BY RAT MAN
On June 6, 1989, Miyazaki persuaded five-year-old Ayako Nomoto to let him take pictures of her. He then asked Nomoto if he could take some pictures of her in the backseat of his car which was parked some eight-hundred

metres away. When he handed her some chewing gum, she remarked on his deformed hands. Enraged, he strangled her.

He took her body home, stripped off her clothes and took photographs of her in lewd poses while he masturbated over her. When Nomoto's corpse began to decompose, Miyazaki dismembered it, abandoning her torso behind a public lavatory in a cemetery. Miyazaki kept her hands, drinking the blood from them, then roasting them and eating them.

He scattered what was left on a hill in front of his house, along with her head. Realizing that it was a risk leaving the body parts so close to his home, he retrieved them and hid the torso and her skull in a storeroom behind his bedroom.

On July 23, 1989, Miyazaki spotted two sisters playing in a park. He told the older sister, who was nine, to stay where she was while he took the younger child down to a nearby river. But the older sister ran home for her father, who sprinted back to find his younger daughter naked, with Miyazaki focusing a camera between her legs. He grabbed him and knocked him down. Miyazaki escaped, but when he returned to collect his car, the police were waiting. They arrested him and charged him with forcing a minor to commit indecent acts. However, they were already convinced they had caught their serial killer.

At his trial Miyazaki blamed his actions on "Rat Man",

an alter ego who possessed him and forced him to kill. His father refused to pay for his defence, saying it would be unfair to the families of the victims, and committed suicide after his son was found guilty. A seven-year wrangle followed, over whether Miyazaki was responsible enough for his actions to merit the death penalty.

He was not much bothered, spending his time in his cell reading manga and watching anime. Eventually, on June 17, 2008, the Minister of Justice signed the death warrant and Tsutomu Miyazaki was hanged the same day.

6

LEE CHOON-JAE
The Korean Zodiac Killer
SOUTH KOREA

Between September 15, 1986, and April 3, 1991, a series of rapes and murders horrified the city of Hwaseong in Gyeonggi Province, South Korea. The victims had all been bound, gagged, raped and, usually, strangled using their own underwear. It spawned the largest criminal investigation in the country's history. The police spent over two-million man-hours on it.

It was not until nearly thirty years later that Lee Choon-jae was suspected. By then the statute of limitations had run out. Meanwhile Yoon Sung-yeo had spent nearly twenty years in jail for what was thought to be a copycat killing which he did not do. The murders only ended when Lee Choon-jae was arrested for something else.

KILLING HIS SISTER-IN-LAW

In December 1993, Lee Choon-jae's wife left him, so he invited his eighteen-year-old sister-in-law over on January 13, 1994, and then proceeded to drug, rape, and kill her. After she had gone missing, Lee went to his father-in-law and offered to help search for her. They told the police that they thought she had been abducted.

Two days later, her body was found under a tarpaulin in a snow-covered hardware store's garage. Her head was in a plastic bag. Her hands were tied with torn underwear and there were multiple wounds all over her body.

Arrested on January 18, Lee denied having anything to do with her death, but gave himself away by asking: "How many years do you serve in prison for rape and murder?"

Although the court overturned this apparent confession on the grounds of police coercion, he was convicted of first-degree murder and sentenced to death in May 1994, though this was commuted to life imprisonment by the Supreme Court of South Korea the following year.

But it was only announced in September 2019 that Lee was identified as the suspect in the Hwaseong serial killings after his DNA was matched to that left on the underwear of some of the victims. Lee confessed to ten of the murders, along with another four unsolved murders thought to have been unrelated. He also confessed to more than thirty rapes and attempted rapes.

COUNTING THE BODIES

The police were counting the bodies as Lee admitted his crimes. The killings began with the disappearance of seventy-one-year-old Lee Wan-im on September 15, 1986, while returning home after visiting her daughter. Her body was found in a field four days later. She had been strangled. A month later on October 20, twenty-five-year-old Park Hyun-sook disappeared after getting off the bus while returning home from Songtan where she had been meeting a prospective marriage partner. Her body was found three days later in a canal. Again she had been strangled and semen was found.

Almost two months passed, then on December 12, twenty-five-year-old Kwon Jung-bon disappeared from in front of her house. Her body was found three months later on an embankment. She had been strangled with her own stockings and gagged with her panties. Again semen had been found.

Twenty-three-year-old Lee Kye-sook was murdered after getting off a bus on her way back from meeting a prospective marriage partner on December 21, 1986. Her body was found on a ridge between paddy fields. She had been strangled. Her hands were tied and her face covered with her girdle. She had been penetrated by an umbrella and semen was found.

Nineteen-year-old high-schoolgirl Hong Jin-young was murdered after getting off a bus and she was found in a rice paddy on January 11, 1987. Her hands were tied and she had been gagged with her socks. She had been strangled and, once more, semen was found.

Then on May 2, 1987, twenty-nine-year-old Park Eun-joo was murdered while delivering an umbrella to her husband. Her body was found a week later. She had been strangled and semen was found.

On September 7, 1987, fifty-four-year-old Ahn Gi-soon disappeared on her way home. Her body was found in a canal the following day. Her hands were tied. She had been gagged with her socks and a handkerchief and strangled. Semen was found.

There was a hiatus after Lee was arrested for breaking into a house on September 26, 1989, and was found to be carrying a weapon. In February 1990, he was sentenced to eighteen months. He appealed on the grounds that he had sought refuge in the house because he was being pursued. The court suspended his sentence. He was given two-years probation and was released in April 1990.

On November 15, 1990, fourteen-year-old schoolgirl Kim Mi-jung was murdered on her way home. Her hands and feet were tied. She had been gagged with her bra and strangled. Once more semen was found.

The four apparently unrelated murders Lee admitted to were those of eighteen-year-old Kim Mi-soon on December 24, 1987, eight-year-old Kim Hyun-jung on July 7, 1989, whose body was never found, fourteen-year-old Park on January 26, 1991, and twenty-seven-year-old Kim on March 7, 1991.

ACTING ON IMPULSE

The murder twenty-two-year-old Yoon Sung-yeo was convicted of was that of fourteen-year-old Park Sang-hee on September 16, 1988. It was considered a copycat killing because the perpetrator had murdered the schoolgirl at 2:00 a.m. while she was sleeping in her bedroom.

Yoon, who was disabled by polio, was released on parole in 2009. After Lee's confession in 2019, Yoon applied for a retrial. In court, Lee expressed surprise that it has taken the police so long to catch him. They had questioned him at the time of the killings for not carrying his ID card, but he was set free soon after.

Lee couldn't understand why he wasn't a suspect, he said: "Crimes happened around me and I didn't try hard to hide things so I thought I would get caught easily. There were hundreds of police forces. I bumped into detectives all the time but they always asked me about people around me."

He said he had no reason to kill the schoolgirls. "It was an impulsive act," he said. "I heard from someone that a person with a disability was arrested but I didn't know which one he was arrested for as I committed many [crimes]."

Lee apologized to the family members of his victims – and to Yoon.

"I heard that many people had been investigated and wrongfully suffered," he said. Four suspects had committed suicide. "I'd like to apologize to all those people. I came and testified and described the crimes in the hopes for the victims and their families will find some comfort when the truth is revealed."

Despite his confession, he could not be tried for the other murders as the statute of limitation had expired on the crimes. Lee Choon-jae remains in jail for the murder of his sister-in-law.

7

YOO YOUNG-CHUL
The Raincoat Killer
SOUTH KOREA

After being convicted of twenty murders, Yoo Young-chul opposed the abolition of the death penalty by the government and their proposal to replace it with life imprisonment instead. "It is the cruellest punishment to isolate hideous criminals, who cannot be reformed, and make them die old. It is also a waste of state funds," he said. "It would be unfair to the world for people like me to continue living. I object to abolishing the death penalty."

Born to poor parents in South Korea, Yoo was fourteen when his father, an epileptic, died. Before he began his killing spree at the age of thirty-three, he had spent eleven years in jail, having been sentenced fourteen times for theft, fraud, forgery, selling child pornography, and crimes of violence. He was serving a sentence for rape in 2002, when his wife of ten years, a masseuse, divorced him. He thought of killing her, but decided not to because of their young son.

HAMMERING THE RICH

During his incarceration, he read an article about Jeong Du-yeong who had murdered nine wealthy people in Busan in 1999 – 2000. Inspired by Jeong Du-yeong he began planning his own killings of the rich. Yoo was released on September 11, 2003, soon after on September 24, he broke into a house in the wealthy Gangnam district of Seoul and bludgeoned to death a seventy-three-year-old emeritus professor and his sixty-eight-year-old wife with a hammer.

On October 9, he broke into another house in western Seoul and killed an eighty-five-year-old grandmother, her sixty-year-old daughter and her handicapped grandson who was thirty-five. His *modus operandi* was to make his attacks during the day when younger and fitter people would be out at work.

A week later, he bludgeoned the sixty-year-old wife of a financier in Gangnam. She died shortly after she was found by her son. The following month, he broke into another fashionable house in the same area and killed the eighty-seven-year-old owner and his fifty-three-year-old housekeeper.

Having cut himself, he set the house on fire to destroy any DNA evidence he had left behind. The police were puzzled because, unlike his inspiration Jeong Du-yeong, Yoo did not take anything. He was not motivated by greed, he simply had a fundamental hatred of the rich.

CUTTING UP THE CORPSES

On December 11, 2003, he met a young woman in a nightclub and asked her to marry him, but she dropped him after she discovered that he was an ex-convict. This further fuelled his resentment of women, spawned by his divorce, and he planned to take his revenge.

On February 9, 2004, he attacked a forty-seven-year-old woman in the street, killing her. On March 16, he choked a twenty-three-year-old woman to death, cut up her corpse and dumped the pieces along a trail near Sogang University.

Then he attacked a forty-four-year-old vendor for selling him fake Viagra, wrestling him into his own van, handcuffing him and murdering him. Yoo cut off his hands and disposed of them elsewhere after setting fire to the van.

From then on he targeted masseuses and bar girls who he took to be prostitutes. There followed a string of eleven horrific murders. He would call an escort or a masseuse, or otherwise lure a young woman back to his one-bedroom apartment. There, he would bludgeon them and decapitate them in the bathroom, hanging the severed head on the toilet-roll holder while he cut up their body. He would then carry the pieces out in bags and bury the remains near Bongwon Temple.

He was caught when he called a masseuse parlour where several girls had gone missing. The owner recognized the phone number and called the police. A rendezvous with Yoo was arranged where several of the employees of the massage parlour grabbed him. They held on to him until the police turned up and handcuffed him. In his flat, they found videos featuring similar murders and dismemberment of corpses.

Yoo feigned an epileptic seizure. When the police loosened his bounds, he escaped, but was recaptured twelve hours later.

CLEANSING HIS SPIRIT

He admitted to at least nineteen murders, but said there were too many to count. If they had not caught him, he said, he would have gone on to kill a hundred more. He also admitted eating the internal organs of four of his victims to "cleanse his spirit".

He said he had killed women because they had betrayed him, and the rich because he grew up in poverty and resented those who lived in a wealthy house nearby. This developed into an abiding hostility to the rich.

There was little physical evidence to link Yoo to the crimes and the prosecution had to rely largely on his confessions. In court he made no attempt to defend himself. However, when asked if he still thought that the victims deserved to die as he had said previously under questioning, he answered no, adding: "Though I did not have adequate opportunity to express it, I am genuinely sorry."

He was convicted and sentenced to death, which was automatically suspended. The case re-opened the debate on whether capital punishment should be retained.

8

CHARLES SOBHRAJ
The Serpent
INDIA

Born in Saigon (now Ho Chi Minh City) in 1944, Hotchand Bhawnani Gurmukh Sobhraj was the son of a Vietnamese peasant girl and a wealthy Indian merchant, who married an Indian woman soon after. When Sobhraj was four years old, his mother married a French soldier. With the French on the retreat in Indochina, the family moved to France in 1953.

While his French stepfather treated him well, Sobhraj was marginalized when more children came along. There were temper tantrums and he became a bedwetter. Sent to a Catholic boarding school, he suffered racist abuse. To mitigate this he changed his name to Charles, after his endearing impression of Charlie Chaplin.

EXPLOITING WEAKNESSES

In his teens he travelled back to Saigon to visit his father – financing his trips by theft – but was rejected. Returning to France, he was jailed for burglary. The conditions in prison were harsh, but Sobhraj made friends with a wealthy prison visitor Felix d'Escogne.

When he was paroled, d'Escogne gave him a place to stay and introduced him to high society, but Sobhraj could not give up his old ways. The evening he proposed to a wealthy young Parisian, Chantal Compagnon, he was arrested driving a stolen car and crashed in an effort to escape.

When it came to sentencing, d'Escogne wrote to the judge saying of Sobhraj: "He exploits 100 per cent the weaknesses of those around him. He has a small conscience, if any … is capable of politeness, but calculatedly so. Impulsive and aggressive."

Nevertheless Chantal stood by him. When he was released after eight months, they married. After a series of burglaries in wealthy homes – along with other scams and cons – Sobhraj decided to leave France. He "borrowed" d'Escogne's car and set off across Eastern Europe, bouncing fake cheques as he went. They had reached Bombay, now

Mumbai, when Chantal gave birth to a baby girl.

He made a living in India by selling stolen cars. This involved a lot of travel and Sobhraj assuaged Chantal by bringing back jewellery from his trips. In the meantime, he ran up gambling debts. To pay them off, he got involved in the armed robbery of a jewellery store in Delhi. This was partially successful, but the thieves had to abandon the stolen jewels while making their escape.

Back in Bombay, he was arrested for driving another stolen car, as well as the jewellery heist in Delhi, and he was taken to Bombay's notorious Tihar jail. There he feigned appendicitis and was taken to hospital. Recovering from needless surgery, he persuaded Chantal to drug the guard while he escaped. They were caught, but after posting bail they fled to Kabul in Afghanistan.

DRINKING HIS OWN BLOOD

Kabul was then on the hippie trail to India. They made a living robbing hippie tourists, but Sobhraj was arrested again. This time, he drank his own blood to make it look like he had an ulcer. Again in hospital, he escaped by drugging his guard. Abandoning his family, he fled to Iran. Vowing never to see him again, Chantal returned to France.

Over the next two years Sobhraj went on the run, travelling around Eastern Europe and Asia using as many as ten stolen passports. In Istanbul he was joined by his half-brother André in a crime spree. When things got too hot in Turkey, they fled to Greece, where they were arrested. Sobhraj escaped again, leaving André to be shipped back to Turkey where he served eighteen years hard labour.

Returning to India, Sobhraj began to pose as a jewel dealer and even a drug trafficker. He befriended young impressionable western tourists, then robbed them. He met French Canadian tourist Marie-Andrée LeClerc who was looking for excitement. After her vacation was over, she agreed to meet him in Bangkok, only to find him with a Thai woman called May who he said was his secretary. Nevertheless she became a devoted follower and together, they met up with an Australian couple, drugged them and ransacked their room, stealing their money, wedding rings, passports, and plane tickets.

Settling for a time in Bangkok, Sobhraj revelled in becoming the leader of a family of hangers-on. He overdosed a French boy named Dominique Renelleau with toxin to give him dysentery, then nursed him back to health, earning his gratitude. He also ingratiated himself with two former French policemen, Yannick and Jacques, "recovering" their missing passports that Sobhraj himself had stolen. Then he teamed up with an Indian criminal named Ajay Chowdhury who became his right-hand man preying on young tourists.

There may have been some murders earlier which

Sobhraj was able to pass off as drug overdoses, but the first known victim of the new team was a young woman from Seattle called Teresa Knowlton. She was found drowned in a tidal pool in the Gulf of Thailand wearing a flowery bikini. Initially it was explained away as a swimming accident after a night of beer and hashish, but forensic evidence showed that someone had held her head under the water. Before her death was discovered, LeClerc willingly posed as Knowlton to cash in the travellers cheques she was carrying which were worth thousands of dollars.

THE BIKINI KILLER

Next Sephardic Jew Vitali Hakim joined the family. He accompanied Sobhraj and Chowdhury on a trip to the beach resort of Pattaya. They returned without him, saying he had decided to stay with friends. Yannick and Jacques were suspicious because Hakim had left all his possessions behind, including his passport and travellers cheques. His body was later found on the road to Pattaya. He had been beaten up and set on fire while he was still alive.

Dutch students Henk Bintanja and his fiancée Cocky Hemker came to stay with the family after meeting Sobhraj in Hong Kong. They were poisoned by Sobhraj, who nursed them back to health. While they were recovering, Hakim's French girlfriend, Charmayne Carrou, came to investigate her boyfriend's disappearance.

Sobhraj and Chowdhury quickly disposed of Bintanja and Hemker. Their bodies were found strangled and burned on December 16, 1975. Their deaths were blamed on bandits. Soon afterwards, Carrou was also found drowned and wearing a similar-styled swimsuit to that of Teresa Knowlton. It was later found she had been strangled. No connection was made at the time, but the murders would later earn Sobhraj the nickname "The Bikini Killer".

On December 18, Sobhraj and LeClerc entered Nepal using Bintanja and Hemker's passports. There they met and murdered Canadian Laurent Carrière and American Connie Jo Bronzich. Sobhraj and LeClerc returned to Thailand using their passports, carrying jewels Sobhraj had stolen from them.

While they had been travelling, Dominique, Yannick, and Jacques had figured out what Sobhraj was up to. They broke into his office and found dozens of passports and identity papers. After informing the police, they headed back to France.

KEEPING AHEAD OF THE LAW

Realizing that the game was up in Thailand and Nepal, Sobhraj, LeClerc, and Chowdhury went to India. In a rundown hotel in Calcutta, Sobhraj drugged and strangled Israeli scholar Avoni Jacob and stole his passport and $300 in travellers cheques. Keeping ahead of the law, they travelled to Singapore, then back to India, then returned to Bangkok.

Meanwhile Dutch diplomat Herman Knipper was looking into the murder of the two Dutch backpackers Henk Bintanja and Cocky Hemker. He got permission to search Sobhraj's apartment where he found the victims' documents, along with syringes and poison.

Sobhraj, LeClerc, and Chowdhury then headed for Malaysia where Chowdhury was sent to steal some gems. After he returned with them, he was never seen again, while Sobhraj and LeClerc headed to Geneva to sell the jewels.

Back in Bombay they picked up two more Western women, Barbara Smith and Mary Ellen Eather. Sobhraj then poisoned Frenchman Jean-Luc Solomon intending to incapacitate him so they could rob him, but Solomon died.

In New Delhi, Sobhraj and the three women persuaded a group of French post-graduate students to take them on as tour guides. Intending to rob them, Sobhraj gave them pills which, he assured them, would prevent dysentery. But the pills took effect too quickly and they began passing out in the hotel lobby. Three of them realized what was going on, overpowered him and called the police.

Under interrogation, Smith and Eather confessed. Sobhraj was charged with the murder of Jean-Luc Solomon and all three were sent to Tihar jail. The conditions were so bad that Smith and Eather tried to commit suicide. But

Sobhraj had concealed seventy carats of precious stones in his body and bribed the guards to get him anything he wanted.

CELEBRITY STATUS

He hired and fired lawyers, eventually representing himself. Found guilty of culpable homicide, he was sentenced to twelve years. LeClerc was convicted of poisoning the French students, but was paroled when it was discovered she had ovarian cancer. She returned to Canada where she died still proclaiming her love for Sobhraj.

For Sobhraj, twelve years was not long enough. Once released, he would be extradited to Thailand where he would face a death sentence for murder. So on the tenth anniversary of his incarceration, he held a party for the guards, drugged them and escaped. He was caught in an upmarket restaurant in Goa and returned to jail to serve another ten years, as he had intended.

When he was released at the age of fifty-two in 1997, the statute of limitation in Thailand had expired and he was returned to France. There he lived a comfortable life, charging for interviews and selling the movie rights to his life story.

It is not known quite why he returned to Nepal in 2003, but he was spotted by a journalist. He was arrested and sentenced to life imprisonment for the murder of Laurent

Carrière and Connie Jo Bronzich.

Sobhraj continues to enjoy his celebrity status. In 2010, he married his twenty-year-old French-Nepali interpreter, Nihita Biswas, in prison, and has been the subject of four biographies, three documentaries, an Indian film titled *Main Aur Charles*, and the 2021 BBC/Netflix drama *The Serpent*.

9

AKKU YADAV
King of the Slum
INDIA

Fearing that serial killer and rapist Akku Yadav was going to walk free from the courtroom in the Indian city of Nagpur, two hundred women burst in and killed him. One hacked off his penis with a vegetable knife and there were some seventy stab wounds on his body. Some of the women were arrested, but eventually they were all released due to lack of evidence.

GANG RAPE

Born Bharat Kalicharan in 1971 or 1972 in Kasturba Nagar,

a slum outside Nagpur in the state of Maharashtra, he was also known as Akku Yadav. He graduated from being a small-time thug to a big-time mobster and king of the slum. He lived largely by extortion and theft, using rape, torture, and murder to intimidate his victims.

Arrested fourteen times, he simply bribed his way out of trouble, though he was once detained for a year under the Maharashtra preventative detention law – The Maharashtra Prevention of Dangerous Activities of Slumlords, Boot-leggers, Drug Offenders and Dangerous Persons Act 1981.

His reign of terror reportedly began with a gang rape in 1991. He allegedly raped over forty women, the youngest being a girl of ten. Such was his savage reputation, he would just take anything he wanted – money, a mobile phone, a motorbike. His gang would beat up anyone who resisted. Yadav himself brutally beat an old man who earned a small amount of money playing a musical instrument called a baja because he could not pay Yadav a hundred rupees. He allegedly murdered at least three other people and dumped their bodies on local railroad tracks.

He murdered a woman named Asha Bai, a daughter of Anjana Bai Borkar, in front of her sixteen-year-old granddaughter. The family were eating dinner when Yadav came to the front door. When she opened it, he dragged her out and stabbed her. He then cut off her ears for her earrings and her fingers to get her rings off. Borkar was one of five women who were later accused of slaying Yadav.

Another woman said Yadav knocked on the door of her house at around 4:30 in the morning, saying he was a police officer. Once inside, he stabbed her husband in the thigh with a knife and locked him in the bathroom, then dragged her away by her hair and raped her, allowing her to return after three or four hours.

Yadav once raped a woman immediately after her wedding. Another was gang-raped by Yadav and his men ten days after she gave birth. Afterwards, she doused herself with kerosene and set herself on fire. His gang pulled another woman from her house when she was seven months pregnant. They stripped her naked and raped her on the road in public view. They also gang-raped a twelve-year-old girl.

Yadav tortured a woman in front of her daughter and several neighbours, cutting off her breasts. He then killed her by slicing her to pieces in the street. One of her neighbours was so horrified that he threatened to report Yadav to the police. Before he could do so, Yadav butchered him too.

GETTING PARANOID

Another man was stripped naked, burned with a cigarette and forced to dance in front of his sixteen-year-old daughter. People were also kidnapped and their homes invaded to terrorize them. But Yadav was getting increasingly paranoid. Thinking people were plotting against him, he prevented people gathering to talk. He even stopped children playing together.

Yadav bought the police drinks and gave them money, so when his victims complained to them they told him who had reported the crime. Women who reported being raped were dismissed as prostitutes. One woman who complained of a gang rape was then gang-raped by the police.

Out of fear, girls were taken out of school and locked away out of sight. Those families that could left Kasturba Nagar. Vegetable vendors avoided the district, so housewives had to go to markets far away to buy their groceries. Things got so bad that, by January 2004, Yadav was banned from entering Nagpur city. But as long as Yadav only targeted poor people, the police did nothing. He still reigned supreme in Kasturba Nagar. Then he went too far.

After raping a thirteen-year-old girl, Yadav and his men went to the house of a woman named Ratna Dungiri demanding money. His gang smashed her furniture and threatened to murder her family. A friend named Usha Narayane told Dungiri to go to the police. Dungiri was too frightened, so Narayane herself filed a complaint. The police told Yadav. Enraged, Yadav and forty of his men surrounded Narayane's house. He was carrying a bottle of acid.

She barricaded the door and called the police. They did not turn up. Meanwhile, Yadav pounded on the door, saying: "I'll throw acid on your face, so you won't file any more complaints!" He described how he would gang-rape her, burn her with acid and murder her. His men then tried to break down the door. So Narayane turned on a cylinder of gas that the family used for cooking and grabbed a match. If they broke into the house, she said, she would blow herself and the rest of them up. Smelling the gas, they left.

THE VENGEANCE OF THE CROWD

Hearing what Narayane had done, the whole neighbourhood turned out and took violent retribution. They pelted Yadav's men with stones, then marched to Yadav's house and burnt it down. He was forced to seek police protection and he was arrested for his own safety.

On the way to court for a bail hearing, he was met with a crowd of five-hundred women. One of his men tried to slip him a knife. But the women saw it and protested. The accomplice was arrested and Yadav was returned to jail. The following day the protesters prevented him from reaching court again.

Five days later on August 13, 2004, he appeared in a courtroom miles from the slum. Hundreds of women marched to the courthouse. When he saw a woman he had raped, he called her a prostitute and said he would rape her again. She hit him with her shoe. Yadav was then lynched by a mob of 200 – 400 women, chili powder was thrown in his face and those of the police protecting him. The police were overpowered by the women and fled, as the vengeance of the crowd took over.

As Yadav was lynched and hacked to death by the crowd, he cried out: "Forgive me! I won't do it again!" They continued stabbing him long after he lay dead. He was just thirty-two.

The women insisted that the butchery had not been planned. There was no formal meeting, but the idea of taking united action passed by word of month. The knife was passed around so each woman could stab him once.

Usha Narayane was arrested and charged with murder, but the crowd would not disperse until she and the others taken into custody were given bail. Narayane was subsequently acquitted. The rest were released without charge.

PART 4

AUSTRALIAN SERIAL KILLERS

1

JOHN BALABAN
The Romanian Maniac

B orn Ioan Balaban in western Romania in 1924, he said his parents separated because his father was cruel, drank excessively and, later, hanged himself. It was not a good start in life.

VISIONS OF GOD
In 1944 during World War II, as Romania split from the Axis and joined the Allies, Balaban read books on philosophy and decided there was no God. Nevertheless, according to an unsworn statement Balaban made after his arrest, one morning the ceiling of his bedroom opened up and

297

God appeared with a grey beard and long white hair and smiled on him.

"John, it is all right if you don't believe in me any more," he said. "You do anything your conscience dictates and you will be happy." Balaban insisted this was not a dream. "Afterwards I thought I could do anything and I was not frightened of the law," he said.

After fighting against the Communists who were taking over the country, he spent a short time in a mental hospital. He claimed to have obtained a degree as an assistant engineer in physics and metallurgy, before spending nine months in the army.

He then escaped to France. In February 1948, he met thirty-one-year-old Riva Kwas, a Polish woman working as a chemist in Paris. He alternately said that he strangled her after they had made love, or that he killed her because he was "in a rage" when she refused him. "I did not have any intention of killing her, but I had the feeling I had to," he said.

Her body lay undiscovered for five days and the case remained unsolved for seven years.

DESERVING TO DIE

Balaban moved home and, soon after, emigrated as one of the "New Australians" – people displaced in the aftermath of World War II who found a new home down under. He travelled on the *Hellenic Prince*, listed on immigration records as a chemist. During the voyage, Balaban had a fight with an immigration official and was locked up in the cells of the ship.

Balaban settled in Adelaide, South Australia. Unable to find work as a chemist – or indeed an assistant engineer in physics and metallurgy – he made a living as a welder, grape-picker and manual labourer. He met a divorcée named Thelma Cadd, who owned the Sunshine Snack Shop, a café in Gouger Street, Adelaide. She lived above the café with her son Phillip. Her widowed mother Susan Ackland often stayed.

They married in September 1952, but split up three months later. Balaban blamed his mother-in-law for the separation. Three days after he left his wife, Balaban met twenty-nine-year-old Yugoslav immigrant Zora Kusic who lived in a shack behind a boarding-house in the suburb of Torrensville. They took a taxi to her place to have a drink. When she asked £5 for sex, he grew angry and started to throttle her.

"I took a knife off the dressing table and cut her throat," he said. "I did not feel sorry for killing Kusic and I think I was quite justified in doing so, because anybody could tell that she was a low woman and deserved to die."

She was found lying on her bed with her throat cut and her body mutilated by knife wounds. A bloodstained pen knife was found by the bed.

Questioned the next day, Balaban denied knowing her,

but when he was arrested two days later he admitted having a drink with her in the hotel and taking a taxi home with her, but he denied going into her room and said he had taken a taxi back to the city. Later, he admitted lying to the police, saying: "It was the only way I could still look after my wife and Phillip, and escape."

Charged with murder, Balaban appeared before a magistrate who decided that there was insufficient evidence to make a *prima facie* case against him. After he was discharged, he returned to his wife, but things were no better between them.

SPLATTERED WITH BLOOD

On Saturday, April 11, 1953, he left the Sunshine café to have a drink. He said his memories were blurred after that and he could not remember clearly what happened. Near the River Torrens, he had a fight with a girl in the woman's lavatory. Then he found an iron bar near the University Bridge. He thought he hit a man sleeping on the ground behind the Adelaide Oval.

Near the Morphett Street Bridge, he saw an Aborigine man with a girl and stopped and had a drink with them, then hit the man with the iron bar. He chased another man near the Torrens tennis courts and hit him with the iron bar.

"I don't know why I hit him, but I disapproved of him, as I do of people lying on the banks of the Torrens and making love," he said.

Tired, dirty, and splattered with blood, he returned to the Sunshine café, believing that the world was against him.

"I went into the bathroom and looked into the mirror to see how hurt I was," he said. "I decided in an instant to kill my wife because she was the cause of my condition, and my fighting that night."

He grabbed a claw hammer, hit his wife around the head and bludgeoned her to death. Then he went into the other bedroom where he attacked Susan Ackland.

"Phillip sat up and cried and I hit him," Balaban said. "I thought it better that he die too."

Café employee twenty-four-year-old Verna Marnie was also sleeping in the flat. "I went out to the sleepout where Verna Marnie slept. I went out to kill her because she had been siding with my wife," he said. "I hit her on the head. I only killed those in the Sunshine café because they deserved to be killed."

But Verna had been woken by the noise of the other murders. When he struck, she raised her arms to protect her head. Balaban suddenly stopped.

"I killed my wife," he said. "Do you want to see her?"

Then he heard a noise from another room.

"Someone's still alive," Balaban said and went to investigate. He bludgeoned the victims again "so they would die quickly".

While he was gone, Verna locked the door and jumped out of the window, dropping seventeen feet to the footpath below. Some young men outside heard Verna's screams and saw her drop. They called an ambulance and the police. Realizing he was in danger of capture, Balaban escaped through a bathroom window. He clambered over the rooftops but was quickly apprehended.

Thelma Balaban was found dead in her bed. Both Susan Ackland and Phillip Cadd were alive, but died of their injuries a few days later. Verna Manie had a fractured skull and back, but survived.

HANGING TOWER

In custody, Balaban admitted the murder of Riva Kwas in Paris in 1948 and that of Zora Kusic. The French police were informed. Balaban was only charged with the murder of Zora Kusic, though the murders at the Sunshine café were taken into consideration when assessing his mental state. As he had admitted Kusic's murder, this was the only bone of contention.

After prolonged arguments, he was found to be sane and sentenced to death by hanging. His appeal was dismissed. Then, in jail, he tried to throttle a prison guard.

At eight o'clock on the morning of August 26, 1953, John Balaban was the first convict to be hanged in the newly converted Hanging Tower at the Adelaide Gaol. The police closed off the roads in case there was a demonstration by anti-capital punishment protesters. They needn't have bothered. There was little sympathy for Balaban and no one turned out.

Balaban was buried in Murderers' Row between the northern walls of Adelaide Gaol. He was just twenty-nine years old.

2

GREGORY BRAZEL
Bluey

On the afternoon of September 20, 1982, Mrs Mildred Hanmer, who was fifty-one, was working alone in the hardware and gift shop she and her husband owned in Mordialloc, a beachside suburb of Melbourne, Victoria. Her husband was not with her that day because he was at home recovering from a hernia operation. At 12:50 p.m., a woman who lived behind the shop heard a loud bang and the voice of a woman calling for help. She entered the hardware and giftware store and discovered Mrs Hanmer grievously injured and lying on the floor. The ambulance and police were called.

Before they arrived, Mrs Hanmer managed to call her husband. He heard her gasping on the telephone and she said: "Dick, I've been robbed and I'm dying."

The paramedics and police officers found Mrs Hanmer bleeding from a gunshot wound to her upper body, but she was still conscious and able to speak. She described her attacker as being a man of around twenty-five years old, five feet seven inches tall with ginger hair – hence his Aussie nickname "Bluey". She described the firearm he was carrying and said that he left through the front door.

Mrs Hanmer was treated at the scene and then taken by ambulance to the Alfred Hospital, where she died at 3:20 p.m. She had been shot once in the right chest between the second and third ribs. The pathologist who conducted the post mortem examination concluded that she had been shot from the front. An extensive police investigation got nowhere and the crime remained unsolved until August 2000.

BLOOD MONEY

Then Gregory Brazel, who was already serving thirty years for murder and other offences, confessed to the killing. He said he had entered the store at around lunch time, carrying a .22 rifle hidden in a sports bag. He asked Mrs Hanmer to cut a key for him. While she was doing that, he closed the front door and locked it, turning around the sign on the door to read: "Back in five minutes".

He took out the rifle and demanded money and got over A\$3,000 from the safe and cash register. Then he told Mrs Hanmer to lie on the floor so he could tie her up. While she was lying on the floor, he shot her in the back. The homemade silencer on the weapon failed and "when the gun went off it sounded like a cannon," he said.

He remembered that blood was seeping through the deceased's clothing and he knew that she was critically injured and would not survive. All he wanted to do was to get away. He did not waste time reloading and firing another shot.

Brazel then said he had been offered A\$30,000 to kill Mrs Hanmer by a former prison inmate and the person who had ordered the hit was none other than Mrs Hanmer's own husband. This was strange as making a hit for money would have attracted a higher sentence than killing as part of an armed robbery gone wrong and, in making his confession, Brazel asked not to be given a life sentence, but only five or ten years on top of the time he was already serving.

Mr Hanmer said that he was angry and disgusted by the accusation that he had ordered the murder of his wife and rejected the allegation. But otherwise the account Brazel gave was accepted. One key fact was that he said he had shot Mrs Hanmer in the back. A re-examination of Mrs Hanmer's clothing by forensic scientists showed that was indeed the case and she had not been shot from the front as the original pathologists had thought.

KILLINGS, KIDNAPS AND CONS

Brazel had an astonishing criminal career. While in the army in 1974, he had taken five soldiers hostage. Shots were exchanged before he was persuaded to release them. He was dishonourably discharged.

He then served sentences for contempt of court and armed robbery. While on early release from prison, he killed prostitute Sharon Taylor on May 28, 1990. Before her body was found, he killed Roslyn Hayward, another sex worker, on September 13. For the first murder, he was given twenty years, reduced to seventeen on appeal. The second murder earned him another twenty years.

Jail did little to reform him. In November 1991, he took a member of the prison staff hostage, earning himself another seven years. He got another two years for arson and two more for bribery. Then he managed to con an elderly woman into depositing A$30,000 into a telephone betting account.

After being attacked by other prisoners he sued the government of Victoria for failing to take reasonable care to protect him and won A$12,000. However, despite his pleas for clemency, the murder of Mrs Hanmer earned him a life sentence.

3

JOHN LESLIE COOMBES
The Phillip Island Killer

When sentencing triple-murderer John Leslie Coombes to life with no possibility of parole, Judge Geoffrey Nettle said he exhibited a "frightening predilection for homicide" and a "dangerous propensity to commit murder". He said he believed that Coombes was not remorseful and if given the opportunity to kill again, he would.

BETTER THAN SEX

Fifty-six-year-old Coombes had killed twenty-seven-year-old childcare worker Raechel Betts. He had strangled her

– or broken her neck – in the house of Nicole Godfrey on Phillip Island off the coast of Victoria. Dismembering her body in the bath, he put the body parts in plastic bags and threw them off a local pier. However, the bags later washed up on nearby beaches.

"I know she was chopped up in the bathroom," Godfrey told police during the investigation. "He took her into the bathroom because I was in bed and I had the TV [on] a little bit and I had my hands in my ears so I couldn't hear anything."

Nicole Godfrey and Coombes then began a sexual relationship and she gave him bogus alibis, claiming later that she had done so for fear of her own safety. Godfrey pleaded guilty to perverting the course of justice and received a suspended sentence in return for assisting the prosecution.

Coombes pleaded guilty to the murder, saying that Betts had enraged him by offering him the sexual service of underage girls in her charge. Coombes' counsel argued Ms Betts was a drug dealer and said his client had "snapped" after she offered him a young girl for sex, having been sexually abused himself as a child. Coombes told police that he murdered Betts after cutting off her breasts as she did not "deserve to die like a f**king woman".

The judge placed little weight on Coombes' claim that Betts had offered him a child for sex, saying he had a propensity to lie for his own advantage. It seems that

Coombes was Betts' drug supplier. Betts' mother Sandra said Coombes was "a cruel monster", who had killed her daughter because she refused to become his mistress.

"Murder to him is better than sex," she said. "May he never be released and never have a chance to harm another human being or animal."

THE FISH CAN FINISH HIM OFF

His first murder had been that of twenty-year-old Michael Peter Speirani who went missing on a fishing trip in February 1984. Coombes had run over him in a motorboat in Port Phillip Bay. He and his accomplice Glen Conlon then pulled Speirani to the side of his boat and "sliced him up a bit so that the fish could finish him off".

That November Coombes and Andrew Opie went to the house of forty-four-year-old Henry Kells with the intention of beating him up, they said. Kells died after the beating and the pair were found guilty of manslaughter. Coombes was sentenced to life, but the possibility of parole was left open.

The judge had been lenient because of his disturbed family background and the breakup of his marriage. He was drinking heavily at the time and was abusing prescription drugs. "I think it would be fair to say that at the time Kells met his death, the applicant was not in a normal and rational frame of mind," the judge said.

In May 1988, the Adult Parole Board was told he did

not pose a threat to the community. That assessment was given by a senior corrections officer who told the panel the convicted killer deserved to have a set term of incarceration.

"In spite of his offence, which did not seem to be pre-meditated, he does not seem to pose a substantial threat to the community," he wrote in his official report. A psychologist also spoke in Coombes' favour, stating to the parole board: "There appears to be no psychiatric contradiction to Mr Coombes release from prison."

But then Coombes and double-killer Dean Ashley broke out of prison. They had found a water pipe left by contractors and placed it across the top of the inner and outer security fences, using it as a bridge. The police said they were extremely dangerous and should not be approached.

After three days on the run, they were found dressed like railway workers at Red Cliffs, Mildura. They surrendered without a struggle when police surrounded the goods train carriage, in which they were hiding. One was carrying a long-handled screwdriver and the other a knife. Coombes was sentenced to another six months.

Coombes was paroled in October 1996, but was arrested again two months later for the murder of Speirani. Incredibly, he was paroled again in 2007. But after the murder of Raechel Betts in 2009, he would never see daylight again.

YOU WOULD KILL AGAIN

Passing sentence, Mr Justice Nettle said: "It passes understanding that a sane human being could hack up and destroy the body of another as if, to use your own words, she were just a lump of meat. The heinousness of that conduct is shocking."

Justice Nettle said Coombes fabricated his reasons for killing Ms Betts to conceal the true nature of his crime. It was also suggested that the murder was sparked by a drug deal gone wrong, and that Coombes had made sexual advances towards Ms Betts.

But the judge could not definitively say any of these reasons were behind the killing. However, there were significant similarities between Coombes' three murders – including the violence with which they were committed and the lies he constructed afterwards.

Summing up Coombes' state of mind the judge said: "It bespeaks an utter disregard of the law and basic norms of society and depraved inhumanity towards the deceased, her family and her loved ones. I am persuaded there is a real risk that if you were afforded the opportunity to kill again, you would kill again."

4

LEONARD FRASER
The Rockhampton Rapist

B efore Leonard John Fraser was sentenced to three indefinite terms for murder in 2003 at the age of fifty-two, he had already spent twenty years in jail for rape of over twenty women and girls, including a terminally ill cancer patient. His daughter Missy Rigby was warned by her grandmother – Fraser's own mother – never to be alone with him. Sometimes she pushed furniture against her bedroom door in a desperate bid to keep her father at bay.

HER FATHER WAS A SERIAL KILLER

Missy had been just two years old when the police first came to her home in Rockhampton, Queensland, which Fraser shared with her mother Pearl, asking to speak to him about the rape of a woman. What her mother did not know was that he was on parole after serving seven years of a twenty-one-year sentence for a series of rapes in New South Wales. In 1985, Fraser was convicted of rape once again and given a twelve-year sentence.

Missy was six when she was reunited with her father on a prison visit. At the age of eleven, she asked her mother why he was in jail and was told that he was a rapist.

"Hearing what he was, it switched off something that would never, ever bring him back into my mind as a dad," she said. At that point, she did not know that her father was a serial killer.

In 2000, he was convicted for the abduction, rape and murder of nine-year-old Keyra Steinhardt in Rockhampton. He then confessed to five murders, apparently in a bid not to be returned to the general population in jail.

The remains of three victims were found – nineteen-year-old Sylvia Benedetti, thirty-six year old Beverly Leggo and thirty-nine-year-old Julie Turner. There may have been more. Among the grisly trophies he kept in his flat were three ponytails that could not be matched to any of the victims that had been found.

The body of hitchhiker Sandy Lawrence, thought to

have been killed in an abandoned crocodile zoo in north Queensland, could not be found, though the police spent days digging.

Fraser also spoke of the murder of a seventeen-year-old girl whose throat he had cut in Kings Cross Street in Sydney in the early 1970s and of murdering two women hitchhikers in separate incidents in New South Wales in the same decade. Some detectives also believe he had a hand in the murder of twenty-one-year-old Rockhampton woman Michelle Coral Lewis who disappeared on January 14, 1989.

Then there was the curious case of teenager Natasha Ryan. He was charged with her murder, but during the trial she was found hiding in a cupboard. She had been living with her boyfriend since she disappeared five years earlier.

QUEENSLAND'S WORST KILLER

The defence argued that the case against Fraser should be thrown out as it relied on the testimony of an undercover informant who had been in jail with him. Nevertheless, the testimony was allowed to stand.

"He was somebody who clearly revelled in or loved killing and also demonstrating how much of a killer he was," said professor of criminology and forensic psychology Paul Wilson. "We know that from the fact that he talked to the informer the police had in prison with him for so long."

It was likely, he said, that Fraser was responsible for more murders of women but police would have a difficult time solving them now.

"It's very unlikely he has been caught for all the murders he has committed," Professor Wilson said. Asked if Fraser was Queensland's worst killer, he said: "I can't think of a worse one. He certainly displayed all the characteristics of a dangerous psychopath."

The judge described him as a sexual predator who was a danger to the community and his fellow inmates. Fraser died in jail in 2007 at the age of fifty-five.

5

PAUL STEVEN HAIGH
The KFC Killer

This man really wanted to get out of jail. After a series of killings in the 1970s, Paul Steven Haigh appealed his sentence in the hope that at some time he would be given parole. In 1986, he had made a submission admitting four murders – though there were probably more. He was then twenty-nine years old.

The killings happened during armed robberies. In his submission he said he walked into a Tattslotto Agency in Melbourne carrying a sawn-off shotgun in a bag, where fifty-eight-year-old Evelyn Adams was working.

"I approached the counter," he said, "and then produced

the shotgun." Haigh thrust a garbage bag at Adams and told her to fill it with money.

Rather than comply, Adams walked towards the door. He shot her dead and fled. After changing his clothes, he had a haircut and shaved off his beard in an attempt to disguise his appearance.

After robbing a Kentucky Fried Chicken outlet, he felt he hadn't garnered enough spoils, so he figured he would rob a nearby pizza parlour. He pulled a stocking down over his face, ran in, and jumped on the counter. Pointing the gun at the proprietor he shoved a bag in his face and demanded all his money.

The owner, forty-five-year-old Bruno Cingolani, went to the cash register and pulled out a very large knife. Haigh shot him. He died a day or two later.

Next he held up another Kentucky Fried Chicken shop, taking A$300. Then he got A$50 from sticking up a Four Seven Eleven, shooting an assistant in the midriff. He then robbed a railway office worker with an accomplice who beat the man around the head with a baseball bat.

He went on to shoot his twenty-seven-year-old associate Wayne Smith – so he "wouldn't look weak" – and his former girlfriend thirty-one-year-old Sheryle Gardner who, he said, knew too much about his crimes. Sheryle's ten-year-old son Danny Michell was in the car with her.

After comforting the boy, Haigh shot him three times in the head, complaining that Ms Gardner was a bad mother for putting the boy in the "terrible situation" of being a witness to her murder. "Danny being present complicated matters greatly," Haigh wrote.

Next came his current girlfriend, nineteen-year-old Lisa Brearley. He got another man to rape and sodomize her at knifepoint so that someone else's DNA would be found, before stabbing her 157 times.

"I only intended to do twenty but I lost count," he said. When her front was covered in wounds, he turned her over and stabbed her back.

"When I was satisfied there was no chance of a miraculous recovery I stopped," he said. "The intensity of her fight fazed me – it wasn't like in the movies. It was the only one I have ever had a nightmare about." Callously adding: "Lisa had become a loose end."

After being jailed for these offences, Haigh "assisted" sex offender Donald Hatherley to commit suicide by putting a noose around his neck, kicking a cupboard out from under him, then pushing down on Hatherley's shoulders. Haigh was convicted of Hatherley's murder.

His appeal was rejected in 2012 and it is thought he will remain in jail until he dies.

6

MATTHEW JAMES HARRIS
The Wagga Wagga Strangler

B orn on June 30, 1968, Matthew James Harris was given up for adoption at the age of ten months. He learnt about this when he was ten years old. It disturbed him emotionally and he began to exhibit behavioural problems, fantasizing from an early age about killing people. After several failed attempts to settle him with foster parents, he left home at the age of fifteen to live as a street urchin and prostitute.

MURDER FANTASIES

Harris admitted that his murder fantasies persisted. "I've always thought I wanted to kill my mother and my family and stuff like that. Just being dirty on the world, you know, being dirty on the fact that I was adopted and I was taken in by this family and then rejected by them ... in the shit with the prostitution and having to lower myself and all that, just all the thoughts."

He also harboured murderous thoughts about his clients. "I went with so many blokes I could have killed a number of them," he said, "but I didn't, I didn't go through with it, but even then I had the thoughts, you know, these blokes that I was sleeping with were using me and I was using them or whatever, I thought, I wanted to kill them, of course."

In 1991, he was sentenced to two-and-a-half years penal servitude for the armed robbery of one of his sex customers. It was while serving this sentence that he came to meet Elaine De Jong through her involvement with Adoption Triangle Organization. She helped him trace his birth mother. He got back in touch with his mother, only to be rejected by her again. Ms De Jong took him in, in an attempt to wean him off heroin.

After six or seven months of living with her, he was admitted to a residential rehabilitation programme. Eventually he moved into his own apartment, but Ms De Jong maintained daily contact with him and they developed a deep friendship.

Harris did not take paid employment but did voluntary work as a driver with the Community Transport Service, an organization which provided transport for elderly and disabled persons in Wagga Wagga, New South Wales. However, approaching thirty, he became depressed, thinking that he was doing nothing worthwhile with his life.

ENERGIZED BY THE HEIST

On June 20, 1998, Harris and Kenneth Scott Frazier knocked on the door of a flat in Nordlingen Drive in Wagga Wagga where Tran Nguyen lived with her three children. They said they were police officers. When she opened the door, she was confronted by two men wearing baseball hats. They were armed with large kitchen knives. She tried to stop them coming in, but they pushed her aside.

They demanded money. Fearing for the safety of her children she took A\$55 from her purse and gave it to Harris. They then held their knives to her throat and asked for her bank card and PIN which she did not have. Nevertheless, they insisted that she give them more money and she handed over about A\$3 in coins.

Frazier then searched the flat, but did not take anything. Harris told Frazier to cut the telephone line. Instead he pulled it out of the wall. As they left, Frazier pushed the knife through the gauze screen at the front door and told Ms Nguyen not to call the police. They spent the money on alcohol. Energized by the heist, Harris decided to scale things up and turn his hand to murder.

THE MURDER SPREE BEGINS

On the evening of October 4, 1998, Geoffrey Hall was on his way to visit his son in Jack Avenue, Wagga Wagga. Sixty-one-year-old Peter Wennerbom, a stroke sufferer, lived next door. Hall noticed that Wennerbom's front door was open and the TV was on. When he entered he found the elderly man lying on the floor and called an ambulance. Wennerbom was dead and a bruise on the side of his throat found at the post mortem was consistent with strangulation.

Then at 9:15 a.m. on October 18, Janice Karen Lowing arrived at Yvonne Jean Ford's home, at 26 Phillip Avenue, Wagga Wagga, with the intention of driving Yvonne to the boarding kennels where she worked as a part-time dog walker. Lowing knocked on the front door but nobody answered. She became concerned and returned to Ford's home at about 11:00 a.m. This time she heard Ford's dog inside the building but she again failed to get any other response. Lowing then went to Wagga Wagga police station and reported her concerns.

When Senior Constable Christopher Jason Hall responded to the report, he found Ms Ford naked in the bath. She was dead. Age thirty-three when she died, she had a mild intellectual disability but was able to look after herself. It appeared that she had been murdered the night before she was found. Again the cause of death was strangulation.

On December 1, 1998, a body was found between six and eight metres from Church Plains Road, Uranquinty, a small town just outside Wagga Wagga. The police found documents on the body that carried the name Ronald Edward Galvin who had gone missing in early November.

On November 24, 1998, Detective Sergeant Spence and another officer had been at his home to investigate his apparent disappearance.

The next day they returned and spoke to Harris who lived next door. He said he had seen Galvin sitting on the stairway with some people, including a "bloke I've never seen before". The police noted that, in Harris's flat, there was a large number of true crime books.

ANGRY AT THE WORLD

Two weeks earlier Harris had told Elaine De Jong that he had tried to kill himself with a heroin overdose, adding that he had something he needed to tell her. They arranged to meet the next day, but he went to Sydney without speaking to her. She came round to his flat on November 15, and they spoke briefly.

At about 3:00 a.m. on November 30, 1998, De Jong received two telephone calls from Harris. In the second conversation he confessed to having killed his next door neighbour. His name was Ronald Galvin. De Jong went to Wagga Wagga police station and reported the confession.

At about 9:30 a.m. on the same day, De Jong received a further telephone call from Harris. He was in Sydney again. This time he confessed to having also killed Yvonne Ford. He said that he knew the victim as a client of the Community Transport Group he worked for.

At about 2:05 p.m. Harris telephoned De Jong again,

saying that he had some heroin and thought it best to "end it all". He then overdosed and was taken to hospital.

The police spoke to him there and, when he was discharged, they arrested him. First they asked him about the death of Ronald Galvin. On November 3, 1998, Harris said he had strangled his neighbour. The following evening he borrowed De Jong's car and drove Galvin's body to nearby Uranquinty. Asked why he had done it, he said: "I think it was just a lot of anger I was getting rid of and it was being projected on him."

When asked about the death of Yvonne Ford, he said that he was out for a walk and, after a few drinks, turned up at her house. Ford let him in, and after some time he made a sexual advance towards her.

"We struck up a bit of a friendship just driving her around, and I obviously could tell she was lonely, she was slightly handicapped," he said. "I didn't come around there for sex, I didn't come around there for anything, I just came around to say hello. I live nearby, but then these thoughts started entering my head that I wanted to kill her."

He persuaded her to have a bath with him, then strangled her and held her head under the water for three or four minutes.

"It could have been her, it could have been anybody. She was just unlucky," he said. "I just thought she would be easy to target, she wouldn't put up a fight or … she would be relatively easy to kill."

Asked how he felt after the murder, he said: "Powerful, angry, just anger, pure anger … Not, not that there was no sex or anything. I was angry at the world. This is why this whole thing has happened, has started, and it was just my total anger building up from, I don't know, from the day I was adopted, it's just all built and built and, and something has set me off and I killed her."

EASY KILLS

Harris then agreed to be questioned about the case of Peter Wennerbom, who not only was Harris's neighbour he was Elaine De Jong's brother. He said he had visited him at his home on a couple of occasions. The day Wennerbom died Harris knocked on his door asking for a drink of water and was invited in. Once inside he strangled Wennerbom. He displayed poor recollection of the exact sequence of events and was inconsistent in his answers regarding his motive.

Asked whether he had gone to Wennerbom's house intending to kill him, Harris said: "I don't know if I went to rob him, I'm not sure, that's what I'm trying to say, I think, I just went there to kill him." Apparently to Harris killing Wennerbom was so easy. "As an old man, there was no resistance at all. I had total, you know, control over the situation, he, he couldn't do anything."

Wennerbom was known to keep large sums of cash at

home, but none was found after the body was discovered.

Questioned again, this time with a solicitor present, Harris said: "At the time I wasn't interested in robbing him, the only thing I wanted to do was to kill, that was my sole purpose … I knew him, I knew he lived on his own and I knew I could kill him."

De Jong said that, after her brother died, Harris had been particularly considerate, helping clear out his house. He went to the funeral, but would not enter the church. He also appeared to be depressed.

I'D STILL BE GOING …

Harris pleaded guilty to all charges. On April 7, 2000, he was sentenced to three concurrent terms of forty years imprisonment with non-parole periods of twenty-five years for the murders and three years imprisonment for the robbery of Tran Nguyen, making him eligible for parole on November 30, 2023.

On May 2, 2000, Harris's sentencing was mentioned in New South Wales Parliament where it was decided the judge had been "far too lenient". After all, Harris had shown no remorse. In a police interview he had said: "To murder and to keep murdering and to get away with it was an achievement … I'd still be going if I hadn't been caught."

The Director of Public Prosecutions appealed. As the Crown Prosecutor had not asked for a life sentence for the murder of Peter Wennerbom, the Appeal Court ruled that it was inappropriate to apply it at that stage. However, he was given life sentences for the other two murders, plus forty years without possibility of parole.

7

EDDIE LEONSKI
The Brownout Killer

E ddie Leonski was an American GI stationed in Australia during World War II, when he became Melbourne's "Brownout Killer", named for the energy-saving power reductions that fell short of a blackout.

Born in Kenvil, New Jersey, USA, in 1917, Leonski was the sixth child of Russian immigrants and was brought up in New York City. His mother was mentally unstable, and by the time he was called up for military service in 1941 two of his brothers had prison records and a third was in a psychiatric hospital. While training with the 52nd Signal Battalion in San Antonio, Texas, Leonski began drinking heavily and he tried to strangle a woman. Nevertheless, the US Army shipped him out to Australia in January 1942.

Stationed at Camp Pell, Royal Park, Melbourne, he continued his heavy drinking and tried to rape a woman in her apartment in St Kilda, a seaside suburb. His drunkenness earned him thirty days in the stockade. When he was released, he went on another bender.

On May 3, 1942, forty-year-old Ivy Violet McLeod was found dead in the doorway of a shop next to the Bleak Hotel in Albert Park, Melbourne. She had been beaten and strangled. She still had her purse so it was evident that robbery was not the motive.

Just six days later, thirty-one-year-old Pauline Thompson was strangled outside a city boarding house after a night out. She had last been seen in the company of a young man who was said to have an American accent.

The next victim, forty-year-old Gladys Hosking, was murdered on May 18, while walking home from work at the Chemistry Library at Melbourne University. Like the other two, she had been left with her genitals exposed, but she had not been sexually assaulted.

A witness said that, on the night of the killing, a dishevelled American man had approached him asking for directions. He was out of breath and covered with mud. His description matched the individual Pauline Thompson was seen with on the night of her murder, as well as the descriptions given by several women who had survived recent attacks.

These survivors and other witnesses were able to pick twenty-four-year-old Private Edward Leonski out of a line-up of American servicemen who were stationed in the city. He was arrested on May 22, and charged with three murders which he then confessed to.

A wrangle over jurisdiction ensued. In the face of stiff opposition and in consultation with the British government, the Australian government allowed Leonski to be court-martialled by the Americans. Following some dispute, he was found sane, and was tried and found guilty on July 17. The execution order was signed by General Douglas MacArthur, then Supreme Commander of Allied Forces in the Southwest Pacific Area, on November 1, 1942.

Held in the city watchhouse, Leonski corresponded with a woman at Eltham, learned Oscar Wilde's *The Ballad of Reading Gaol* and became a communicant of the Catholic Church. He was hanged in Pentridge prison on November 9, 1942, only the second US serviceman to be executed during World War II. His body was temporarily interred, until it was returned to Honolulu where it was buried in Schofield Barracks Post Cemetery in an area reserved for prisoners who had died in military custody.

8

LINDSEY ROBERT ROSE
The Contract Killer

H aving got away with five murders over ten years, Lindsey Robert Rose was not even a suspect until a police officer who Rose had corrupted told detectives in New South Wales that he had boasted of at least two murders.

Born Lindsey Robert Lehman in North Sydney in 1955, his parents separated before he was born and he took the surname Rose from his stepfather after his mother remarried. He served an apprenticeship as a fitter and turner before joining the New South Wales Ambulance service in 1976. The following year he was one of the first responders at the Granville Train Disaster where eighty-four people died and 213 were injured.

He quit the ambulance service in 1979 to become a licensed private eye, which was largely a cover for his criminal career as a contract killer. On January 20, 1984, he broke into the home of Edward John "Bill" Cavanagh in Sydney's Hoxton Park and shot him dead, ostensibly for beating up one of his friends some time before. Cavanagh was running a trucking business with drugs baron Robert Trimbole. Rose also killed Cavanagh's girlfriend Carmelita Lee so there would be no witness.

Three years later, Rose was burgling the home of wealthy businessman William "Bill" Graf in West Ryde. He was disturbed by Graf's girlfriend Reynette Holford. Before making his escape he stabbed her with a vegetable knife and a screwdriver, and tied her up. She died from her injuries.

Then on February 14, 1994, Rose shot and killed Fatma Ozonal, then shot and stabbed Kerrie Pang to death at "Kerrie's Oasis," the massage parlour Pang owned in Gladesville. Knowing that Pang would not let him in, Rose offered Ronald Walters A$500 to knock on the door. The murder had been ordered by Pang's partner Mark Lewis because of difficulties in their relationship and Lewis did not like the line of work she was in. Rose disliked Pang too. Ozonal was not part of the murder plan and was simply in the wrong place at the wrong time.

After the police came to question Rose, he left Sydney and made for Adelaide in South Australia, where he reverted to his birth name Lehman. He was on the run for forty weeks until a member of the public recognized him from a mugshot shown on TV news.

Returned to New South Wales, he pleaded guilty to five murders and was sentenced to five consecutive life sentences without the possibility of parole. Later he was given another forty years after confessing to conspiracy to pervert the course of justice, robbery, kidnapping, robbery while armed, malicious wounding, larceny, and supplying a prohibited drug. On New Year's Day in 1983, Rose and his criminal associates had hijacked a semi-trailer containing cigarettes valued at $600,000 and held two truck drivers hostage for several hours.

Rose was one of the first six inmates of Goulburn Gaol's High Risk Management Unit after it was opened in 2001. He complained about the number of inmates converting to Islam and the lack of educational opportunities, particularly after inmates were deprived of the use of computers.

9

JOHN "SNOWY" ROWLES
The Murchison Murders

The so-called Murchison Murders are part of Australian folklore. They were three murders committed by itinerant stockman John "Snowy" Rowles in 1929 – 30 near the Rabbit-Proof Fence, the State Barrier Fence of Western Australia, constructed between 1901 and 1907 to keep rabbits and other agricultural pests from the east out of Western Australian.

The murders inspired Arthur Upfield's detective novel *The Sands of Windee*. Upfield had already written several novels while he was working as a boundary rider on the Rabbit-Proof Fence and was writing a new one in which he wanted to feature the perfect murder. The problem was: how to dispose of the body?

He discussed the matter with colleague George Ritchie who came up with a foolproof method. Ritchie's method was to burn the victim's body along with that of a large animal, sift any metal fragments out of the ashes, dissolve them in acid, pound any remaining bone fragments into dust, then scatter the remains into the wind. The problem then was: how could the murder ever be detected. Upfield offered £1 if he could come up with an answer. Trying to figure it out, Ritchie mentioned the problem to Rowles who was also riding the boundary along the fence.

On December 8, 1929, Rowles left Camel Station with James Ryan and George Lloyd. A few days later, George Ritchie said he had met a prospector named James Yates, who told him he had seen Rowles driving a car. During the meeting Rowles told Yates that Ryan and Lloyd were both walking through scrub, gathering timber. Neither Yates, Ritchie, nor Upfield saw anything odd in this behaviour. But, significantly Yates said he had only seen Rowles. Ryan and Lloyd were never seen again.

On Christmas Eve 1929, Arthur Upfield was in the small gold mine town of Youanmi in Western Australia when he too met Rowles who told him that Ryan had decided to stay in Mount Magnet, and had lent Rowles his truck.

A New Zealander calling himself Louis Carron had arrived in the Murchison area and had found a job at

Wydgee sheep station. In May 1930, Carron left his job there in the company of Snowy Rowles. Carron's pay cheque was cashed by Rowles at the town of Paynesville, east of Mount Magnet.

Louis Carron had corresponded regularly with a friend, who noticed that Carron had disappeared. Carron's friend sent a reply-paid telegram to Rowles at Youanmi asking for information about Carron, but Rowles did not reply. There was a large transient population in the area at the time so for someone to disappear was in no way remarkable. Indeed, by that point, no one had yet noticed that Ryan and Lloyd were missing. Snowy Rowles had killed them and disposed of their bodies by the method described by George Ritchie.

What caught Rowles out was that, when he had disposed of the bodies, he had dissolved the ashes in acid but had not removed the metal. At the 183-mile hut on the Rabbit-Proof Fence a wedding ring was found.

Before their wedding, Louis Carron's wife had taken the ring to an Auckland jeweller to have the ring resized. In a rush, the jeweller had used nine-carat solder to rejoin the ends of the ring which was eighteen-carat. The difference in colour was easily spotted and the ring was identified as Carron's

Although it was clear that Rowles had killed all three men and disposed of their bodies using Ritchie's method, he was only charged with the murder of Carron. Meantime, it was also discovered that Rowles was actually a convicted burglar named John Thomas Smith who had escaped in 1928 from a lock-up in Dalwallinu. The jury brought in a guilty verdict for the murder of Louis Carron, and Snowy Rowles was hanged at Fremantle Prison on June 13, 1932.

10

CHRISTOPHER WORRELL & JAMES MILLER

The Truro Murderers

On Anzac Day 1978, a young man out looking for mushrooms in the fields around Truro, fifty miles northeast of Adelaide, found the body of a young woman, who was later identified as Veronica Knight. The following year bushwalkers found the body of Sylvia Pittman nearby. Five other women had gone missing in that area, so the police searched the whole region. They then found the bodies of Vicki Howell and Connie Iordanides, but the bodies were so badly decayed they provided few clues to the killer's identity.

The police put out an appeal for help, offering a reward of A$30,000. They were contacted by a woman named Amelia. She said that her friend James Miller knew the dump site well. Miller described the victims as "rags" and had said to her that one of the girls had enjoyed being raped and murdered.

Police tracked down Miller to a shelter for the homeless. He completely denied knowing Amelia until they confronted him with a photograph showing the two of them together with another man. After six hours of questioning, Miller finally told the police that the third person in the picture, Christopher Worrell, was responsible for the murders. Miller claimed he had simply driven Worrell around, saying he was powerless to do otherwise as they were lovers. The only one who could confirm this story was Worrell, who had died in a car crash in February 1977.

LOOKING FOR PREY

With a record of over thirty convictions – including breaking and entering, and robbery – Miller had been in an Adelaide jail for breaking into a gun shop where he shared a cell with Worrell, who was on remand for rape. He already had a two-year suspended sentence for armed robbery.

A sexual relationship developed between them. When they got out, Miller would perform oral sex on Worrell, while Worrell perused bondage magazines. However, Worrell really preferred women, and he had no trouble getting them either. Miller helped drive him around cheap hotels, bus stops, and train stations, looking for prey.

After they picked up the girls, Miller would drive them to a remote spot and go for a walk while Worrell had sex with the girls. Sometimes Worrell would tie them up, but release them afterwards.

On December 23, 1976, they spotted eighteen-year-old Veronica Knight in a shopping centre. She had become separated from a friend while doing their last-minute Christmas shopping and she accepted a lift from them. They drove her out to the foothills near Adelaide. But this time when Miller returned from his customary walk, he found that Worrell had raped and murdered her. Miller said that he was not happy about it, but Worrell pulled a knife and threatened to kill him if he did not help dispose of the body.

They were out on the prowl again on January 2, 1977, when Worrell picked up fifteen-year-old Tania Kenny. Soon after, Miller found her dead, wearing just a shirt, bound with rope and with a plaster gag over her mouth. Again Miller helped Worrell dispose of the body.

The pattern continued. Usually Worrell simply had sex with the girls and let them go. Then on January 21, they picked up sixteen-year-old Juliet Mykyta. She resisted and Miller witnessed her murder. He claimed he had tried to stop Worrell strangling her, but he was too strong.

BLESSING IN DISGUISE

On February 6, Worrell killed sixteen-year-old Sylvia Pittman, strangling her with her own tights. The following day, he picked up twenty-six-year-old Vicki Howell. Miller said he was sure that Worrell would not murder the older woman, but he was wrong. Then Worrell raped and murdered sixteen-year-old hitchhiker Connie Iordanides on February 9, and twenty-year-old Deborah Lamb on February 12. Her tights had been wrapped around her mouth and jaw seven times and she had possibly still been alive when they buried her.

The murders always left Worrell in a foul mood. He went away for the weekend with Miller and a friend, Debbie Skuse, who had just split up with her boyfriend. On their way home, Skuse had an argument with Worrell while he was driving. He flipped the car, killing the two of them. At the funeral, Miller explained to Amelia that the accident had been a blessing in disguise.

Miller protested to the police that he had killed no-one, but the prosecution argued that, after the first killing, he must had known what was going to happen. Convicted of six of the seven murders in March 1980, Miller was sentenced to life imprisonment.

11

DEREK PERCY
Sadistic Child Murderer

When he died in prison on July 23, 2013, having been the longest serving prisoner in the state of Victoria, Derek Percy took his secrets with him to the grave. He had not even been convicted of any offence, though his murder and mutilation of twelve-year-old Yvonne Elizabeth Tuohy was not in doubt. He had been found not guilty by reason of insanity in April 1970. Unlike others who had been handed the same verdict, he was never transferred to a mental hospital as it was considered that he had an untreatable personality disorder.

TORTURED TO DEATH

Yvonne Tuohy had been at the beach in the small town of Warneet, in Western Port Bay, Victoria, on July 27, 1969, with her friend eleven-year-old Shane Spiller. Derek Percy, then a twenty-one-year-old naval rating, grabbed Tuohy, putting a knife to her neck. He probably would have abducted Spiller as well, but the boy was carrying a tomahawk which he thrust at Percy to warn him off as he approached.

Percy drove off with Yvonne Tuohy in the car. Spiller described the car to the police and told them it had a naval badge on it. This led the police to HMAS *Cerberus*, the Australian Navy's training base nearby. Percy had been on weekend leave. Three hours later, they found him there washing blood from his clothes. The horror of what he had done meant the memory was quickly receding from his mind, but Detective Sergeant Richard Knight took Percy through the process in reverse, allowing the police to find the little girl's body six miles from the beach. She had been molested, tortured, and murdered.

UNSOLVED CHILD MURDERS

Over the previous four years, there had been a spate of unsolved child murders and abductions for which Percy was implicated, fitting the description of the killer.

Mary Sharrock and Marianne Schmidt, both fifteen, were murdered on Sydney's Wanda Beach on January

11, 1965. Nine-year-old Jane Beaumont, her seven-year-old sister Arnna and four-year-old brother Grant were abducted from Glenelg Beach near Adelaide on January 26, 1966.

Six-year-old Allen Redston was murdered in Canberra on September 28, 1966. Three-year-old Simon Brook was killed in Sydney on May 18, 1968. And seven-year-old Linda Stilwell was abducted from the St Kilda foreshore in Melbourne on August 10, 1968.

In all these unsolved cases, a man answering Percy's description had been seen nearby, or there was evidence that Percy had been in the vicinity. Also there had been an attempted abduction of a twelve-year-old girl near the *Cerberus* base on April 1, 1969. The victim identified Percy after the Tuohy incident led to his arrest.

Detective Knight had already concluded that the murder of Yvonne Tuohy was not Percy's first attack and took the unusual decision to put a rookie cop on the case. The young policeman had been on the force for just six months, but he had been at school with Percy. Sobbing, Percy told him: "Looks like I've f**ked up this time." Knight asked if there had been others, but Percy said he could not remember.

Percy admitted being in St Kilda on the day that Linda Stilwell went missing. He also said that he had driven by the spot Simon Brook was found on the day he had been killed. And he has been near the beach in Adelaide on the day the Beaumont children went missing.

He said he could not remember if he had killed the children and volunteered no further information. Nevertheless, over the years, cold-case investigations have turned up other evidence that points to Percy as the perpetrator in all these cases.

SLASHING WOMEN'S UNDERWEAR

Derek Ernest Percy was born on September 15, 1948, in Strathfield, New South Wales. He was the eldest son of a railway electrician who moved his young family to Warrnambool on the coast of Victoria. Father and son shared a passion for sailing. The Percys took caravan holidays, often travelling from state to state for yachting competitions in their V8 Studebaker.

In 1961, they moved to Mount Beauty, near Bright in Victoria. Derek went to Mount Beauty High School where he had few friends. He wore a green and gold striped tie like the other pupils, but his was made from a cheaper, coarser fabric.

He was intelligent, but shy and never had a girlfriend. He also carried a sharp pocket knife, which was not unusual in the countryside of Victoria. However, it was noted one time when he accidentally stabbed himself deeply in the thigh he did not cry out or show any emotion.

In 1964 in Mount Beauty, women's underwear began to go missing from washing lines. Percy was thought to be the culprit. Out near a local swimming pond, two teenagers saw what they thought was a girl in a petticoat. It turned out to be Percy in a negligee. He then began slashing at the clothing and stabbed at the crotch of a pair of knickers.

"I would describe Derek's eyes as being full of excitement, a glazed look, but I recall there was something very cold and sinister in the look," one of the teenagers told police much later.

Underwear and dresses were stolen from the wardrobes of two little girls who lived next door. Some were found under bushes along with a doll whose eyes had been "blinded" and pictures of women in bikinis whose eyes had been pencilled out and whose bodies were slashed with a razor blade.

In his entry in the Mount Beauty school magazine Percy said his favourite saying was: "It depends." Perpetual occupation: "Isolating himself." Ambition: "Playboy." Probable fate: "Bachelor." Pet aversion: "Girls."

Despite his high IQ Percy failed his exams and moved with his family to Khancoban. Noticeably the underwear-stealing stopped in Mount Beauty and began again in Khancoban.

BIZARRE VIOLENT FANTASIES

Things took a more serious turn when he lured a six-year-old girl into the family caravan and sexually assaulted her. Her father took it up with Derek's dad, who was already worried about his son after finding him dressed in women's clothing. And it was found he was committing bizarre and violent sexual fantasies to paper, a practice he would continue for the rest of his life.

Having dropped out from school, he joined the Navy in 1967, graduating at the top of his entry class. But it was soon found that he wasn't suitable officer material.

Some forty years later, the police pieced together the details of his family holidays which showed he was near the places where children had been abducted and murdered in the late 1960s.

On January 11, 1965, the teenagers Marianne Schmidt and Mary Sharrock had gone to Sydney's popular Cronulla Beach area with Marianne's four younger siblings. After a picnic, the younger children stayed in a sheltered area at Wanda Beach and the two fifteen-year-olds started talking to a fair-haired youth who was carrying a knife in a sheath and a spear. The two girls' mutilated bodies were found the next day, partially buried near a sand dune.

As in the Tuohy case, the victims were taken from the beach and their bodies dumped nearby. The crotch area of one of the girls' swimming costumes had been cut open, just as Percy had been seen slashing female underwear at Mount Beauty.

WE KNOW IT WAS YOU

Neighbours confirmed that the Percys had gone to Sydney for a holiday that summer. They had gone to attend the national yachting regatta at Botany Bay Yachting Club, near Wanda Beach. Percy's grandparents lived a short distance from the West Ryde railway station where the two girls had caught the train on their way to the beach.

After police arrested Percy, they found he had a diary which described his evil urges to sexually abuse, torture, murder, and mutilate children. One excerpt said he would force a victim to drink beer. The post mortem showed that Mary Sharrock had a blood-alcohol level equivalent to drinking about half-a-pint of beer. He also wrote about abducting and killing "Two girls at Barnsley", a beach in northern New South Wales. Police believe this was code for Wanda Beach.

When Percy started a new school that year, a classmate spotted his resemblance to the photo-fit released in the case of the missing girls from Wanda Beach. Fellow students taunted him, saying: "We know it was you that killed those girls in Sydney. You have the same haircut and we know you were there." Percy went berserk and challenged them to a fight.

HOG-TIED AND PLASTIC-WRAPPED

The day the three Beaumont children went missing they were seen talking to a man at about 11:00 a.m. Forty-five minutes later they bought a pie and two pastries with a pound note – which was more than the pocket money their mother had given them. Percy also wrote about giving children food before kidnapping and killing them. His brother confirmed that the family had been in Adelaide at that time.

Asked by detectives if he was in Adelaide when the Beaumont children went missing, he said: "I don't know." He was then asked if he was blocking out thoughts "because something horrible happened in Adelaide and you don't want to remember it?" He said it was possible.

On September 27, 1966, six-year-old Allen Geoffrey Redston left his home in the Canberra suburb of Curtain to go to a nearby milk bar to buy an ice-cream. The next day his body was found in reeds by a local creek. The body was hog-tied and had plastic wrapped around the throat. In the days leading up to the murder, a fair-haired teenager had been forcing boys to the ground, tying them up and placing plastic bags over their heads in an apparent attempt to suffocate them.

Percy had written about tying up victims and using plastic to asphyxiate them. Yvonne Tuohy was bound and gagged when she was found. When Percy was a child, as a punishment, his grandmother would lock him in a room and hog-tie him the way Allen Redston's body had been found.

The identikit composed from witness accounts closely resembled Percy and a man in the vicinity was seen riding a red bike with "ram's horn" handlebars, exactly like the one Percy owned and took with him on caravan holidays.

He admitted that the family were in Canberra at the time. They had a relative there. A green and gold striped tie made of a coarse cloth was found at the scene of the crime. Percy no longer needed his Mount Beauty tie as he had changed school.

SIMON BROOK DISAPPEARS

After three months in the Navy, Percy was posted on sentry duty on the aircraft carrier HMAS *Melbourne* which was undergoing a refit in Cockatoo Dry Dock at Sydney Harbour. On his daily commute from the naval base on Garden Island he had to pass through the suburb of Glebe. On May 18, 1968, three-year-old Simon Brook disappeared from the front yard of his family home in Glebe.

The house was next to Jubilee Park where a truck driver said he saw a small boy matching Simon Brook's description holding hands with a young man. The identikit closely resembled Percy. When an inquest into Simon Brook's death was reopened in 2005, Percy refused to give evidence on the grounds of self-incrimination.

On August 10, 1968, seven-year-old Linda Stilwell's mother told her to go and find her brother and sister. They returned without her. Two days later, a woman called to say that she had seen a girl matching Linda's description rolling down a grassy hill near Melbourne's Lower Esplanade. There was a man nearby wearing "a deep navy blue, almost black, spray jacket, similar to that worn when sailing".

Percy had transferred to the troop ship HMAS *Sydney*, which was based in Melbourne, on July 1, 1968. He was on leave at the time Linda disappeared. After he was arrested for the Tuohy abduction, the woman came forward again, saying that she was absolutely sure that Percy was the same man she had seen in the spray jacket.

LIBRARY OF SEX CRIMES

In the forty-four years Percy was in jail he was paid his Navy pension, amassing A$200,000, some of which he used to pay for his defence. He also paid for the storage of thirty-five boxes of newspaper articles on sex crimes, pictures of children, a video with a rape theme, and handwritten stories on sex offences involving abduction and torture. Among them police found a 1978 street directory with a line drawn through the St Kilda Pier where Linda Stilwell was abducted and a pornographic lesbian cartoon on which Percy wrote the word "Wanda" across the top.

There was one final unsung victim – Shane Spiller. He was just eleven when, after his friend Yvonne Tuohy was abducted, he was asked to pick out the man he had seen from a police line-up.

"I had to walk up and point right at his nose. The look he gave me. I can still remember it," he said years later.

In 2000, Shane applied for criminal compensation. He was awarded A$5,000, increased to A$50,000 on appeal.

Two years later, he disappeared from his house in the town of Wyndham, New South Wales, where he had lived for years. His car was still parked at the front and squatters had moved into the house.

A resident who knew him said: "He was always saying someone was after him. No one knows what happened to him." A local publican said: "He was really scared. He told me that one day he might just take off."

PART 5

SOUTH AFRICAN SERIAL KILLERS

1

STEWART WILKEN
The Boetie Boer

When twelve-year-old Henry Bakers did not return home on January 22, 1997, his mother Ellen was not immediately worried. He often stayed over with his grandmother in Missionvale, not far from their home in Algoa Park, a suburb of Port Elizabeth, South Africa. However, when he still did not come home the next night, she grew concerned. The following morning she went to see her mother, who said that Henry had left for home two days before.

Ellen contacted the Child Protection Unit and Sergeant Ursula Barnard set about investigating the case. Henry had been seen in a nearby park with Stewart Wilken who had lived with his mother for a short time.

While trying to track down Wilken, Sergeant Barnard discovered that Wilken's ten-year-old daughter by his first marriage, Wuane, had disappeared two years earlier. Wilken was also under investigation for two counts of sodomy filed by his parents-in-law concerning the two sons of his second wife.

Wilken had no fixed abode but when Sergeant Barnard caught up with him, he seemed genuinely concerned about Henry. He admitted that he had been with the boy on the day the child had gone missing, but knew nothing of his whereabouts as he had spent the night with a lady friend. His alibi proved to be false.

SEND HER SOUL TO GOD

On January 31, 1997, Wilken was arrested and the CPU called in Sergeant Derrick Norsworthy of the Murder and Robbery Unit. He had been trained by Dr Micki Pistorius, South Africa's first psychological profiler, in the investigation of serial murder, including advanced interviewing and interrogation techniques.

When Wilken was brought to Sergeant Norsworthy's office, he introduced himself as "Boetie", meaning "Brother Farmer" in Afrikaans. Norsworthy pointed out the certificates he had been awarded for the completion of his training in the investigation of serial killers, but Wilken was more interested in the picture of Norsworthy's young daughter that the sergeant kept on his desk.

Norsworthy then accused Wilken of killing both Henry Bakers and his daughter Wuane. Wilken admitted both murders. "I'm sick," he said, adding that he had returned to Henry's body to have sex with it.

Fifteen months earlier, on September 29, 1995, Wilken had visited his first wife. Later Wuane's half-sister, the daughter of a previous relationship, said she had seen Wuane sitting on the pavement fifty yards from their home. She was never seen alive again.

Wilken said that he was worried about Wuane's welfare. He was convinced that her stepfather was molesting her and she was not being fed properly. Her stepsister agreed that they were often short of food and their stepfather did not like them. Wilken said that Wuane had told him that she wanted to run away.

That day he took her to Happy Valley, an amusement park populated by fairy-tale characters. He said that some of his happiest memories were playing there as a child. He was also living in the bush nearby after leaving his second wife.

Wilken then said that he had inspected Wuane's vagina and found that she was not a virgin. He strangled her to "send her soul to God" and protect her from the abuse he had suffered as a child. He kept her naked body, talked to it and slept next to it. As the body decomposed, he wrapped it in a tarpaulin and kept her clothes close to him.

Then there was Henry Bakers. Wilken said the boy had asked him about sex, so he took him to an open field, told him to take off his clothes and performed fellatio on him. Then he sodomized him. When Henry protested and cried out, Wilken strangled him. He ejaculated as the child died.

Wilken took the police to the places he had left the bodies. Sergeant Norsworthy then asked if there were more bodies. Wilken said there were at least ten. He then made a full confession.

SODOMIZED AND STRANGLED

His first confirmed victim was fifteen-year-old street urchin Monte Fiko, who he had murdered in February 1990. Wilken had sodomized him at Cillié High School in Sydenham and strangled him. In October that year, after an argument with his first wife, Wilken picked up a twenty-five-year-old prostitute named Virginia Gysman. He paid her and took her to Dagbreek Primary School, where they had sex. But when he penetrated her anally, she complained, so he strangled her with her clothing, again ejaculating as she died. He left her body in the schoolyard.

In January the following year, Wilken was solicited by thirty-seven-year-old Mercia Papenfus at the Red Lion Hotel. They went to St George's Park to have sex. When Mercia demanded her payment beforehand, Wilken flew into a rage and strangled her. Then he sodomized her dead body and left it in the park.

On October 12, 1991, Wilken met a fourteen-year-old street boy, who he said agreed to have sex with him for money. Again Wilken took the boy to St George's Park. When the boy asked for the money, Wilken got angry. The boy tried to flee, but Wilken overpowered him and sodomized him, ejaculating as he strangled his victim.

Between June and September in 1993, Wilken picked up another young street boy. They went to Target Kloof, where Wilken sodomized and strangled the boy, hiding his dead body in the ravine.

On July 27, 1995, Wilken killed forty-two-year-old prostitute Georgina Boniswa Zweni in Prince Alfred's Park. He sodomized and strangled her, then sexually assaulted her dead body with a knife. A forensic pathologist later testified that he had "stuck in the knife, pulled it out, stuck it in and pulled it out" repeatedly.

He had counted at least twenty stab wounds, including a cluster of five next to her navel. Wilken then cut off her nipples and ate them. Her clothes were thrown into a fish pond. That September he murdered his ten-year-old daughter Wuane.

On May 25, 1996, he picked up twenty-two-year-old prostitute Katriena Claassen. They went down to the beach. Wilken shoved a piece of plastic bag down her throat to keep her from screaming and sodomized and strangled her.

Between May and August of 1996, he met another street urchin. After the boy masturbated him, Wilken told the boy to undress and sodomized him. When the boy threatened to tell the police, Wilken strangled him though he said he would probably have killed the boy anyway. Next, on January 22, 1997, Wilken murdered Henry Bakers.

CHILDHOOD OF SUFFERING

Wilken told Sergeant Norsworthy that he returned to the bodies of the boys he had murdered. He rubbed vinegar and butter on the boys' feet to hide their scent from the police dogs. He also inserted rolled up pieces of newspaper into their anuses to keep the maggots out, so that he could commit necrophilia with them later. However, he denied having any sort of sex with Wuane, either before or after she was dead.

Though nothing can excuse what Stewart Wilken had done, there may be some explanation in the appalling childhood he had suffered. Born on November 11, 1966, in Boksburg, he and his two-year-old sister were abandoned in a phone booth when he was about six months old. They were found by a domestic worker, who took them to the home of her employer. This man, known only as "Doep", subjected the boy to terrible abuse. He burned his genitals with cigarettes and forced him to eat from the same bowl as his dogs. Doep also engaged in acts of bestiality with his pets and made the boy lick his penis afterwards. This went on for a year-and-a-half. After a while his sister disappeared and he did not know what happened to her.

When he was two years old, the neighbours, Mr and Mrs Wilken, adopted him. He was undernourished and infested with lice. They named him Stewart Wilken and took him with them when they moved to Port Elizabeth.

He did not do well at school, where he was mocked by the other pupils and beaten by the teachers. At home he fared little better. His stepmother locked him in his room and sometimes a cupboard. He wet the bed. When he fought back after a boy attacked him, his stepmother did not take his side. After that he decided he would be his own "mother, father, sister and auntie," Dr Pistorius said.

At eight, he started smoking marijuana. At nine, he was sodomized by a deacon after Sunday school. After his stepfather died, he was sent to a reformatory. There he was locked up naked as punishment and the older boys sodomized him. When he was old enough he enlisted in the Army, but was discharged after four months when he attempted to commit suicide.

GHOSTS OF HIS VICTIMS

Wilken met a woman named Lynne in a nightclub. She became his first wife. They had a daughter, Wuane. After Wuane's birth, Lynne said Wilken would only have anal sex with her, often in very uncomfortable positions. Wilken claimed that Lynne turned to prostitution at that time.

The marriage was not a happy one. Wilken assaulted his wife on many occasions. She retaliated by having him arrested for smoking marijuana. After they divorced, Wilken vowed that he would never have sex with a white woman again for fear that it might be his long-lost sister.

He met a biracial woman named Veronica, who already had two sons. They married and had two daughters. When the marriage faltered, Veronica's parents accused Wilken of sodomizing the two boys. It was then that he left home and went to live in the bushes near Happy Valley.

Wilken appeared in court on February 3, 1997, charged with the murders of Wuane and Henry Bakers. Over the months that followed, more charges were added. The final charge sheet listed ten counts of murder and five of sodomy.

Sergeant Norsworthy managed to track down Wilken's biological mother. She had been reunited with Wilken's sister shortly after she had disappeared. His mother asked Sergeant Norsworthy to tell Wilken that she loved him in spite of everything he had done. Wilken broke down when he heard this. When they spoke on the phone, he called her "Mummy", a name he had never used before.

Wilken was found guilty on seven counts of murder in the Port Elizabeth Supreme Court on February 27, 1998, and received seven life sentences, which he is serving in a prison in Bloemfontein. He claims to be haunted by the ghosts of his victims.

2

MOSES SITHOLE
The ABC Killer

After the end of apartheid there was an explosion of serial killers in South Africa. The most prolific was Moses Sithole who was convicted of thirty-eight murders, along with forty rapes and six robberies. The murders began in Atteridgeville, continued in Boksburg and finished in Cleveland, a suburb of Johannesburg, making him the ABC Killer.

THE PLACE OF GOLD
The eventual capture of Moses Sithole began with the discovery of a mass grave at the Van Dyk Mine near

Boksburg. One of the bodies, that of forty-three-year-old Amelia Dikamakatso Rapodile, was identified by the contents of her handbag which was found at the murder site. She was last seen alive on September 7, 1995, when she left work to see a man named Sithole who had promised her a better job. Her hands were tied behind her back and then to her neck with her pantyhose.

Another victim found at the Van Dyk Mine was twenty-six-year-old Makoba Tryphina Mogotsi who had gone missing on August 15 that year. A man who said he was from Youth Against Human Abuse, a bogus charity run by Sithole, had visited Kids' Haven where she worked and spoken to her about a job with his organization.

She thought he was legitimate because he had once delivered two destitute teenage girls to the home, accompanied by a photographer from Johannesburg newspaper, *The Star*. On a second occasion he came to show her the resulting newspaper article and said he was organizing a fund raiser. Soon after, Tryphina Mogotsi disappeared.

Despite the publicity surrounding the discovery of the bodies at the Van Dyk Mine, the killings did not stop. Just a week later Agnes Sibongile Mbuli, aged twenty, was on her way to meet a friend when she went missing. On October 3, her dead body turned up at Kleinfontein train station near Benoni. That day, a man called the offices of *The Star* and spoke to reporter Tamsen de Beer. The caller claimed that he was the "Gauteng serial killer" – Gauteng means "place of gold" and is the name of the province containing both Johannesburg and Pretoria.

"I am the man that is so highly wanted," he said, and told her that he wanted to turn himself in. The reporter contacted the police who recorded three more calls from the man. In each conversation, he gave information about the murders that could not have been gleaned from the media.

He also said he had started killing because a woman had falsely accused him of rape. In jail, he suffered abuse by fellow prisoners. Now he was getting his revenge.

"I force a woman to go where I want and when I go there I tell them: 'Do you know what? I was hurt, so I'm doing it now.' Then I kill them," he said. He admitted using the victims' clothing, particularly underwear, to strangle them so he would leave no fingerprints.

In cooperation with the police, Tamsen de Beer arranged a meeting with the caller, but he managed to elude the police. However, they had identified him as Moses Sithole and on October 13, they released a picture of him to the media, appealing for help.

After two more murders, Sithole contacted his sister's husband, Maxwell, who worked at the Mintex factory in Benoni, saying that he needed a gun. Maxwell arranged to meet him at his factory. The police had installed Inspector Francis Mulovhedzi as a security guard, but when

Sithole arrived he grew suspicious and fled. Inspector Mulovhedzi gave chase and cornered him in an alley. But it took gunshot wounds to Sithole's legs and stomach before Mulovhedzi could arrest him. Sithole was rushed to hospital and survived.

LEAVE NO VICTIM ALIVE

Sithole was born in 1964 in the black township of Vosloorus. Unable to support her five children, his mother abandoned them at a local police station. He was sent to an orphanage in KwaZulu, Natal, where he suffered systematic abuse.

Handsome and charming, Sithole was sexually precocious from an early age, but his relationships were short-lived. There was speculation that his mother's abandonment of her children might have sparked his aggressive attitude towards woman. However, he told some of his rape victims about the bad experiences he had had at the hands of a previous girlfriend.

This girlfriend was Buyiswa Doris Swakamisa who Sithole attacked in February 1989. She reported the assault to the police. He was convicted of rape and sent to Boksburg Prison for six years. Even though he maintained his innocence, he was released after four years for good behaviour. Prison taught him a brutal lesson – in future he would leave no victim alive to testify against him.

While he was in jail, Sithole met a woman named Martha Ndovu who had been visiting another inmate.

When Sithole was released in 1993, he moved in with her. On December 5, 1994, Martha gave birth to a baby girl. In February 1995, after his killing spree had started, Sithole paid *lobola* – the traditional bride-price – for Martha. But they soon separated.

During questioning Sithole was unforthcoming until a female detective was brought in. Then he began describing his crimes, masturbating while he did so.

According to *The Star*, Sithole told the detective: "In Atteridgeville I killed many – about ten. I caught them with my hands around the neck and strangled them. I thought of something to tie them up ... I used stockings. I placed it around their necks."

He chose the locations for his rapes and murders before he picked his victims, claiming that he only raped the pretty ones. He also said he forced the women to avert their gaze while he raped and killed them, and he would masturbate while he watched them die.

After it was determined that he was fit to stand trial, he was charged with forty counts of rape, six counts of robbery and thirty-eight counts of murder, including four that the Cleveland killer David Selepe, who had died in custody, had previously been charged with.

RAPE TESTIMONIES

Sithole's trial began on October 21, 1996, and he pleaded not guilty to all of the charges. The first three cases to be heard concerned rapes from 1987 and 1988. Twenty-nine-year-old Patricia Khumalo said that, in September 1987, she had been looking for work and her sister introduced her to a man named "Martin" who they both identified as Moses Sithole. Martin said he had work for Patricia and she got on the train with him in Boksburg. Alighting at Geldenhuis station, Martin said that he knew a short cut through the veldt. There he attacked her.

"He grabbed me by the clothes in front of my chest," she said. "I was frightened. He ordered me to lie on the ground and raped me … I pleaded and cried and asked him not to kill me. He said he wouldn't, because I have the kind of eyes that makes him feel sorry."

On September 28, twenty-six-year-old Dorcas Kedibone Khobane accompanied the man, who called himself "Samson", to Cleveland. Again they stopped at Geldenhuis station and took a shortcut through the veldt. There he hit her and pulled a knife.

"He threatened to kill me with it and to cut me into pieces unless I did as he asked," she said. "He pushed me on the ground and took my panties off. He dropped his pants to his knees and he raped me."

He said he had a girlfriend in Vosloorus named Sibongile. "He then asked if we could sleep together again," Dorcas Khobane said. When she refused, he raped her again. In court, she identified Moses Sithole as Samson.

Sibongile Nkosi then took the stand, saying she was

seventeen years old in 1988 when she got involved with the twenty-four-year-old Sithole, who again called himself Martin. Sibongile told the court that he had often hit her and had threatened to kill her family if she left him. When the defence said Sithole had never laid a finger on her, she asked if she should strip naked so that the court could see the scars.

Sibongile's younger sister Lindiwe Nkosi then testified that, in October 1988, "Martin" had invited her to visit her sister in Soweto. She was fifteen at the time. On the way, they got off the train at Geldenhuis station. Luring her into the veldt he asked Lindiwe if she wanted to have sex with him. When she said no, he pulled out a bottle of petrol and said he would kill her and burn her body if she did not. Then he beat her, raped her and throttled her until she lost consciousness. When she came round, he said he would kill her if she told anyone what had happened.

MODUS OPERANDI

Although the rape of Buyiswa Doris Swakamisa had been dealt with at his trial in 1989, she appeared in the 1996 trial to testify about his *modus operandi*. It was pointed out that Sithole's subsequent victims seem to have been selected for their resemblance to Buyiswa Swakamisa and that the attacks had stopped between 1989 and 1993 when Sithole had been in jail for her rape.

Buyiswa Swakamisa testified that Sithole had called

himself "Lloyd Thomas" when he offered her a job in February 1989. Walking through the veldt near Cleveland, he produced a *panga* or machete from a rolled-up newspaper and said he was going to have sex with her.

Then he "threw the *panga* to one side and said if I did not want to have intercourse with him, I could run away, but had to make sure that he did not catch up with me or he would kill me. I just stood there. He came towards me and slapped me and ordered me to take off my clothes."

After he raped her he said that "he hated women because he once had a child with a girlfriend in Alexandra and that his girlfriend had poisoned the child". Then he tied her up, took her money and left.

Sithole had been charged with the theft of the cash card of murder victim Amanda Thethe. It had then been used to withdraw money from a cash point after her death and the man using it had been caught on security camera. Sithole's sister Kwazi Sithole identified the man in the photograph as her brother.

Sithole had known Amanda Thethe before he killed her. Dan Mokwena, a work colleague of nineteen-year-old Elizabeth Mathetsa, said Elizabeth had introduced him to her boyfriend "Sello". She was found dead on June 16, 1995. In court Mokwena identified the man he knew as "Sello" as the prisoner in the dock.

Mary Mogotlhoa knew Sithole as "Charles". They had had a brief relationship shortly before his arrest. He had given her a watch, which Tryphina Mogotsi's mother identified as her daughter's.

The grandmother of Monica Vilakazi testified that a man calling himself Moses Sithole had phoned her home on September 11, 1995, the day before her granddaughter went missing. The following day she left her grandmother's house to become another one of the women whose bodies were found at the Van Dyk Mine. Three days after Monica disappeared, there was another phone call. Monica's grandmother recognized his voice as Sithole's. He taunted her, saying that Monica got what she deserved.

Throughout the testimony, Sithole sat smiling. The only time he cried was when his wife Martha entered the court to testify against him with their one-year-old daughter Bridget.

RAMBLING INCOHERENCE

A voice identification specialist identified the voice of the man who had called *The Star* reporter Tamsen de Beer as Moses Sithole's.

On December 3, in the sixth week of the trial the prosecution introduced a video made in Boksburg Prison not long after Sithole's arrest, showing him speaking about the women he had murdered.

In July 1995, he said a woman he killed had shouted at him when he asked for directions. But he turned on the charm and arranged to meet her for a date. Then he strangled her. "I cannot remember her name," he said. "I killed her and left her there. I went straight home and had a shower."

He then relayed in detail how he had killed twenty-nine women. He said he did not want to see the faces of his victims as he took their lives, so he strangled his victims from behind. All his victims had reminded him of Buyiswa Swakamisa, he said, the woman he claimed had "falsely" accused him of rape in 1989. He also maintained that he had not raped any of his victims, but some had offered to have sex with him to save their lives.

One victim that stuck in his mind was Amelia Rapodile. "She started to fight," he said. "I gave her a chance to fight and I tell her, if you lose, you die … She was using her feet and kicked me. Then she tried to grab my clothes, but she could not grab me. I just tell her bye-bye."

Sithole took the stand in his own defence, claiming that he was totally innocent of all charges. But he was not convincing under cross-examination and *The Star* said his testimony was "rambling, often incoherent".

Finally, on December 4, 1997, Moses Sithole was found guilty on all thirty-eight counts of murder, forty counts of rape and six counts of robbery. He was sentenced to 2,410 years in prison – fifty years for each of the murders, twelve years for each rape and five years for each count of robbery. These sentences were to run consecutively, so that there would be no possibility of parole for at least 930 years.

He is currently incarcerated in Mangaung Correctional Centre in Bloemfontein.

3

JIMMY MAKETTA
The Jesus Killer

During his killing spree of 2005, rapist and serial killer Jimmy Maketta would stand on a hill in Philippi in the Western Cape on Fridays and watch the farm workers leaving their jobs for the weekend. He picked out his targets and lay in wait until nightfall, holding back until they got so drunk that they did not even realize what was happening to them. In court, he admitted nineteen rapes, sixteen murders, six housebreakings, three assaults, one kidnapping, one theft and one attempted murder. Later he said he gave his heart to Jesus – hence the name the Jesus Killer.

PSYCHOPATH WITH NO REMORSE

His nine-month reign of terror, which lasted from April to December 2005, ended after the police arrested the wrong person. Pointing this out, Maketta wrote one letter to his wife Janetta and two to Captain Jonathon Morris, who had recently taken over the investigation, giving details of the rapes and murders.

On two occasions, he even telephoned the police to tell them where the bodies could be found. Maketta also wrote to *Die Son* and the *Voice* newspapers, saying he was responsible for the killings. He even provided a map to show where he had left his victim's bodies.

While revisiting the crime scenes, Captain Morris found a cellphone. Eight calls had been made to the same number. Morris called it again. The number turned out to be that of Maketta's son who lived in Grabouw. Morris went to see him and the son gave him Maketta's address in Mitchells Plain. He no longer lived there, but Captain Morris tracked him down to nearby Constantia where Maketta was painting a house. Together they went to Steurhof railway station which was near where Maketta lived in the bush.

After collecting his clothes and food, Morris took him in for questioning. Maketta denied everything until Morris produced the cellphone and the letters he had written. Then he admitted all the rapes and murders, along with murders the police knew nothing about. Maketta showed them where the bodies could be found. Further DNA evidence and cellphone records confirmed Maketta's confession.

Most of the victims had been beaten to death with a wooden pole. In May 2005, farm worker Nolusindiso Sono had been raped and murdered on Weltevrede Farm, Weltevrede Road, Philippi. Also that month, farm worker Mina Javas was raped and murdered on Highlands Farm, Weltevrede Road. Her body was thrown into an irrigation ditch.

In July, farm worker Richard Cornelius was murdered on the Bernie Oelof Farm in Punt Road, Philippi. Then farm worker Hilton Augustead was murdered on a farm bordering Philippi and Westridge.

In October, the body of an unidentified man was found on the Bernie Oelof Farm. Later in the same month Maketta murdered farm worker Petrus Marks, whose body was found in a ditch on Onverwacht Farm, Punt Road. Then the naked body of a farm worker, Magriet Koela, was found in the bush on the Brock Sandmine Farm, Old Weltevrede Road in Philippi. The following month, the body of farm worker Jennifer Petersen was found in an irrigation ditch on the Geduld Farm, off Weltevrede Road.

Before Maketta was asked to plead, the state withdrew seven charges, including those of indecent assault and attempted murder. When Justice Essa Moosa asked him what he would plead to the remaining charges, Maketta looked confused.

"To make this easier on me I will take it all on me and plead guilty," Maketta answered. He was convicted of all forty-seven charges.

A psychiatrist at Valkenberg Hospital testified: "Maketta had been categorized as a serial killer because he's just killed so many people. A serial killer is someone who kills more than two or three victims [followed by] a cooling-off period. During that time he reflects in and enjoys moments of the murder."

"He's a psychopath with a typical childhood. He often fought with others, set things alight, ran away from home and was involved in incidents of bestiality. He is mild-mannered, soft spoken and pleasant-looking but he lacks remorse. When I asked what he felt about all this he just shrugged his shoulders. There is zero possibility of him being rehabilitated. It is hopeless. If a person has killed so many victims it's impossible to say he's not dangerous."

WE WANT HIS BLOOD

In mitigation, Maketta's attorney said that his client had come from a dysfunctional family in Grabouw and had lived in the bush after completing Grade 6.

"He was one of fifteen children and he left home. He started stealing and later the serious crimes started," his lawyer said. "He left for Cape Town where he stayed with his sister in Mitchells Plain. He couldn't get a permanent job but did try to make something of his life."

Captain Morris said: "He also wrote to me, to thank me for the way I had treated him. In this letter he says no matter what happens to him, he always wants to stay in touch with me. He says he's given his heart to Jesus, and has turned a new leaf."

It made no difference. Adjudged a "dangerous psychopath lacking remorse", Maketta would go to jail "for ever".

That did not satisfy the victim's relatives. Outside the court building, more than fifty of them gathered on the steps chanting: "We want Jimmy. He raped and killed our people. We want his blood."

4

MADUMETSA JACK MOGALE
The West End Killer

Dubbed the West End Killer, Madumetsa Jack Mogale lured black African women into open areas near a West-End brick and clay factory close to his home in Waterworks, Westonaria, and in various locations in Lenasia, south of Johannesburg, in 2008 and 2009 where he raped and murdered them.

PREACHER AND PROPHET

One victim who miraculously survived was nineteen years old when she accepted a lift from Mogale. He told her that he was a preacher and prophet with the Zion Christian

Church (ZCC) and prophesied over her as he drove. She only realized that she was in danger when he took a wrong turn. When she asked where they were going, he became aggressive.

Mogale battered her face with a brick while raping her in an open veldt at Westonaria. After the rape, he left her unconscious and bleeding in the veldt. She came round the following day and crawled to a nearby road where she was able to get help. Her jaw had been dislocated and there were maggots on her wounds.

Mogale murdered Hanyeleni Mhangwani who had testified against him in a fraud case at Westonaria magistrate's court. He also raped and killed Dipuo Mogadi, Umanikazonke Sindane, Sonto Tsotetsi, Nothembela Ndabisa, Dipuo Denese, Mamikie Tlallo and nine other women whose bodies have not been identified. They were later linked to Mogale by DNA evidence.

Most of his victims' bodies were found decomposing in the veldt. The murders shared a similar *modus operandi*, circumstance, victim profiles, and location, according to forensic analyst Professor Gerard Labuschagne, who headed the police's investigative psychology unit.

Mogale's victims were either strangled or killed with blunt force injury, and fourteen were sexual in nature, which Professor Labuschagne said in his testimony was indicative of a serial killer. He concluded that in all the cases "undoubtedly the same offender" was involved.

EXORCIZING EVIL SPIRITS

When police officers arrested Mogale in his shack near Zuurbekom in March 2009, they handcuffed his hands in front of him, but then he pulled out his penis and tried to urinate on the arresting officers. His hands were then handcuffed behind his back. He also swore at members of the public who had gathered at the scene.

A SIM card belonging to Mogale was found in a cellphone taken from the nineteen-year-old rape victim who had survived. It was found in his shack. The accused could not explain how it had got there when he was questioned. It was found along with a white g-string and some sangoma beads. The police located him after looking for a ZCC preacher who wore sangoma beads and drove a white Volkswagen Golf with a registration number they had been given after the teenage rape victim went missing.

Another woman who survived also said that Mogale had claimed to be a ZCC preacher and prophet. She had been given a herbal "tea" for uterine problems. She said he put herbs into her vagina and said he needed to have sexual intercourse to exorcize evil spirits from her. He maintained they were having an affair and the sex was consensual. The two surviving victims identified his ZCC badge and the sangoma beads he wore.

Forty-one witnesses testified against him, including his common-law wife Charlotte Manaka who contradicted all his testimony. Forty-two-year-old Mogale said they were conspiring against him. "I didn't do anything," he said. "You know how life is, this is a challenge, I didn't do any of those things. I don't even know those women."

NAKED AND RAPED

Judge Frans Kgomo described Mogale as a liar who contradicted himself numerous times and tried to shift blame every time he was cornered.

"I can safely say that the accused was an untruthful witness whose evidence cannot be relied on. He contradicted himself and came up with new versions. I formed the impression that he was not telling the whole truth," said Kgomo. "The accused did also not bring in witnesses to back up statements made during cross-examination by the State."

The judge went on to say that evidence indicates that the murders were the work of a serial killer and it all pointed to Mogale.

"In the light of the totality of evidence, much of which is uncontested such as the DNA evidence, the admissions and testimonies, it can be confirmed that in all the bodies, except the one of a child, the cause of death was strangulation. Bodies were left in sexual positions, naked and raped," said the judge.

"On the day he was arrested, the accused displayed hatred for women, he behaved like a psychopath and even showing his manhood to the female police officer. When he met the same policewoman at the station he said 'when I come out of here you will be the first person I rape and kill.'"

He concluded that Mogale had been proved guilty beyond all reasonable doubt. Judge Kgomo found Mogale guilty of fifty two of the sixty-one charges against him, including nine kidnappings, nineteen rapes, sixteen murders, an attempted murder, three robberies with aggravating circumstances, a fraud or theft, an assault with intent to cause grievous bodily harm, a sexual assault, and escape from lawful custody. He was sentenced to sixteen life sentences to run concurrently, plus twenty-three years without possibility of parole.

5

ANDRIES MAKGAE
The Township Killer

According to Andries Makgae, he developed a hatred towards women when sixty-year-old Maria Pilore accused him of giving her HIV. His wife, a Zimbabwean woman, is thought to have died of AIDS after he was arrested. He said he also hated her because she was a prostitute.

Maria Pilore was last seen visiting a tavern in Onderstepoort, Pretoria, on January 1, 2012. Then it seems she was on her way to fetch water when Makgae overpowered her. He denied raping her, saying they were having a relationship.

When Maria's remains were found seventeen days later by police divers after being dumped off Bon Accord Dam fifteen miles north of Pretoria, all that remained was a skull and her bones. Her family only identified her by her shoes.

A few weeks later, Makgae killed again. This time his victim was sixty-nine-year-old Juliet Mokgatla. She had been sent by her husband to a nearby shop on February 4, 2012, and never returned. Her body was discovered a few days later in dense bush. She had been raped and her underwear was around her neck. It had been used to strangle her.

It is thought that twenty-nine-year-old Praise Mpatsi suffered the same fate at Makgae's evil hands. Her husband testified that his wife was at home when he left for work on January 3, 2013. When he returned she was missing. Her body was discovered nearly three weeks later with her underwear tied around her neck. The cause of death could not be established as the body was in an advanced state of decomposition.

About a week after he had killed Mpatsi, and while the police were still searching for her body, Makgae claimed his final victim. He broke into the home of forty-four-year-old Selina Eva Matjela on a smallholding near Onderstepoort. He brutally raped her twice and the next morning demanded cash. Though badly wounded, she survived.

Her brothers alerted the police, who arrested Makgae. The doctor who examined her said she could barely talk after being throttled. She died soon after the attempted murder, her demise brought on by the vicious attack.

Makgae was also charged with the murder of his friend

Sam Mufuleka. It is thought that he had found out about the murders, so Makgae threw petrol over his house and set it on fire with him inside.

Three of the bodies were found on the same small-holding, where mostly illegal immigrants lived. Makgae confessed that he would walk with his victims to or from one of the drinking places in the township and then pin them down, rape them, and strangle them.

He accompanied the police to the murder scenes after his arrest and pointed out the places where he killed the women. He also led the police to other places in Kameeldrift and Villieria where he claimed he had committed more murders. The area was combed by the police and a dog unit, but they could not find any remains or bones. No bodies or missing persons were reported in the area.

Makgae said that he had forgotten how many women he had killed. The police thought the total was maybe about ten, including his wife who had gone missing.

After being found to be sane, Makgae stood trial on charges of raping and killing Pilore, Mokgatla, Mpatsi, and Mufuleka. He was also charged with the rape of Matjela. He was convicted on the rape charges, two of which he denied, and three of the murders, which he admitted. He was acquitted of the murder of Sam Mufuleka due to lack of evidence. It was the judge's opinion that Makgae was not only a danger to society but he was also unable to be rehabilitated. He was given three life sentences.

AFTERWORD

THE LETTERS OF JACK THE RIPPER

What we do not know about Jack the Ripper probably outweighs what we do know. In fact much of what is accepted as the truth about the Ripper killings is the result of historical speculation about the culprit which has arisen from contemporary journalistic guesswork.

Murder had always been a feature in Victorian newspapers, but the constant updates on the Whitechapel murderer transformed the way news was being reported at the time. It started when the Central News Agency of London was a sent a letter from the killer on September 27, 1888, almost a month after the first murder of Mary Ann Nichols. The agency did not forward the letter to the police until September 29, the day before the double murder of Elizabeth Stride and Catherine Eddowes.

The writer of the "Dear Boss" letter, as it is known,

was the first person to coin the *nom de guerre* "Jack the Ripper," or trade name as he called it. Many now doubt the authenticity of the letter, but at the time it caused quite a stir. Written in red ink it taunted the efforts of the police to catch him:

Dear Boss,

I keep on hearing the police have caught me but they wont fix me just yet. I have laughed when they look so clever and talk about being on the right track. That joke about Leather Apron gave me real fits. I am down on whores and I shant quit ripping them till I do get buckled. Grand work the last job was. I gave the lady no time to squeal. How can they catch me now. I love my work and want to start again. You will soon hear of me with my funny little games. I saved some of the proper red stuff in a ginger beer bottle over the last job to write with but it went thick like glue and I cant use it. Red ink is fit enough I hope ha ha. The next job I do I shall clip the ladys ears off and send to the police officers just for jolly wouldn't you. Keep this letter back till I do a bit more work, then give it out straight. My knife's so nice and sharp I want to get to work right away if I get a chance. Good Luck.
Yours truly
Jack the Ripper

Dont mind me giving the trade name

PS Wasnt good enough to post this before I got all the red ink off my hands curse it. No luck yet. They say I'm a doctor now. ha ha

The day after the double murder on October 1, 1888, the Central News Agency received another communique from the killer, this time they passed it straight to the police without delay. The "Saucy Jacky" postcard contained enough significant information to persuade investigators it was an authentic piece of correspondence from the killer, in among the hundreds of other hoax letters they were receiving. They published it in the hope someone would recognize the handwriting, and it caused another sensation:

I was not codding dear old Boss when I gave you the tip, you'll hear about Saucy Jacky's work tomorrow double event this time number one squealed a bit couldn't finish straight off. Had not time to get ears off for police thanks for keeping last letter back till I got to work again.

Jack the Ripper

The "double event" refers to the killing of Elizabeth Stride and Catherine Eddowes. At the scene of the crime, police did indeed find a piece of Catherine Eddowes' ear which got cut off during the Ripper's frenzied attack.

On October 16, George Lusk, leader of the Whitechapel Vigilance Committee who had been assisting police enquiries in the community, received another letter from the Ripper. This time the letter was accompanied by half a human kidney – a gruesome trophy taken from Catherine Eddowes – the killer had fried the other half and eaten it. The letter "From Hell" with its shocking contents and littered with spelling errors looked like the real deal to Lusk, and he passed it to Dr Frederick Wiles, a doctor on the Mile End Road.

From hell.
Mr Lusk,
Sor
I send you half the Kidne I took from one women prasarved it for you tother piece I fried and ate it was very nise. I may send you the bloody knif[e] that took it out if you only wate a whil[e] longer
signed
Catch me when you can Mishter Lusk

Wiles took the package to the leading pathologist Dr Thomas Openshaw at the London Hospital in Whitechapel. Openshaw was getting frequent press mentions and was something of a Ripper celebrity. The pathologist identified it as a left kidney. Then on October 29, 1888, he received his own Ripper letter. The "Openshaw Letter" is now on display in the Royal London Hospital's museum in Whitechapel:

> *Old boss you was rite it was the left kidny i was goin to hoperate agin close to your ospitle just as i was going to dror mi nife along of er bloomin throte them cusses of coppers spoilt the game but i guess i wil be on the job soon and will send you another bit of innerds*
> *Jack the Ripper*

> *O have you seen the devle*
> *with his mikerscope and scalpul*
> *a-lookin at a kidney*
> *with a slide cocked up.*

Although police spent many man-hours trying to identify the senders of the Ripper Letters, very few people were ever held responsible. Investigators were eventually convinced that the letters were hoaxes and the work of imaginative journalists trying to keep the story in the headlines for as long as possible to sell newspapers. Little did anyone realize at the time, that over 100 years later, the world would still be fascinated by the unsolved Whitechapel murders and the unidentified Jack the Ripper – probably the most notorious serial killer of all time.

CREDITS

Cover images pictured clockwise from top left: Ridgway / Ramirez / Miyazaki / Mogale.

Text: 8 fbi.gov/stats-services incorporating public domain material / 114 news4jax.com.

Images: The images throughout the book are included for visual identification of the person in question in each biographical article and are in the public domain.

13 Los Angeles Police Department/San Quentin State Prison, California Department of Corrections and Rehabilitation / 21 Texas Department of Criminal Justice, Huntsville / 30 Tahoe City Police Department, California / 38 Bergen County Prosecutor's Office, Hackensack, New Jersey / 45 Sacramento County Sheriff, California / 51 Waushara County Sheriff, Wautoma, Wisconsin / 58 Federal Bureau of Investigation, Washington DC / 65 Los Angeles Police Department, California / 72 Los Angeles Police Department, California / 85 Joshua Trujillo/ seattlepi.com / 94 Los Angeles Police Department/San Quentin State Prison, California Department of Corrections and Rehabilitation / 108 Florida Department of Corrections, Tallahassee / 115 Fulton County Police, Atlanta, Georgia / 129 examinerlive.co.uk / 135 HM Prison Full Sutton, Yorkshire / 143 West Yorkshire Police, Dewsbury, 1981 / 162 HM Prison Wakefield, West Yorkshire / 169 Strathclyde Police, Glasgow / 194 lpiccolo.net / 201 oavcrime.com.br / 204 politie.be/nl / 216 psycho-criminologie.com / 221 Ministry of Justice, Zhytomyr Prison, Ukraine / 233 serial-killers.ru/karts/jumagaliev.htm / 241 leparisien.fr / 251 news.cgtn.com / 256 japantimes.co.jp / 261 Tokyo Metropolitan Police Department / 269 youtube.com / 275 newsnpr.org / 280 indiatimes.com / 289 ati.com / 297 Adelaide News 9 Dec 1952 / 304 heraldsun.com.au / 308 police.vic.gov.au/city-port-phillip Victoria Police / 313 police.qld.gov.au/ Queensland Police / 317 police.vic.gov. au Victoria Police / 329 imdb.com / 332 news.com.au / 335 Arthur William Upfield, National Library of Australia / 339L police.sa.gov.au / South Australia Police / 339R heraldsun.com.au / 343 nzherald.co.nz / 357 saps.gov.za South African Police Service / 365 biography.com / 376 saps.gov.za South African Police Service / 381 sowetanlive.co.za.

Cover images are all credited as internal images.

This edition published in 2022 by Canary Press
an imprint of Canary Press eBooks Limited
236 Berglen Court
7 Branch Road
London E14 7JZ
UK

10 9 8 7 6 5 4 3 2 1

ISBN 9781908698551

Printed in UK

AUTHOR

Nigel Cawthorne is a journalist and author specializing in history and crime. Several of his books are bestsellers such as The Mammoth Book of the Mafia and The World's Most Notorious Cults.